The Longman Companion to

Napoleonic Europe

Longman Companions to History

General Editors: Chris Cook and John Stevenson

Now available:

THE LONGMAN COMPANION TO NAPOLEONIC EUROPE
Clive Emsley

THE LONGMAN COMPANION TO THE MIDDLE EAST SINCE 1914
Ritchie Ovendale

THE LONGMAN COMPANION TO COLD WAR AND DETENTE,
1941–91
John W. Young

The Longman Companion to

Napoleonic Europe

Clive Emsley

Longman
London and New York

Longman Group UK Limited
Longman House, Burnt Mill,
Harlow, Essex CM20 2JE, England
and Associated Companies throughout the world.

*Published in the United States of America
by Longman Publishing, New York*

© Longman Group UK Limited 1993

First published 1993

0582 07224 7 CSD
0582 07225 5 PPR

British Library Cataloguing in Publication Data

A catalogue record for this book is
available from the British Library

Library of Congress Cataloging in Publication Data

Emsley, Clive.
  Longman companion to Napoleonic Europe / Clive Emsley.
    p.   cm. – (Longman companions to history)
  Includes bibliographical references and index.
  ISBN 0-582-07224-7. – ISBN 0-582-07225-5 (pbk.)
  1. Europe–History–1789–1815. I. Title. II. Series.
D308.E48 1993
940.2'7–dc 20   92-12764
                                                   CIP

Set by 7LL in 10/12 pt New Baskerville
Produced by Longman Singapore Publishers (Pte) Ltd.
Printed in Singapore

Contents

List of maps and genealogical tables

Maps

Tables

Preface

Napoleon was regarded by his contemporaries with admiration and adulation or with fear and loathing; sometimes, it would seem, with a mixture of all four. The fascination with him as an individual and with the colossal changes wrought by his wars across Europe has continued among historians, and many others, ever since. This guide is designed to provide readily accessible information on Napoleonic Europe. While it attempts to provide detail on rather more than the ever-popular military aspects of the period, and to cover the whole of Europe, it is by no means exhaustive. I have, for example, not included a biography of every Napoleonic marshal, but I have tried to include something on the principal monarchs and statesmen of the period and, given the various embargo acts and the Anglo-American War, I have included material on the United States. In several instances also, I have run chronologies on beyond 1815 to give an impression of the immediate legacy of the Napoleonic years. Economic and population statistics for the period are not particularly reliable, and I have been very selective here seeking to give suggestive comparative material and/or the kind of detail which I believe will be of the most value.

Any book of this sort relies heavily on the detailed research of others. But in addition to published works my particular thanks are due to John Breuilly for help on Germany, to Charles Esdaile who generously provided me with advice and detail on the Iberian peninsula and to Tim Blanning who cast a critical eye over the manuscript. The errors which remain, and the omissions, are, of course my own.

As ever, I owe an enormous debt to my wife, Jennifer, and to Mark and Kathryn, who put up with me.

Acknowledgements

The publishers would like to thank the following for permission to reproduce copyright material: Economica, Paris for table 5 from *L'économie britannique et le blocus continental*, 2nd edn, François Crouzet (1987); Kluwer Academic Publishers for table 14 from *Michael Speransky: Statesmen of Imperial Russia, 1772–1839*, Marc Raeff (1957).

For Kathryn and Mark

Chronologies: international affairs and military campaigns

1. The wars of the French Revolution and the rise of General Bonaparte, 1792–1801

1792 April 20 The French declare war on the King of Hungary and Bohemia (i.e. the Holy Roman Emperor), leading to the invasion of France by Austrian, Prussian, Hessian and *émigré* armies.

July 29 A Manifesto signed by the commander of the invading Austrians, the Duke of Brunswick, threatens Paris with destruction if the royal family are harmed. This leads to

August 10 The Parisians storm the Tuileries Palace and imprison the royal family in the Temple.

September 20 French victory over the Prussians at Valmy.

21 First meeting of the National Convention; suspension of the monarchy; beginning of Year I.

November 6 French victory over Austrians at Jemappes.

1793 January 21 Execution of Louis XVI.

February 1 National Convention declares war on Britain.

24 Levy of 300,000 men decreed for French army leading to the uprising in the Vendée and the beginning of the war against the *Chouans*.

March 7 National Convention declares war on Spain.

August 10 Decree of the *levée en masse* requires every Frenchman to play a part in fighting for 'his nation.'

27 French seaport and naval arsenal of Toulon surrenders to the British.

September 22 Beginning of Year II.

October–December Succession of defeats for Vendéan rebels.

December 19 British evacuate Toulon; Captain Bonaparte noted for his role in commanding the artillery at Toulon.

1794 June 26 French victory at Fleurus leads to conquest of Belgium.

July 27 Overthrow of Robespierre (9 Thermidor).

September 22 Beginning of Year III.

1795 January 20 French army enters Amsterdam.

February 17 'Pacification' of the Vendée at La Jannaye.

April 5 French make peace with Prussia.

22 Peace of La Prevalaye with the *Chouans*.

May 16 French make peace with Holland.

July 22 French make peace with Spain.

September 23 Beginning of Year IV.

October 1 French annex Belgium.

5 Revolt in Paris of 13 Vendémiaire suppressed by General Bonaparte's 'whiff of grapeshot'.

10 Bonaparte appointed commander of the Army of the Interior.

26 Dissolution of the National Convention.

November 3 Directory established.

1796 February 23 General Bonaparte appointed commander of the Army of Italy.

March 9 Bonaparte marries Josephine de Beauharnais.

11 Bonaparte leaves Paris to take command of the Army of Italy.

April–May Bonaparte fights a brilliant campaign (battle of Lodi, 10 May) forcing the Austrians to withdraw to the Adige. Intervening elsewhere in the peninsula he establishes the Ligurian Republic (6 June) and the Cisalpine Republic (9 July).

September 4 Coup of Fructidor in Paris establishes a more radical tone to government.

November 15–18 Bonaparte wins the battle of Arcola.

1797 January French expedition to Ireland dispersed by gales.

14 Bonaparte wins the battle of Rivoli.

February 12 Bonaparte enters Mantua and

19 imposes the Treaty of Tolentino on the Papacy.

April 19 Bonaparte agrees to the preliminary Peace of Leoben with the Austrians.

May Bonaparte occupies the Venetian Republic.

October 18 Peace of Campo Formio between Austria and France.

26 Directory authorises the creation of the Army of England under the command of Bonaparte.

December 5 Bonaparte returns to Paris from Italy.

1798 February Bonaparte persuades the Directors that the best way to beat Britain would be a thrust at India and plans are made for the expedition to Egypt.

May 19 Bonaparte embarks with his Egyptian expedition from Toulon.

July 1 The French army begins to disembark at Alexandria.

21 Bonaparte wins the battle of the Pyramids.

31 Nelson destroys Bonaparte's fleet in the battle of the Nile.

August French expedition under General Humbert lands in Ireland; it enjoys initial success, but is too small, and too late to assist the main Irish rebellion.

September 5 Jourdan Law establishes conscription in France.

9 Bonaparte's Egyptian successes lead to Turkey declaring war on France.

November War renewed in Italy; an anti-French coalition established between Britain and Russia, later to be joined by Austria and Naples.

1799 March 12 War renewed with Austria and there follows a succession of French reverses (Stockach in Baden, 25 March; Magnano in Italy, 5 April; Russian troops enter Milan, 28 April, Turin, 27 May; French also defeated at Novi in Italy, 15 August). Most of Bonaparte's Italian gains are lost. Conscription sparks off internal disorder in France.

August 22 Bonaparte leaves Egypt.

27 Anglo–Russian landing in Holland.

September 25–27 Masséna wins battle of Zurich.

October 9 Bonaparte lands in France, and

16 arrives in Paris.

18 British agree to evacuate Holland by the Convention of Alkmaar.

23 Tsar Paul withdraws from the anti-French coalition.

November 9–10 Coup of 18–19 Brumaire establishes the provisional Consulate.

1800 May 6 Bonaparte leaves Paris and heads for Italy crossing the Great St. Bernard Pass (15–23).

June 14 Bonaparte wins the battle of Marengo and agrees an armistice with Austria.

July 2 Bonaparte returns to Paris.

November 28 Armistice with Austria expires.

December 3 Moreau beats the Austrians at Hohenlinden.

16 Tsar Paul organises the Armed Neutrality.

1801 February 9 Peace of Lunéville between Austria and France.

March 21 British army defeats the remains of Bonaparte's army in Egypt.

23 Assassination of Tsar Paul, together with

April 2 Nelson's victory at Copenhagen, undermines the Armed Neutrality.

October 1 Preliminary peace treaty of London between Britain and France.

1802 March 27 Treaty of Amiens ends war between Britain and France.

See maps 1 and 2 on pages 000 and 000.

2. The Napoleonic Wars, 1803–15

The Anglo–French War, 1803–14

The principal opponents throughout the wars were Britain and France. The British, supreme at sea, financed a succession of European coalitions against Napoleon's Empire. Napoleon, supreme on land, contemplated the invasion of England particularly between 1803 and 1805, but never succeeded in controlling the Channel to enable such an enterprise to be launched. Both sides sought to cripple the economic power of the other. The chronology of the Anglo–French War therefore largely becomes subsumed in that of other conflicts.

1803 16 May Britain declares war on France seizing all French ships in British ports. Napoleon arrests all British residents in France (*détenus*) and sends troops to occupy Hanover (ruled by George III as elector) and ports in southern Italy. French troops begin massing around Boulogne for the invasion of England.

1804 12 December Spain declares war on Britain.

1805 March–April French and Spanish fleets attempt to draw British warships from the Channel to enable Napoleon to mount his invasion, but the fleets miss their *rendez-vous* in the West Indies and return to their home ports. The British warships also fail to be drawn.

 April 11 Treaty of alliance between Britain and Russia (not ratified by the Tsar until July); the former promises to pay £1.25m annually for every 100,000 Russian soldiers in the field. The treaty constitutes the beginning of the Third Coalition.

 August 9 Austria secretly joins the Anglo–Russian alliance.

 October 21 French and Spanish fleets, having put to sea again, meet Nelson's fleet off Cape Trafalgar and are decisively defeated. Nelson is killed, but the battle largely destroys the French naval threat to Britain.

1806 January British capture Cape of Good Hope from Dutch.

 February British capture San Domingo from French.

March–April British government makes tentative suggestions about peace negotiations.

May 16 A British Order in Council declares a blockade of Europe.

June A small British fleet under Commodore Sir Home Popham with 1200 British troops commanded by Lt. Gen. William Carr Beresford arrives off the River Plate (having sailed from the Cape of Good Hope) hoping to raise the Spanish colonists in revolt. The weak Spanish viceroy in Buenos Aires surrenders the city without a fight, but the colonists are not keen to rise up on Popham's urging, especially after he seizes over 1m. dollars from the public treasury and ships them back to Britain.

June–July Acting on the authority of the British government, Lord Yarmouth, one of many Englishmen under restraint in France, begins tentative and ultimately unsuccessful negotiations in Paris.

July 6 A small British force, raiding the Italian mainland from Sicily, defeats French troops at Maida.

August 12 The Spanish colonists in Buenos Aires, led by a French officer in Spanish pay, drive Beresford from their city. Popham is called home to face a court-martial.

November 21 Napoleon issues the Berlin Decree declaring a blockade of Britain.

1807 February British troops in Spanish America, now reinforced, capture Montevideo.

March 17 In an attempt to take Turkish pressure off the Russians 5000 British troops land in Alexandria, but the campaign against the Turks under Mehemet Ali is a succession of disasters.

July 5 A new attack on Buenos Aires fails. British troops withdraw from South America. Gen. Whitelock, in command of the unsuccessful attack, is court-martialled and dismissed the service.

September 14 The remnants of the British expedition to Egypt evacuate Alexandria.

1808 May–June British expedition commanded by Sir John Moore is sent to Sweden to aid Gustavus IV against Franco–Russian attack. Moore refuses to agree to the King's demands for an offensive to regain Finland and Pomerania. Moore is arrested but escapes, and the British army, most of which has never left its ships, returns home.

August 1 Sir Arthur Wellesley lands in Portugal marking the beginning of the British involvement in the Peninsular War.

1809 August–October Disastrous British expedition to Walcheren Island. The objectives of the expedition, to destroy Dutch shipping and naval facilities in the Scheldt, are never clearly defined or planned. Flushing surrenders on 18 August, but large French reinforcements deter any attempt to invade the mainland. Many troops are struck down with fever.

(For remainder of conflict see pages 12–16, Peninsular War and page 20, Waterloo campaign)

The Austerlitz campaign, 1805

1804 November 6 A secret agreement is made between Austria and Russia to oppose Napoleon's Italian policies.

1805 April–August The Third Coalition is organised, with Britain agreeing to finance Russian and Austrian armies against Napoleon.

August 24 Napoleon signs a defensive treaty with the Elector of Bavaria.

26 Napoleon abandons the camp at Boulogne and prepares to march his army into Germany.

September 2 Austrian armies begin to mobilise: Archduke Ferdinand and General Mack begin their march towards Ulm as a warning to the Elector of Bavaria; Archduke Charles prepares to attack Masséna's French army in Italy. Three Russian armies prepare for a juncture with the Austrians and a drive on Strasbourg.

25 The first French troops cross the Rhine. Napoleon leads the main body of his army in a march towards the Danube; the river is crossed east of Ulm thus cutting Mack's lines of communications and seeking to prevent any link up with the Russians. A series of minor engagements are fought (Albeck on 11 October and Elchingen on 14) until

October 15 Mack is completely surrounded at Ulm.

17 Mack opens negotiations and, hoping for the arrival of the Russians, agrees to lay down his arms if he is not relieved in 21 days. Trouble breaks out between Austrian and French troops in the town; Napoleon sends in troops to restore order and as a consequence

22 Mack is compelled to agree to an unconditional surrender with 23,000 men. Another 10,000 Austrians subsequently surrender at Heidenheim.

29 Masséna attacks Archduke Charles at Caldiero; he is checked, but it is the Austrians who withdraw.

Napoleon presses further along the Danube, fighting two minor actions (Dürrenstein on 11 November and Hollabrün on 16)

November 15 Napoleon enters Vienna without resistence. The Austro–Russian armies begin to concentrate around Olmütz.

17 Leaving a garrison in Vienna Napoleon marches north from the city hoping to tempt the Austrians and Russians to battle.

December 2 Battle of Austerlitz. Napoleon crushes the Austrian and Russian armies.

4 Austria signs armistice. Russian armies withdraw homewards.

26 Peace of Pressburg between Austria and France.

The Prussian campaign, 1806

1805 September French troops violate Prussian territory by passing through Ansbach. Prussia threatens to mobilise.

October 1 Prussian army is mobilised.

November 3 Prussia signs the Treaty of Potsdam with Austria and Russia offering armed mediation with France; if Napoleon refuses the mediation, Prussia promises to join the allies.

Prussian envoy Haugwitz leaves for meeting with Napoleon.

December 13 Haugwitz meets Napoleon at Schönbrunn.

15 Haugwitz signs Treaty of Schönbrunn with Napoleon; under the terms of this treaty Prussia is promised Hanover.

1806 July 12 Napoleon establishes the Confederation of the Rhine. Prussia, alarmed by this and angered by Napoleon's discussions with Britain (wherein he offered to return Hanover to George III) enters into a rapprochement with Russia.

August 26 Prussia issues an ultimatum to Napoleon requiring him to withdraw his armies to the west bank of the Rhine by 8 October.

The Prussians plan an advance into Bavaria but

October 8 Napoleon forestalls them by advancing into Thuringia.

14 Napoleon inflicts a crushing defeat on the Prussian army at Jena, while Davout, with the vanguard of the *Grande Armée*, withstands a series of attacks from a second Prussian army at Auerstädt; Davout is also victorious when additional troops under Bernadotte arrive.

25 Davout enters Berlin.

27 Napoleon enters Berlin. There follows a mopping up operation.

November 7 The last major Prussian army under Blücher surrenders at Lübeck. A smaller force under Kalckreuth retires into Danzig, while another under Lestocq joins up with the Russians in Poland. Frederick William III of Prussia takes refuge with the Tsar.

The Prussian campaign then merges into

The Polish campaign, 1806–7

1806 November 2 Concerned about the Russian alliance with Prussia Napoleon orders his army forward into Poland.

28 French occupy Warsaw, but the Russians are beginning to harry their lines of communication. Napoleon attempts to cut off the Russian army in front of him but, partly because of the terrain, the appalling weather, and the exhaustion of his troops, his manoeuvre fails.

December 26 The Russians fight a rearguard action at Pultusk, and sucessfully withdraw.

1807 January The two armies retire into winter quarters after Pultusk, but foraging by the French brings confrontations with Russian outposts. The Russians believe the French are reopening hostilities and fighting recommences.

February 8 Indecisive battle of Eylau fought in appalling weather with heavy casualties on both sides. Both sides withdraw, once again, into winter quarters.

March 18 French begin siege of Danzig.

April 26 Convention of Bartenstein by which Prussia and Russia agree to continue the war against France and invite Britain, Sweden, Austria and Denmark to join them. Only the two former respond.

May 27 Danzig falls to the French.

June 5 Fighting is renewed in Poland, particularly in the area aroung Königsberg where the main Russian supplies are.

10 Battle of Heilsberg; a French attack is repulsed but the Russians withdraw.

14 Battle of Friedland; Napoleon orders Lannes to seize the town but the Marshal comes upon the whole Russian army. Napoleon comes to his support and inflicts a decisive defeat.

15 Königsberg surrenders to the French.

19 Napoleon occupys Tilsit. The Russians seek an armistice.

23 Armistice signed.

25 Napoleon and Alexander meet at Tilsit on a raft in the middle of the Niemen.

July 7–9 Treaties of Tilsit.

The Peninsular War, 1808–14. See map 3, p. 299

(In Spain this war is more commonly known as 'the War of Independence'.)

1807 August Napoleon orders Portugal to comply with his blockade of Great Britain and British goods or face his army.

October 19 Junot leads a French army into Spain en route for Portugal.

27 France and Spain agree, by the Treaty of Fontainebleau, to divide Portugal between them.

November 30 Junot's army enters Lisbon.

1808 January Napoleon orders more troops into Spain, ostensibly to assist Junot, but they promptly occupy the Spanish fortresses of San Sebastien, Pamplona, Figueras and Barcelona.

March 26 Murat occupies Madrid.

May 2 *Dos de Mayo*, the people of Madrid rise against the French occupation and are brutally suppressed. The example of the *Madrileños* provides the spark for similar uprisings in the provinces and a series of juntas are established. The French are forced to attempt to pacify the whole country fighting a series of Spanish provincial armies and mounting a series of sieges (notably of Gerona, Valencia and Zaragoza).

July 14 The Spanish army of Galicia is decisively defeated at Medina de Rio Seco.

26 A French army under Dupont is forced to surrender at Bailén, and gradually the French are compelled to withdraw to the Ebro River.

August 1 A British army led by Sir Arthur Wellesley lands at Mondego Bay, Portugal.

17 Wellesley defeats a small French force at Roliça.

21 Junot attacks Wellesley at Vimeiro and is defeated, but Wellesley's superiors arrive (first Sir Harry Burrard, then Sir Hew Dalrymple) and rather than pursuing and destroying Junot's army on

30 they sign the Convention of Cintra allowing the French to take ship back to France. Burrard, Dalrymple and Wellesley are recalled to face a court-martial. Sir John Moore takes command of the British army in Portugal.

September Napoleon begins reorganising the French army on the Ebro. The Spanish also reinforce their armies, but they are weakened by a lack of central command, by provincial jealousies and pride; many generals will not co-operate with each other.

October Moore begins marching from Portugal to link with the Spanish troops on the Ebro.

November 6 Napoleon takes personal command of the French army on the Ebro and a succession of battles fought by his marshals (Espinosa, Gamonal, and Tudela) break the Spanish armies.

28 Moore, at Salamanca, receives the news of the Spanish defeats and decides to return to Portugal.

30 Napoleon captures the pass at Somosierra opening his way to Madrid.

December 4 The French reoccupy Madrid.

19 Napoleon sets off in pursuit of Moore.

20 Beginning of the second siege of Zaragoza.

1809 January 1 Napoleon hands the pursuit of Moore over to Soult.

11 Moore's depleted army reaches Corunna to embark on board ship, but bad weather has delayed the troop transports.

14 Moore's ships arrive.

16 Soult attacks Moore at Corunna but is beaten off; Moore is killed, but his army escapes.

January–March A series of new French successes against the Spanish at Uclés and Medellin. Zaragoza is captured on 20 February after a terrible siege. Soult invades Portugal and captures Oporto.

But the French are spread thinly over the whole peninsula.

April 22 Wellesley, exonerated over the Convention of Cintra, returns to Portugal to take command of the British and Portuguese armies.

May 12 Wellesley attacks Oporto and forces Soult to retreat leaving behind his artillery.

July 17 Having joined with the Spanish General Cuesta, Wellesley begins a march along the Tagus to Madrid. But there is much wrangling between the two armies until, confronted by a French army under Joseph and Victor, they agree to withdraw.

27–28 The battle of Talavera: Wellesley repulses Victor's attacks and is eager to advance once again but Cuesta refuses. Threatened by a new army under Soult, Wellesley separates from the Spanish and withdraws to Portugal. As a reward for his victories Wellesley is created Viscount Wellington of Talavera.

October In winter quarters in Portugal Wellington gives orders for the construction of a line of fortifications 25 miles north of Lisbon – the Lines of Torres Vedras.

November Having embarked on a winter campaign the Spanish are defeated at Ocaña and Alba de Tormes.

1810 In the new campaigning season, and following his success over the Austrians in the Wagram campaign, Napoleon pours heavy reinforcements into Spain intent on both pacifying the country and driving the British from the peninsula.

April 17 Masséna is appointed commander of the French Army of Portugal; he arrives in Salamanca to take command of his army one month later.

June Masséna launches his army into Portugal capturing the Spanish fortress of Ciudad Rodrigo (10 July) and the Portuguese fortress of Almeida (26 July). Wellington withdraws before him.

September 27 Wellington, in a strong defensive position at Busaco, repulses Masséna's attack, and then continues to withdraw.

October 10 Wellington enters the lines of Torres Vedras. Masséna camps before them for a month, and then withdraws 30 miles to winter at Santarem.

1811 March 5 Sir Thomas Graham, having led a combined force of British, Portuguese and Spanish out of the besieged port of Cadiz, lands behind the French army surrounding the city and wins the battle of Barrosa.

Masséna, his army starving and demoralised, begins his retreat from Portugal, pursued by Wellington.

April Wellington, concerned at the French occupation of the frontier fortresses of Almeida, Badajoz and Ciudad Rodrigo, begins the siege of the two former.

May 3–5 Masséna, attempting to relieve Almeida, is beaten by Wellington at Fuentes de Oñoro.

10 The French garrison escapes from Almeida destroying the fortifications. Napoleon replaces Masséna with Marmont.

16 Soult, attempting to relieve Badajoz, is driven back at Albuera by the British under Beresford.

The remainder of the year sees the French continuing to attempt to pacify the country, but with little success against the increasing number of guerrilla bands – the exception is the army under Suchet in Aragon. French armies continue to menace Wellington, but fight no major actions with him. Wellington remains on the Portuguese–Spanish frontier planning the reduction of the fortresses.

1812 January 8 Wellington begins the siege of Ciudad Rodrigo.

19 Ciudad Rodrigo is stormed and captured; the French siege train is captured with it.

March 17 Wellington begins the siege of Badajoz.

April 5 Badajoz is stormed and captured; the French pontoon train is captured with it. The British troops suffer heavy casualties in the attack (about 5000 men) and run amok in the city for two days.

Wellington advances into Spain.

July 22 Wellington defeats Soult at Salamanca.

August 12 Wellington enters Madrid. But French armies from all over Spain begin to converge on him and he withdraws back towards Portugal.

September 22 Anglophile deputies in the Cortes succeed in having Wellington appointed supreme commander of the Spanish armies, but the move is not popular with some Spanish generals.

November 19 Wellington re-enters Ciudad Rodrigo bringing the year's campaigning to an end.

1813 May 22 Wellington's army marches out of winter quarters. The French under Joseph and Jourdan withdraw before him.

June 21 Joseph attempts to make a stand at Vitoria, and is decisively defeated. Wellington turns his attention to the fortresses of Pamplona and San Sebastien.

July 13 Soult takes command of Joseph's beaten army, reorganises it and

20 launches a counter-attack towards Pamplona.

26–August 1 The battle of the Pyrenees; Soult is repulsed with heavy losses.

August 31 An attempt by Soult to relieve San Sebastien is beaten back by Spanish troops on the heights of San Marcial. San Sebastien is stormed and captured. Soult withdraws to defensive lines along the River Bidassoa.

October 7–9 Wellington crosses the Bidassoa driving Soult before him.

25 Pamplona captured.

November 10 Wellington attacks Soult's position on the River Nivelle and pushes him back into France. Wellington's army crosses into France. Soult withdraws to the River Nive, south of Bayonne.

December 9–13 Wellington strikes across the Nive; Soult counter-attacks but is repulsed and withdraws further to a position on the Adour.

1814 January 9 Napoleon's overtures to the Spanish government are rejected.

February 17–24 Wellington manoeuvres Soult out of his positions on the Adour; part of the Anglo–Spanish army is left to invest Bayonne while Wellington sets off with the major part in pursuit of Soult.

27 Soult turns to face Wellington at Orthez but is defeated, enabling Wellington to occupy Bordeaux.

March 26 Soult's army reaches Toulouse.

April 10 Wellington attacks Toulouse and in spite of the heavy casualties inflicted on the Anglo–Spanish army...

12 Soult evacuates Toulouse. Wellington hears of Napoleon's fall and informs Soult, leading to an end to hostilities between the two armies.

14 Unaware of the events in Paris the garrison at Bayonne make a sortie; about 1000 casualties are suffered on both sides. This is the last action of the war.

The Wagram campaign, 1809

1809 April 6 Archduke Charles issues a proclamation to the German people announcing the Austrian aim of restoring German independence and national honour.

10 Austrian troops cross the River Inn and invade Bavaria.

13 Napoleon leaves Paris to take command of his army in Germany.

17 Napoleon joins his army at Erfurt and repulses Charles in a series of battles notably

22 Eckmühl, and

23 Ratisbon, from where he continues his march on Vienna.

May 13 Napoleon enters Vienna unopposed, but the Austrians have destroyed the bridges across the Danube.

17–20 A bridge of boats is constructed downstream of Vienna to enable the army to cross the river.

20–21 French troops led by Masséna and Lannes cross the Danube by the pontoon bridge and occupy Aspern-Essling.

21–22 The Austrians attack and drive the French from Aspern-Essling; Lannes is killed.

The defeat is the cue for a series of uprisings against the French and their allies in Germany, notably that of Andreas Hofer in the Tyrol.

June 14 An Italian army commanded by Eugène de Beauharnais defeats Archduke John at Raab and joins with Napoleon.

July 4–5 The French successfully cross the Danube.

6 Napoleon defeats Archduke Charles at Wagram.

12 An armistice is signed between Austria and France.

October 14 Peace of Schönbrunn.

The Russian campaign, 1812. See map 4, page 300

1812 April Concerned by Napoleon's behaviour in developing the Grand Duchy of Warsaw and about the serious effect which the Continental System was having on Russian trade, Alexander issues an ultimatum to Napoleon: Russia is to be allowed to trade with neutrals and French troops are to evacuate Prussia. Following Napoleon's acceptance of these terms, Alexander is prepared to negotiate an indemnity for his brother-in-law (the Duke of Oldenburg, whose lands had been taken by Napoleon) and a reduction of the Russian customs dues on French goods.

June 24 The first units of the *Grande Armée* (some 600,000 strong) cross the Niemen at Kovno. The Russians withdraw before them; probably at this stage they withdraw because they are reluctant to face Napoleon rather than because they are following any scorched earth policy.

August 16 The French attack Smolensk.

17 The Russians withdraw from Smolensk; but following this the Russian government orders Kutusov to block the French advance on Moscow.

September 7 Inconclusive battle of Borodino fought between Napoleon and Kutusov; the Russians withdraw again.

14 The French enter Moscow, but Alexander refuses to negotiate.

October 19 The French evacuate Moscow intending to withdraw south but on

24 at the battle of Maloyaroslavets, Kutusov forces Napoleon to retreat along the same route by which he had invaded.

27 The first frost of the winter.

November 9 The French reach Smolensk where they rest.

16 The French withdraw from Smolensk.

The temperature falls to −20°C, sometimes to −30°C.

26–28 The French cross the Berezina on pontoon bridges under attack from the Russians.

December 5 Napoleon leaves the army at Smogorni and travels to Paris (arriving on 18).

18 Remnant of the *Grande Armée*, about 18,000 strong, crosses the Niemen.

The German War of Liberation, 1813

1812 December 30 Convention of Tauroggen between the Prussians under Yorck von Wartenburg (technically part of the *Grande Armée*) and a Russian army under Diebitsch.

1813 February 26 Treaty of Kalisch creates a military alliance between Prussia and Russia, but not made public until 13 March.

April 25 Napoleon reaches Erfurt and assumes command of the French army in Germany.

May 1 Napoleon marches into Saxony and occupies Lützen.

2 A Russian attack on the French at Lützen is beaten, and Napoleon sets off in pursuit of the Russian and Prussian armies.

20 Napoleon victorious at battle of Bautzen.

June 4 Armistice of Poischwitz signed between the allies and Napoleon, to last for two months.

14–15 Treaties of Reichenbach between Britain, Prussia and Russia; the former promises subsidies, and the latter two states promise not to make a separate peace with France.

26 Napoleon meets Francis I and Metternich at Dresden but will not accept their mediation.

27 Austria signs a new Treaty of Reichenbach with Britain, Prussia and Russia.

August 11 Austria declares war on France.

Napoleon begins to advance on Berlin.

26–27 Napoleon beats an allied army at Dresden, but his subordinates lose a succession of minor battles: Oudinot at Grössbeeren (23 August); Vandamme at Kulm (29 August); Ney at Dennewitz (6 September). These defeats force him to withdraw and concentrate around Leipzig.

October 16–19 The 'battle of the Nations' at Leipzig; Napoleon is heavily defeated by the Austrian, Prussian and Russian armies supported by many of his former German allies who now turn against him.

30 A largely Bavarian army impeding Napoleon's retreat is swept aside at Hanau.

November 5 Napoleon's retreating army reaches Mainz.

The campaign in Northern France, 1814. See map 12, detail page 312

1814 January 1 Prussian troops begin crossing the Rhine and moving into France.

25 Blücher enters Nancy and

28 links with the Austrian advance guard at La Rothière.

February 1 Napoleon attacks the allies at La Rothière and forces them to retire to Arcis-sur-Aube, but

2 his follow-up attack is checked by bad weather and he is forced to withdraw.

4 Blücher resumes his advance, but his forces are widely spread out and Napoleon is able to launch a series of successful attacks at Champaubert (10), Montmirail (11), and Vauchamps (14). Napoleon then turns on the Austrians, inflicting defeats in a trio of minor actions at Mormant (17), Montereau (18), and Méry (21).

March 7 Blücher's Prussians had joined with Bernadotte's Swedish army, when Napoleon attacks and beats their advance guard on the plateau of Craonne.

10 Napoleon attacks the main Prussian and Swedish force at Laon, where he is forced to retreat towards Rheims.

Napoleon determines to attempt to cut the communications of both the Prussian and the Austrian armies.

20–21 He clashes with the Austrians and Russians at Arcis-sur-Aube and is forced to withdraw. At the same time his plans fall into allied hands and these, together with reports of dissatisfaction within Paris, decide the allies to march directly on the capital.

31 Marshal Marmont, having tried to defend Paris from the heights of Montmartre, decides further resistance is impossible and agrees to an armistice.

The Waterloo campaign, 1815

Following Napoleon's return from Elba the allies plan a general invasion of France for early July 1815. An Anglo–Dutch army under Wellington and a Prussian army under Blücher are to invade from Belgium; Austrian and Russian armies are to invade from the east. Napoleon seeks to forestall this by destroying his enemies piecemeal, beginning with those in Belgium.

June 11 Napoleon leaves Paris for his army on the Belgian frontier.

14 The French army crosses the frontier.

16 Two indecisive battles fought at Quatre Bras (between Ney and Wellington) and at Ligny (between Blücher and Napoleon). Blücher is forced to withdraw; this leaves Wellington exposed and forces him to withdraw also. Napoleon sends Grouchy in pursuit of Blücher, but contact is lost with the major part of the Prussian army.

18 Grouchy fights a minor action with a Prussian corps at Wavre. Napoleon attacks Wellington's position at Waterloo, but fails to break the British infantry lines, and the arrival of Blücher's main army in the afternoon ensures a crushing defeat for the French.

3. The Anglo–American War, 1812–15

Trouble developed between Britain and the US from the rupture of the Peace of Amiens as the Americans took more and more of the European carrying trade and as the Royal Navy sought to enforce the blockade and the control of neutral shipping. At the same time the Royal Navy was concerned about British seamen sheltering in the US and on US ships, while the Americans protested about the British pressing their nationals to serve on warships.

1807 June 27 HMS Leopard fires on USS Chesapeake, forces it to surrender, and seizes four crewmen as British deserters. This is the most notable incident in the continuing quarrel over seamen and impressment.

December 22 The Embargo Act prohibits trade with countries outside the US. This is a disaster for US trade; it especially angers New England merchants and is openly broken in spite of a succession of additional acts to strengthen it.

1809 March 1 The Embargo Act is replaced by the Non-Intercourse Act prohibiting trade with Britain and France and their allies until one or both repeal their blockade decrees (Berlin and Milan Decrees, and Orders in Council). Thomas Jefferson's term as president ends; he is replaced by James Madison. David Erskine, the new British minister in Washington, suggests to Madison that US ships could be exempt from the Orders in Council if the US repeals the Non-Intercourse Act with reference to Britain.

July–August Canning repudiates Erskine's suggestion and recalls him. Madison re-establishes the Non-Intercourse Act against Britain.

1810 May Congress repeals the Non-Intercourse Act, but proposes to stop trade with whichever belligerent fails to modify its blockade decrees. Napoleon promises the Berlin and Milan Decrees will no longer apply to US shipping.

November 2 A US proclamation imposes non-intercourse against Britain if the Orders in Council are not repealed within three months.

1811 Friction continues throughout the year. The French continue to act against US ships; the British will not repeal the Orders in Council and continue to press seamen who claim to be American.

1812 June 18 US declares war on Britain.

There are isolated engagements at sea throughout the war and the British mount a blockade of the US east coast disrupting coastal traffic and severely impeding foreign trade. At the same time American privateers have a serious impact on British commerce. Elsewhere the fighting is initially confined to Lakes Erie and Ontario and the land border between the US and Canada around these lakes.

July A US incursion into Canada under Gen. William Hull is checked; Hull withdraws to Detroit.

August 15 The British capture Fort Dearborn (site of modern Chicago); the US garrison is massacred by Indians.

16 Hull surrenders to British and Indians at Detroit.

October 13 US troops under Gen. Stephen Van Renssellaer cross the Niagara River to attack Queenstown. But his New York militiamen refuse to move from the soil of their own state; Van Renssellaer's 900 regular troops are forced to surrender.

November Gen. Henry Dearborn leads an abortive invasion of Canada along Lake Champlain, but withdraws without engaging the British.

1813 April 27 A new US incursion into Canada results in the burning of York (Toronto).

September 10 The US flotilla on Lake Erie defeats its British counterpart.

October 5 A mixed force of Canadians and Indians is beaten by the Americans at Thames River. Tecumseh, the Indian leader, is killed.

1814 July US troops, under Gen. Jacob Brown and Gen. Winfield Scott, cross the Niagara River, capture Fort Erie and defeat the British at Chippewa (5). The drawn battle of Lundy's Lane (25) leads to the Americans withdrawing to Fort Erie where they are besieged.

August British troops, now reinforced with men from Europe following Napoleon's defeat, land in Chesapeake Bay, defeat the Americans at Bladensburg (24) enter Washington, burn the White House and other public buildings (25), then re-embark on their ships to do the same to Baltimore.

September 11 British troops had begun to advance from Montreal down Lake Champlain, but the defeat of their accompanying flotilla off Plattsburg compels them to withdraw.

12 British troops land close to Baltimore, but their attack is checked and they withdraw.

17 US troops break out of Fort Erie.

December 13 British troops land close to New Orleans.

15 Angry at the way in which their trade has been hit and their protests have apparently been ignored by the government, delegates from New England meet at the Hartford Convention in Hartford, Connecticut, and propose amendments to the Constitution (the radicals had sought secession from the union but this is not adopted).

24 Treaty of Ghent ends the war.

1815 January 8 Unaware of the peace, British troops launch an attack on New Orleans and are driven off with heavy losses.

4. European diplomacy, 1815–22

1815 June 9 Final Act of the Congress of Vienna.

18 Napoleon defeated at Waterloo.

September 26 Alexander I's plan for a Holy Alliance agreed to by Austria, Prussia and Russia.

November 20 Treaty of Paris finally ends the Napoleonic wars. France is to pay an indemnity of 700m francs and to support an allied army of occupation for five years. The four powers Austria, Britain, Prussia and Russia establish the Quadruple Alliance and resolve to hold future congresses to settle European problems.

1817 July 28 Convention agreed in London between Britain and Portugal for the prevention of the slave trade.

September 23 Treaty concluded in Madrid between Britain and Spain for the abolition of the slave trade.

1818 May 4 Convention agreed at The Hague between Britain and The Netherlands for preventing the slave trade.

September–November Congress of Aix-la-Chapelle, at which the former allies agree to withdraw their army of occupation from France (1 Oct), to invite France to join their deliberations (4 Nov) and to enlarge the Quadruple Alliance into the Quintuple by the addition of France (15 Nov)

1819 August Meeting of German monarchs at Carlsbad leads to the drafting of the reactionary Carlsbad Decrees. Metternich seeks the backing of the Quintuple Alliance for his measures but Britain and Russia are critical.

1820 October–November Congress of Troppau. Concerned by revolution in Spain and an uprising in Naples, Austria, Prussia and Russia agree to the Protocol of Troppau (19 Nov) which threatens first, exclusion from the European alliance of any states which have undergone a change as a result of revolution, and second, military action against them. Britain publicly protests against the Protocol.

1821 January–May Against a background of the deployment of Austrian troops to suppress the risings in Naples and Piedmont, the powers meet at Laibach where Austria, Prussia and Russia reaffirm the Protocol of Troppau (12 May) in spite of British protests.

February–March The Greek rising against Turkish rule prompts Austrian and British concerns about Russian involvement in the Balkans.

October Castlereagh and Metternich meet at Hanover to co-ordinate their policies to prevent first, Russian involvement against Turkey, and second, French involvement in Spain.

1822 October–December The powers meet at Verona where Metternich seeks to act as a broker. All except Britain agree to send notes of protest to Madrid (see also page 266). Britain, where Canning is now Foreign Secretary, separates herself from the others. Co-operation between the four remaining powers collapses soon after the congress and French troops march into Spain (April 1823). Verona is the last of the post-war congresses.

Chronologies: domestic and national affairs

SECTION II

Cross-boundary diplomacy
and external affairs

1. Austria

1801 February 2 Peace of Lunéville ends Austria's participation in the French Revolutionary wars. In the aftermath of the wars Archduke Charles is made President of the *Hofkriegsrat* (the military council) and introduces reforms into the army. Charles also persuades the Emperor Francis (his brother) to create ministers to supervise the different departments of state with these ministers meeting in a cabinet under Francis – the *Staats- und Konferenzministerium*. The new system replaces the old advisory council of the Emperor, the *Staatsrat*. Under the new system Charles is appointed Minister of War.

1802 May The Hungarian Diet meets and there is a confrontation between it and Francis over his demands for men and money (Charles's military reforms having demonstrated that Hungary does not contribute proportionately to the armed forces). Matters are not resolved to the satisfaction of either party.

1803 May War between Britain and France; Francis seeks to stay neutral.

September 3 An enlightened recodification of the criminal law reintroduces the death penalty (abolished by Joseph II), but reduces the severity of other sentences and separates crimes from civil misdemeanours. This is one of a series of enlightened enactments designed to foster stability; educational reforms follow (1805), and there are continual modifications of the manorial system.

1804 August 10 Francis assumes the title of hereditary emperor of Austria. He does this in the belief that the Holy Roman Empire will shortly come to an end, and because of Napoleon's assumption of an imperial title. Francis considers that if the Holy Roman Empire goes, then the Habsburgs in Austria will appear inferior to the imperial monarchs of France and Russia. He assures the Hungarians that this will not change the position of their country within the Empire.

November 6 Secret treaty agreed with Russia to resist any new moves by France in Italy.

1805 March The *Hofkriegsrat* is re-established as a rival to Charles. It is symptomatic of Francis's ignoring of his ministers and his desire to run things himself.

August 9 Austria joins the new coalition against Napoleon.

September A new meeting of the Hungarian Diet forces concessions from Francis especially over use of the Hungarian language.

December 2 Battle of Austerlitz.

26 Treaty of Pressburg, by which Austria makes peace with France. The treaty is very severe. Francis's new Foreign Minister, Stadion, proposes social and political reforms to awaken German national feeling for a war of revenge. Francis rejects the reforms; but he eventually sanctions a propaganda campaign – but carefully directed only at the German Austrians and not at other subject peoples.

1806 February 10 Charles is appointed 'Generalissimus' and exempted from the control of the *Hofkriegsrat.* He begins further reforms of the army with the idea of a new war against France. He sacks 25 generals, moderates military punishments, and establishes a reserve.

August 6 Francis renounces title of Francis II, Holy Roman Emperor, and becomes Francis I, Emperor of Austria.

1807 January 4 The competence of the *Staats- und Konferenzministerium* is restricted to internal affairs only.

April 13 Death of the Empress Maria Theresa.

1808 January 6 Francis marries Maria Ludovica of Este; Italian by birth she is nevertheless keen to promote the German national feeling urged by Stadion, Charles, and Archduke John.

April 1 The right of towns to elect their own aldermen and burgomasters is abolished; henceforth these are to be central appointments.

A new Hungarian Diet ('the Accursed Diet') agrees to increase Hungary's military contribution to the imperial army and the nobles promise a voluntary gift to the exchequer.

June 6 The *Staats- und Konferenzministerium* is abolished and the old *Staatsrat* re-established.

9 Charles establishes the *Landwehr* with service compulsory for all men in the hereditary Habsburg lands and Bohemia aged 18–45, unless otherwise serving in the army, the reserve, or officially exempt.

31 A new Hungarian Diet is summoned on the pretext of the crowning of Maria Ludovica. 'The Handsome Diet' is carefully selected, feted and showered with honours; it agrees to a further increase in Hungarians for the army.

1809 January Andreas Hofer, the Tyrolean patriot, visits Vienna for negotiations.

April 9 Austria declares war on France.

May 15 Napoleon issues a manifesto urging the Hungarians to rise and establish their independence.

21–22 Charles's victory over the French at Aspern- Essling is the cue for Hofer's rising in the Tyrol.

29 Francis promises never to make peace with France without the Tyrol being reunited with Austria.

July 6 Battle of Wagram.

October 14 Peace of Schönbrunn ends the war; Francis increasingly centres government upon himself; Stadion is dismissed and Francis turns to Metternich as his principal advisor.

November 20 The Tyrolean uprising is finally crushed. Hofer escapes, but is subsequently captured.

1810 February 20 Hofer is executed in Mantua.

April 2 Francis's favourite daughter, Marie Louise, marries Napoleon. Francis is initially reluctant about the match, but takes Metternich's advice.

1811 February 20 The deepening financial crisis, worsened by the wars, necessitates the *Finanzpatent*, a drastic deflationary measure recalling old currency and replacing it with paper redemption bonds at a rate of one new for five old of the same face value. The measure is unpopular throughout the Empire.

June 1 A new General Civil Law Code is promulgated for the Empire to come into force on 1 January 1812.

August The *Finanzpatent* leads to a new confrontation with the Hungarian Diet.

1812 May 30 Dissolution of the Diet.

September 1 Francis introduces the *Finanzpatent* into Hungary 'provisionally', pending the convocation of the next Diet; but he does not call the next Diet for 13 years.

1813 June 26 Metternich meets Napoleon at Dresden offering to act as a mediator between him and the allies. Napoleon refuses.

27 Austria signs the treaty of Reichenbach with Russia and Prussia, and with British agreement. The treaty remains secret.

31

August 11 Austria formally declares war and joins the allied coalition.

1814 October 1 Formal opening of the Congress of Vienna.

1815 June 9 Final act of the Congress. Austria regains virtually all of the territory which she has lost in the wars since 1792, the main exception being the Austrian Netherlands (Belgium). The whole empire is reorganised on the principle of centralised rule by the Emperor and his closest advisors: the restored Italian lands (Lombardy and Venetia) are given to Francis's brother Rainer as viceroy and they are permitted to use the Italian language, but they enjoy little self government; Hungarian autonomy is equally truncated.

The harvest of 1815 in the Empire is poor, as is that of 1816, and the next two years are marked by serious famine.

1816 July 1 The state repudiates 60 percent of its national debt as Stadion (in charge of the Empire's finances since 1814) attempts to restore order to the national finances. The following year he creates a national bank with the power to issue its own notes. Between 1814 and 1821 he succeeds in raising the national revenue from 50m. to 110m. gulden a year.

August 16 The reactionary Count Joseph Sedlnitzky is appointed Police Minister; he works closely with Metternich to preserve the state for the next thirty years until both are thrown out of office by the Revolution of 1848.

2. Britain

1800 January Pitt rejects Napoleon's peace overtures.

July Second Combination Act passed modifying some of the features of its predecessor of 1799, but still restricting the right of organisation among workers.

August The Act of Union unites Ireland and Britain abolishing the separate Dublin Parliament.

1801 February–March Confrontation between Pitt and George III over Catholic emancipation with the former urging its introduction and the King insisting that this would require him to break his coronation oath. The King becomes ill, leading to talk of a regency; Pitt resigns.

A new administration is formed by Addington.

October 1 Treaty of London; a preliminary peace treaty signed with France.

1802 March 25 Peace of Amiens signed with France.

May Health and Morals of Apprentices Act passed – the first Factory Act. This puts a limit of 12 hours on the daily labour of pauper apprentices in textile mills, and requires inspections by local magistrates; the latter proves largely ineffective.

November 16 Arrest of Col. E.M. Despard and others in London suspected of plotting insurrection.

1803 February 21 Having been found guilty of treason Despard and six others are executed.

May 18 Britain declares war on France.

July 23 Insurrection in Dublin against British rule led by Robert Emmet. The insurrection is defeated; Emmet is arrested, tried the following October, and executed.

1804 April 29 Addington's ministry resigns, and is replaced in May by a new government under Pitt.

1805 October 21 Nelson defeats the Franco–Spanish fleet at Trafalgar.

1806 January 23 Death of Pitt.

February A new administration is organised led by Lord Grenville (First Lord of the Treasury) and Fox (Foreign Secretary); known as the 'Ministry of All the Talents'.

March–June Fox seeks to negotiate a peace with France.

September 15 Death of Fox.

November 21 Napoleon issues the Berlin Decree stepping up the economic warfare between Britain and France; Britain responds with the Orders in Council.

1807 March 24 Resignation of 'All the Talents' following a confrontation with George III over Catholic emancipation.

25 The final piece of legislation of the 'Talents' is rushed through parliament – the act abolishing the Slave Trade.

A new administration is organised under the Duke of Portland.

1808 August The first British troops land in Portugal beginning British involvement in the Peninsular War.

1809 January A parliamentary committee is appointed to investigate charges against the Duke of York (a son of George III) of involvement in the corrupt sale of army commissions.

June A Whig member (J.C. Curwen) introduces a bill to prevent the sale of parliamentary seats by requiring an oath from members that no money has changed hands. The bill is taken over by the government, amended and passed.

Sir Francis Burdett's motion for parliamentary reform is defeated.

August–October The Walcheren expedition.

September Ill health forces the resignation of the Duke of Portland; a new administration is organised under Spencer Perceval. Disagreement between two former ministers (Canning and Castlereagh) leads to them fighting a duel (22 September).

1810 February–March A parliamentary enquiry into the Walcheren expedition meets, and produces a report critical of the government's handling of affairs.

April 6–9 Perceval's attempt to have the radical MP Burdett sent to the Tower for a libel on the House of Commons provokes rioting in London.

A Whig member (Thomas Brand) introduces a bill for parliamentary reform aimed at extending the franchise. It is defeated.

November Following the death of his youngest daughter, Princess Amelia, George III suffers a renewed bout of his illness which leads to plans for a regency under his son, George, the Prince of Wales.

1811 February 5 The Regency Act establishes the Prince of Wales as Regent, but with limited powers for 12 months.

March Luddite disturbances begin in the Midlands.

1812 January Luddite disturbances spread to Lancashire and Yorkshire; the government responds by making frame-breaking a capital offence.

February 18 The restrictions on the Prince Regent's powers come to an end.

March Widespread petitions are organised against the Orders in Council.

April The Luddite disorders reach their peak with the attack on Rawfolds Mill and the murder of a mill owner, William Horsfall.

May 11 Spencer Perceval assassinated by John Bellingham, which leads to a new government being organised under Lord Liverpool.

June Liverpool's government revokes the Orders in Council, but too late to prevent a declaration of war by the United States.

1813 August–September A bumper harvest brings a fall in grain prices; farmers demand protection; parliament establishes a Corn Committee to investigate the problem.

1814 April The abdication of Napoleon brings an end to war in Europe.

December 24 Treaty of Ghent ends war with United States.

1815 March Beginning of the Hundred Days and resumption of war against France.

Parliament passes a Corn Law prohibiting the sale of foreign corn in Britain until the domestic price reaches 80s. (£4) a quarter.

June 18 Napoleon defeated at Waterloo.

For much of the summer and early autumn a seamen's strike paralyses the east coast; the strikers use their recent war service in their arguments against the owners' proposals to maintain low manning levels and to reduce pay. The end of the war brings widespread economic dislocation to those industrial areas (coal and iron) which had done well out of military demand.

1816 April The wartime measure of income tax is abolished by parliament.

Beginning of widespread unrest over high food prices, notably in East Anglia.

December A mass meeting by radical reformers in London ends in the Spa Fields riots.

1817 January An attack on the Prince Regent's coach on the way to the opening of parliament leads to a suspension of the Habeas Corpus Act and restrictions on public meetings.

March Plans for a hunger march of Lancashire weavers to London with a petition for the Prince Regent to relieve their distress; but few of the 'Blanketeers' ever set off, and few get far.

June Rising in Pentrich, Derbyshire.

1818 March Repeal of suspension of Habeas Corpus Act.

1819 July 2 The Cotton Factories Regulation Act, a watered-down version of a bill first introduced by Sir Robert Peel in 1815, prohibits the employment of children under nine years and imposes a maximum working day of 12 hours for those aged 9–16.

August 16 The 'Peterloo Massacre'; cavalry (some of whom are wearing the Waterloo medal) kill 11 and wound several hundred at a reform meeting on St. Peter's Fields in Manchester. The name 'Peterloo' is coined from an amalgamation of St. Peter's Fields and Waterloo.

December 'The Six Acts' are introduced following a panic about radical activities.

1820 January 29 Death of George III.

3. France

1799 September 23 Beginning of Year VIII.

October 9 General Bonaparte returns to France from Egypt; he arrives in Paris 16 October.

November 9–10 The coup d'état of 18–19 Brumaire overthrows the Directory and inaugurates the Consulship.

December 13 'Election' of three Consuls (Bonaparte, Cambacérès and Lebrun).

15 (24 Frimaire) The Constitution of the Year VIII is put into effect.

28 Sunday services recommence in churches.

1800 February 7 (18 Pluviôse) Publication of the results of the plebiscite accepting the Constitution of the Year VIII: 1,280,000 ayes; 1250 noes.

13 Bank of France established.

17 Law of 28 Pluviôse establishes the departmental prefects and a new administrative system in France.

19 Bonaparte installs himself in the Tuileries Palace.

March 5 and 29 Bonaparte's meetings with Cadoudal.

18 Law of 27 Ventôse establishes a new judicial system.

August 12 Creation of the preparatory commission for the drafting of the Civil Code.

September 23 Beginning of the Year IX.

October 10 The 'Opera Plot'; attempted assassination of Bonaparte.

20 The list of proscribed *émigrés* is modifed to enable more to return to France.

November 5 Negotiations with the Papacy open over the Concordat.

December 24 Crime of 3 Nivôse; attempted assassination of Bonaparte by a bomb in rue Saint-Nicaise – 'the infernal machine'.

1801 February 9 (20 Pluviôse) Treaty of Lunéville with Austria.

July 15 (26 Messidor) Concordat agreed.

23 Discussions begin on the Civil Code in the Council of State.

September 23 Beginning of the Year X.

October 1 (9 Vendémiaire) Preliminary Treaty of London with Britain.

9 Decree creating the rue de Castiglione launches the rebuilding of central Paris.

1802 March 25 (4 Germinal) Treaty of Amiens with Britain.

April 8 Bonaparte adds the Organic Articles to the Concordat without informing the Papacy.

18 Concordat published.

26 The list of proscribed *émigrés* is reduced to 1000.

May 1 Law of 11 Floréal establishes a new education system and, notably, the *lycées*.

19 (29 Floréal) The Legion of Honour established.

August 2 (14 Thermidor) Napoleon is proclaimed Consul for life, and henceforward he only uses his christian name.

4 The Constitution of the Year X is approved by plebiscite: 3,200,000 ayes; 7200 noes.

September 23 Beginning of the Year XI.

Work begins on the Ourcq canal to improve the Paris water supply.

1803 February 26 Napoleon offers the Comte de Provence an annual pension of 2m. francs in return for his renouncing all claim to the throne of France on behalf of himself and his heirs.

April 12 Law of 22 Germinal establishes a regulatory system for labour in manufacturing and prohibits workers' unions.

14 The Bank of France is granted the privilege of issuing banknotes.

May 18 Britain declares war on France.

23 (2 Prairial) Napoleon orders the arrest of all British males in France between the ages of 18 and 60; this leads to the apprehension of 700–800 civilian *détenus*.

September 23 Beginning of the Year XII.

October 1 Napoleon orders work to begin on the Vendôme Column.

December 1 (9 Frimaire) Introduction of the worker's passbook (*livret ouvrier*), to be carried by all working men so that any employer might know details of a man's previous employment.

1804 February 13 Discovery of a royalist plot to kidnap Napoleon.

19 Arrest of Gen. Moreau.

28 Arrest of Gen. Pichegru.

March 9 Arrest of Cadoudal.

15 Arrest of the duc d'Enghien; executed on 21 March.

April 6 Pichegru found strangled in prison.

May 18 (28 Floréal) Napoleon is proclaimed Emperor. Constitution of the Year XII. Proclamation of the Civil Code.

19 The first 18 marshals of the Empire are created.

June 28 Execution of Cadoudal. Banishment of Moreau.

September 23 Beginning of the Year XIII.

November 6 Announcement of the plebiscite on the Empire: 2,500,000 ayes; 1400 noes.

December 2 (11 Frimaire) Napoleon's coronation.

1805 March 19 A press bureau is created to supervise publications and theatrical performances.

May 30 Annexation of the Ligurian Republic.

August–September The Third Coalition is organised against France. Napoleon breaks up the camp at Boulogne preparing for the invasion of Britain and marches his army against Austria.

September 23 Beginning of the Year XIV.

October 21 Battle of Trafalgar; Franco–Spanish fleet defeated.

December 2 Battle of Austerlitz; Austro–Russian army defeated.

December 31 (10 Nivôse) Termination of the Revolutionary Calendar.

1806 March 18 The first of the councils of *Prud'hommes* (wise men or skilled men) are created to settle employer–employee disputes involving not more than 60 francs, and to seek to effect reconciliation if the amount was greater.

May 10 University of France established and entrusted exclusively with public teaching and education throughout the Empire.

August 14 Entailed estates (*majorats*) established for members of the new imperial nobility.

September 26 Industrial exhibition opens in Paris.

October Defeat of Prussia.

December 10 Opening of the Grand Sanhedrin made up of 41 rabbis and 26 laymen to consider whether Mosaic law is compatible with civil law and the duties of French citizenship. This leads to

1807 March 2 Decrees on the civil status of Jews which help to promote assimilation.

September 11 Proclamation of the Commercial Code.

December Completion of the Simplon road between France and Italy.

1808 March 1 Two decrees issued systematising the imperial nobility.

17 A decree is issued outlining the centralised system of education under the University.

June 9–10 Arrest of Gen. Malet and others in Paris charged with conspiring to bring down the regime.

September 10 Married men and widowers with children are exempted from conscription.

1809 April–July War with Austria.

November 30 Napoleon resolves to divorce Josephine.

December 15 A decree is issued announcing the divorce.

1810 January 12 The Church Court of Paris annuls the marriage between Napoleon and Josephine.

February 5 A general directorship of printing and bookselling is established better to control the press.

March 30 The *Ecole Normale Supérieure*, responsible for the training of teachers, is reorganised.

April 1 Napoleon marries Marie Louise of Austria.

July 1 Lucien Bonaparte abdicates as King of Holland and Holland is annexed to France.

August 3 A decree limits the number of newspapers to one in each department.

December 13 The annexation of north-west Germany leads to the French Empire reaching its maximum extent: 130 departments.

1811 March 20 Birth of the King of Rome, a son for Napoleon.

1812 March–April High bread prices provoke disorder; the most serious riot is at Caen (2 March). The trouble leads to

May 8 Price controls for grain.

June 24 Beginning of the Russian campaign.

October 22–23 Gen. Malet escapes from confinement and attempts a second coup.

29 Malet executed.

December 18 Napoleon arrives back in Paris.

1813 March 30 Before leaving for war Napoleon organises a Council of Regency to ensure the rights of his heir.

December 25 The *Corps législative* adopts a resolution critical of further war, except in defence of French territorial integrity, and urging Napoleon to uphold the laws guaranteeing political liberties. Napoleon refuses to let the resolutions be published and adjourns the body.

1814 January Allied armies invade France.

24 Joseph Bonaparte is appointed Lieutenant-General of the Empire.

March 12 At Bordeaux the duc d'Angoulême proclaims the restoration of the Bourbons.

28 Joseph arranges the departure of the imperial family from Paris.

April 1 A provisional government is established under Talleyrand.

3 Napoleon is deposed by the Senate.

6 Napoleon abdicates in favour of his son, the King of Rome.

11 Napoleon abdicates unconditionally and the Senate summons the comte de Provence to be Louis XVIII.

May 2 Louis issues the declaration of Saint-Ouen promising to establish a representative government.

3 Louis enters Paris.

4 Napoleon lands on Elba.

30 First Treaty of Paris.

June 4 Louis issues the Constitutional Charter.

1815 March 1 Napoleon returns to France.

20 Napoleon arrives in Paris; Louis XVIII flees to Ghent.

22 Promulgation of the Additional Act.

April 8 The duc d'Angoulême signs the Convention of La Palud ending the resistance of his royal army to the Bonapartists.

June 18 Battle of Waterloo.

22 Second abdication of Napoleon.

June–November A sporadic white terror is directed against Bonapartists in different parts of France – among the victims, in Avignon on 2 Aug, is one of Napoleon's marshals, Guillaume Brune. In some areas of the south, where the terror is especially violent, it also takes on an anti-Protestant hue.

July 8 Louis XVIII returns to Paris.

15 Napoleon leaves France on the British warship HMS Bellerophon.

August 14–22 Elections resulting in the *Chambre introuvable* (the 'incredible chamber'), so-called because of its majority of reactionary deputies.

November 20 Second Treaty of Paris.

December 8 Execution of Marshal Ney.

1816 January The beginning of a grain crisis which is to continue until the harvest of 1817 and provokes rioting.

September 5 Dissolution of the *Chambre introuvable.*

October 25 Election results in success for the constitutional monarchists.

November–December A wave of food riots.

1817 May–June A second wave of food riots.

September 20 Election successes by liberals enable them to form an independent political grouping in the chamber.

1818 March 10 New law on army recruitment taking its name from the Minister of War, Marshal Gouvion St. Cyr.

November 30 Departure of the allied armies of occupation.

1819 September 11 New successes by liberals in elections.

1820 January 13 Assassination of the duc de Berry (son of the comte d'Artois) leads to a political reaction directed particularly against the press.

4. Germany

Germany had been profoundly affected by the wars of the French Revolution, especially the Rhineland where there had been considerable fighting and where scores of tiny principalities had been abolished. The authority of the Habsburg Holy Roman Emperor had been undermined by French victories, and the princes of the larger territories in the south and west especially saw the opportunity to enlarge their territories at the Empire's expense. See maps 6 and 7 on pages 304 and 305.

1801 February 9 Peace of Lunéville between France and Austria (ruled by the Habsburg Holy Roman Emperor) results in the left bank of the Rhine becoming French territory. Over the next 18 months the princes of the south and west negotiate individual terms with Napoleon.

August 24 Treaty between Bavaria and France enlarging the former's territories in compensation for French acquisitions on the left bank of the Rhine.

September The Imperial Diet (*Reichstag*) accepts a proposal from the Emperor Francis II to establish a committee (*Reichsdeputation*) to negotiate with France for compensation (*Entschädigungsplan*) for losses on the left bank.

1802 May 20 Treaty between France and Württemberg extending the latter's territory and resolving disputes following the French occupation of the left bank of the Rhine.

23 Similar treaty between France and Prussia.

August 2 An imperial decree summons the *Reichsdeputation* to begin its work, which it does on 24 August on the basis of a plan drawn up by France and Russia.

1803 February 25 Main resolution of the *Reichsdeputation* (the *Reichsdeputationshauptschluss)* is accepted by the *Reichstag.*

April 27 Francis II accepts the *Reichsdeputationshauptschluss.*

May–June Following the resumption of war between Britain and France, the French seize and despoil Hanover.

1804 March 14–15 French troops seize the duc d'Enghien at

Ettenheim in Baden and take him to France.

September Napoleon holds court in Mainz.

October 24–25 French troops seize the British *chargé d'affaires* in Hamburg and take him to France.

1805 January 1 *Dienstpragmatik* in Bavaria abolishes the sale of offices, lays down rules for appointment and promotion and the qualifications for officials.

September 23 Bavaria signs treaty of alliance with France against Austria.

October 1 Baden signs treaty of alliance with France.

8 Württemberg signs treaty of alliance with France.

December 2 Battle of Austerlitz.

12 Treaty of Brno between France, Baden and Württemberg.

26 Treaty of Pressburg between France and Austria, also involving Bavaria. These treaties end the power of the imperial knights and hasten the abolition of the imperial *Reichstag* (20 January 1806).

1806 January 14 Eugène de Beauharnais marries Augusta of Bavaria (daughter of the Elector Max Joseph); later in the year the other middle-sized German states are similarly linked to Napoleon when Stephanie de Beauharnais (Josephine's niece) marries Crown Prince Charles of Baden, and Jerome Bonaparte is betrothed to the daughter of Frederick of Württemberg.

March 15 Napoleon creates the Grand Duchy of Berg to be ruled from its capital, Düsseldorf, by Marshal Murat.

July 17 Napoleon creates the Confederation of the Rhine headed by Karl von Dalberg as Prince Primate. Napoleon keeps supervisory control and is named as protector. The Electors of Bavaria and Württemberg become kings; the Electors of Baden and Hesse-Darmstadt become grand dukes; others are similarly honoured.

August 6 Francis II, Holy Roman Emperor, forsakes this title and becomes Francis I, Emperor of Austria.

26 Execution of Johann Philip Palm for publishing anti-French literature.

October 14 Battles of Jena and Auerstädt.

December 11 Treaty of Posen converts Saxony into a kingdom, now enlarged by territory taken from Prussia.

1807 July 9 Treaty of Tilsit leads to the creation of the new Kingdom of Westphalia for Jerome Bonaparte from the lands of princes who had sided with Prussia (Hesse-Cassel, Brunswick, southern Hanover, some lesser territories, and some Prussian lands).

22 Treaty of Dresden establishes the Grand Duchy of Warsaw out of Polish lands, to be supervised by the King of Saxony.

August 23 Jerome Bonaparte marries Catherine of Württemberg.

November 15 A constitution for Westphalia is issued at Fontainebleau on the Napoleonic model, establishing equality before the law, equal liability of taxation, and religious freedom, and also abolishing serfdom. Conscription is a 'fundamental law'; the Code Napoleon is to be introduced on 1 January 1808.

December 7 Jerome Bonaparte arrives in Cassel as King of Westphalia.

1808 May 1 A constitution is introduced into Bavaria on the French model.

August 31 The legal status of serfdom abolished by edict in Bavaria.

December 11 The legal status of serfdom abolished in the Grand Duchy of Berg.

1809 January 11 Feudal dues are abolished in the Grand Duchy of Berg.

April 2–3 Abortive uprising in Stendal (north of Magdeburg) by Friedrich von Katte, a former lieutenant in the Prussian army.

22–23 Abortive uprising by Wilhelm von Dörnberg, a colonel in the Westphalian Guards.

28 Major von Schill leads his regiment out of Berlin on manoeuvres, and starts an uprising in northern Germany.

May 24 Von Schill, in retreat, captures Stralsund in Swedish Pomerania and contacts a British fleet offshore.

31 Von Schill is killed when Stralsund is stormed.

June 9 Rising led by the Duke of Brunswick-Oels and his Black Hussars captures Dresden.

19 Brunswick captures Leipzig, but is confronted by a much larger Westphalian army and forced to withdraw (June 26).

July 31 Having defeated another Westphalian army Brunswick enters his hereditary capital, but he cannot prompt a mass uprising.

August 1 Brunswick defeats the advance guard of King Jerome's army, but faced with overwhelming numbers he withdraws to the mouth of the Weser where he and his men are picked up by a British fleet.

October 12 Friedrich Staps, a Saxon student, attempts to assassinate Napoleon at a review at Schönbrunn (Austria).

1810 February 16 Napoleon obliges Dalberg to sign away the succession of the Grand Duchy of Frankfurt to Eugène de Beauharnais.

1811 June 10 Death of Grand Duke Charles Frederick of Baden; succeeded by his grandson Charles.

1812 December 30 Convention of Tauroggen.

1813 March 17 Frederick William of Prussia's proclamation *An mein Volk* begins the German War of Liberation, though initially it is more of a German civil war with Baden, Bavaria, Hesse-Darmstadt, Saxony and Württemberg on Napoleon's side.

August 11 Austria declares war on France.

October 8 Treaty of Ried, Bavaria joins anti-French coalition and Austria guarantees her full sovereign rights at the end of the war.

17–19 Battle of Leipzig. Some Saxon and Württemberg troops desert Napoleon. Frederick Augustus I of Saxony is captured and the Russians take over the government of Saxony for a year.

November 2 Austria guarantees the sovereignty and territory of Württemberg and Hesse-Darmstadt in response to their breach with France.

15 At Frankfurt the monarchs of Austria, Prussia and Russia agree a common policy towards former members of the Confederation of the Rhine, guaranteeing their sovereign rights and their existing or former territories; this leads to treaties with Baden, Nassau and Hesse-Darmstadt (24 Nov), Saxe-Coburg (24 Nov) and Hesse-Cassel (2 Dec).

21 With the collapse of the Kingdom of Westphalia, Brunswick, Hesse-Cassel and Hanover are restored as independent states.

From the close of the year and on through the Congress of Vienna, the allies discuss the settlement of Germany at the end of the war.

1814 May 30 First Treaty of Paris includes a statement to the effect that all German territories between Austria and France are to be independent and united in a federation.

October–June 1815 The Congress of Vienna decides the final shape of restoration Germany. There are to be 38 states (39 with the restoration of Hesse-Homburg in 1817). By virtue of their size Austria and Prussia dominate – the latter much enlarged with new provinces on the Rhine, parts of Saxony, and western Poland. There are a group of medium-sized states, some of which (notably Baden, Bavaria and Württemberg) keep the territories secured under Napoleon, one of which (Saxony) is reduced for having remained loyal to Napoleon for too long, and some of which have been restored (Brunswick, Hanover). Only six of these states acquire and develop parliamentary constitutions in the restoration period: Nassau (enacted in 1814 and renewed in 1816); Saxe-Weimar (5 May 1816); Bavaria (26 May 1818); Baden (22 Aug 1818); Württemberg (25 Sep 1819); and Hesse-Darmstadt (18 Mar 1820).

1815 June 8 The new German Constitution, the Federative Act, is promulgated, establishing the 38 independent states as a confederation leagued in diplomatic alliance.

1816 November 5 The Federal Diet, the negotiating body of the new Confederation, meets at Frankfurt. It is designed to co-ordinate the policy of the independent governments, and voting is arranged so that no single state can dominate.

1817 October 18 The German Students' Associations (*Burschenschaften*) organise a liberal, nationalist festival at the Wartburg Castle at Eisenach. This is to celebrate the tercentenary of Martin Luther's 95 theses (the first act of the Protestant Reformation) and the fourth anniversary of the battle of Leipzig. The festival ends with the burning of modern symbols of reaction (a wig, a corporal's cane, a cavalry belt) which causes outrage and fear among the political authorities.

1819 March 23 A German student, Karl Sand, murders a conservative Russian state councillor and author, August Kotzebue. This prompts Metternich to seek strong measures against liberalism in the press and within the universities.

July 30 Frederick William of Prussia agrees to support Metternich's proposals.

August 6 Opening of a conference of the German rulers at Carlsbad where Metternich wins sufficient support to have a series of reactionary decrees carried by the Federal Diet.

September 20 The Federal Diet confirms the Carlsbad decrees.

5. Italy

At no time during this period was Italy united as a single state. Before the French Revolution much of the north of the peninsula had been under Habsburg influence; in the north-west were Piedmont (part of the Kingdom of Sardinia) and the small Republic of Genoa; the north-east and the Adriatic coast constituted the Republic of Venice; the centre was dominated by the Papal States; to the south were the twin Kingdoms of Naples and Sicily. During the Revolutionary wars Habsburg influence had been undermined (and this was cemented by the Treaty of Campo Formio, Oct 1796); the French Republic had also established a series of sister republics: the Cisalpine (north centre), the Ligurian (Genoa), the Roman (Papal States), and briefly the Parthenopian (Naples). The war begun in 1798 by the second coalition resulted in many of these changes being reversed.

1800 May Bonaparte invades Italy via the Great St. Bernard Pass.

June 2 Bonaparte occupies Milan.

14 Bonaparte defeats the Austrians at Marengo.

1801 February 8 Treaty of Lunéville largely restores the situation agreed at Campo Formio. The Cisalpine and Ligurian Republics are formally restored.

March 21 Treaty of Aranjuez between France and Spain establishes the Kingdom of Etruria out of Tuscany for Louis, the son of Ferdinand of Bourbon, Duke of Parma, and the son-in-law of Charles IV of Spain. Louis does not become king until his father's death in 1802.

28 Treaty of Florence between France and Naples permits French troops to be on Neapolitan territory and closes Neapolitan ports to British ships.

1802 January The Italian Republic is created out of the Cisalpine, and the committee appointed to select a president chooses Bonaparte. The vice-president, chosen by Bonaparte, is a Milanese nobleman, Francesco Melzi d'Eril who had served under the Austrian Habsburg rulers of northern Italy but has liberal sympathies.

Melzi is entrusted with the government in Bonaparte's absence and embarks on a series of reforms.

June Charles Emmanuel IV abdicates his throne in Piedmont in favour of his brother Victor Emmanuel I; he retires to Rome and joins the Jesuit Order. Victor Emmanuel maintains close links with the British who, in turn, keep a strong influence over, but never occupy, Sardinia.

August 13 Napoleon introduces military conscription into the Italian Republic.

September 21 Piedmont is annexed to France; the local population are informed two weeks later.

1803 May 27 Death of Louis I, King of Etruria. His wife, Marie Louise, daughter of Charles IV of Spain continues to rule, but Napoleon is concerned that she is more attached to Spain than to France and shortly begins negotiations for her removal.

1804 May Melzi organises a meeting in Milan to frame a constitution transforming the Italian Republic into a kingdom. Melzi's candidate for the throne is Joseph Bonaparte who he knows to be liberal. Napoleon rejects the constitution; at the same time his confidence in Melzi is shaken by the revelation that he has been in communication with the Austrians. Melzi is gradually squeezed out of positions of power, though he remains in government and continues to receive honours.

1805 January Joseph finally refuses the Italian crown.

February Melzi and other leaders of the Italian Republic accept a constitution prepared by Napoleon.

March 18 Napoleon takes the title King of Italy.

May 26 Napoleon is crowned king in Milan. Eugène de Beauharnais becomes viceroy.

June The Ligurian Republic is annexed to France.

December 2 Napoleon defeats the Austrians and Russians at Austerlitz and following this he declares that the Bourbons of Naples, who sided with the coalition against him, have ceased to reign.

26 Treaty of Pressburg between France and Austria recognises the French settlement in Italy. Austrian Venetia becomes part of the Kingdom of Italy (from 1 Jan 1806) and French troops occupy Istria and Dalmatia.

1806 January 1 The Code Napoleon is introduced into the Kingdom of Italy.

February 4 Armistice between France and Naples.

11 The Neapolitan Bourbons, Ferdinand IV and Maria Caroline, retire to Sicily under British and Russian protection.

14 French troops enter Naples.

March 30 Joseph Bonaparte is crowned King of Naples and begins reforms of the economy, the fiscal and legal systems.

July 1 Small British expeditionary force lands in Calabria winning the battle of Maida (4 July). It fails to spark off a national rising but it does provoke increased guerrilla activity against the French and discourages Napoleon from invading Sicily.

August 2 Joseph announces the abolition of feudalism in Naples, but the reform is bound with a cluster of caveats.

November 2 Fra Diavolo, the most successful of the Calabrian guerrillas is captured, and executed (11 Nov). With Diavolo's death the scale of guerrilla/bandit activity is brought under greater control, but it continues at least until 1812 with atrocities on both sides.

1807 May 22 Joseph's police chief, Saliceti, orders a series of arrests in Naples thus pre-empting a conspiracy planned to link with a landing of Bourbon troops from Sicily. The leaders of the conspiracy are executed; Saliceti's policy of police terror continues until he is sure that the threats are neutralised.

July 23 Joseph proclaims a general amnesty for political offences.

November 27 Marie Louise, Queen of Etruria, is invited to leave Florence and return to Spain.

December 27 A French official is sent to administer Etruria.

1808 February 2 Rome is occupied following papal refusal to sanction Jerome Bonaparte's divorce and because Napoleon sees it as a means of further strengthening the continental system.

March 15 Etruria (Tuscany) is annexed to the French Empire.

July 8 Joseph abdicates as King of Naples.

15 Treaty of Bayonne makes Marshal Joachim Murat King of Naples from 1 August.

September 6 Murat (King Gioacchino Napoleone) enters Naples.

October 4–18 Murat attacks the British garrison on the Isle of Capri (under Hudson Lowe) and forces it to surrender.

1809 March 27 The Kingdom of Italy introduces a new tax (*dazio di consumo*) on wheat, flour, meat and wine to pay for the war against Austria. It provokes widespread discontent.

April Austrian troops invade Italy.

May Encouraged by the Austrian invasion and the example of Andreas Hofer in the Tyrol, uprisings break out notably in Lombardy and the Veneto. They are soon suppressed once the Austrians withdraw.

16 Napoleon declares the annexation of Rome. Pope Pius VII prepares a bill of excommunication but is arrested and exiled (5 July).

July 1 A new milling tax comes into effect provoking further peasant uprisings throughout the kingdom. The risings are suppressed, but the tax is repealed.

1810 January 1 The Code Napoleon is introduced into Naples.

February 17 Rome is formally annexed into the French Empire and declared its second city.

August–September Murat prepares for the invasion of Sicily, but the small force which does manage to cross the straits (under Cavaignac) is forced to withdraw after only a day (18 Sep).

1811 July Lord William Bentinck arrives as British minister to the court at Palermo and shortly embarks on a programme of reforms which he believes will maintain the Bourbon dynasty; his actions are opposed by Maria Caroline who suspects that the British have designs on Sicily.

1812 June The Sicilian parliament meets and prepares a constitution.

December Murat's agents begin discussions about the survival of his kingdom with Metternich (Murat himself was then commanding the *Grande Armée* retreating from Russia, Napoleon himself having already left it for France).

1813 January 17 Murat leaves the *Grande Armée* in Posen to return to Naples.

June Bentinck has Maria Caroline removed from Sicily.

August–September Austrian troops, aided by local uprisings, take Illyria and then invade the Kingdom of Italy.

November 5 Murat issues a proclamation to his army saying that he will never again fight in foreign lands but henceforth only in Italy and only for Italian independence. He then marches his army northward, though it is unclear on whose side he intends to fight. Bentinck will not agree to an armistice with him, but the Austrians continue to negotiate.

1814 January 11 Murat signs a treaty with the Austrians promising to support them in Italy and renouncing his claim to Sicily in return for a guarantee of the throne of Naples. Murat now styles himself the 'Liberator of Italy' entering Rome (24 Jan) and Bologna (31 Jan).

February During fighting between Austrians and French under Eugène de Beauharnais, Murat refuses to commit his troops.

March 14 Bentinck lands in Livorno with an Anglo–Sicilian army, issues a proclamation calling on the Italians to rise up in defence of their liberties, and snubs Murat.

April 14 Murat finally moves against Eugène, but news arrives of Napoleon's abdication.

16 Eugène signs the Convention of Schiarino-Rizzino with the Austrians.

17 The Senate of the Kingdom of Italy in Milan recognises Eugène's government and sends delegates to Paris to negotiate with the victorious allies, but there is disorder over the next two days with radicals and members of the *Carbonari* protesting that the Senate has elected Eugène as king.

20 The Senate is broken up by a crowd which sacks the building; this gives the Austrian army the excuse to restore order.

26 Eugène issues a farewell proclamation handing his Italian army over to Austrian control; he leaves Italy the following day.

May 14 Victor Emmanuel returns to Piedmont and

21 declares the old constitution restored.

June 12 Austrian government announces the annexation of Lombardy.

July Bentinck leaves Sicily.

1815 February Murat demands that Louis XVIII recognise him as King of Naples or be attacked, and requests permission of the Austrians to march his army north to the French border. The Austrians refuse.

March 4 Murat hears news of Napoleon's return from Elba and eventually decides to attack the Austrians in the belief that while they are busy with Napoleon they will withdraw their troops from northern Italy and leave him alone.

19 Murat marches north.

30 At Rimini Murat declares Italy to be independent.

May 2–3 Murat is defeated by an Austrian army at Tolentino and his withdrawal becomes a rout.

13 Queen Caroline agrees to surrender to a British fleet when Austrian troops arrive in Naples.

18 Murat returns to Naples, but the situation is such that the following day he has to depart in civilian clothes.

21 Queen Caroline embarks on HMS Tremendous.

23 The Bourbon monarchy is restored in Naples.

October 8 Having spent months in France and Corsica Murat returns to Italy landing at Pizzo in Calabria with a small force. He attempts to raise the population but is captured after a skirmish.

13 Murat is tried by a Neapolitan Council of War, and shot.

With the death of Murat the Napoleonic period in Italy comes to an end; most of the old regimes have already been restored under the settlement agreed by the Congress of Vienna.

Venetia and Lombardy are combined and brought under Austrian rule.

Marie Louise, Napoleon's Austrian wife, becomes ruler of Parma, Piacenza and Guastalla maintaining some of the Napoleonic reforms.

Modena is restored to the rule of the reactionary Francis IV (an Austrian Habsburg prince).

Tuscany is restored to the more liberal Ferdinand III (an Austrian Habsburg prince).

The Kingdom of Sardinia is restored to include both Piedmont and Sardinia, and now with the addition of Liguria.

The Papacy is restored to Rome and its control of the surrounding territory is also re-established. Initially, with Cardinal Consalvi as minister, there are some liberal reforms.

Ferdinand IV is restored as King of both Sicily and Naples. In 1815 he takes the title Ferdinand I, and at the end of the following year he abolishes the constitution and declares Sicily and Naples reunited as the Kingdom of the Two Sicilies. His rule is marked by harsh reactionary policies, but he has especial problems in Sicily as a legacy of Bentinck's reforms.

In the five years following Murat's death liberal ideas and secret societies, notably the *Carbonari,* spread across the peninsula. June 1817, a rising in Macerata; July 1820 – March 1821, a rising in Naples; March – April 1821, a rising in Piedmont.

6. The Netherlands

1800 April–June Bonaparte is keen to get better financial support from the Dutch, and believes he can do this with a new constitution, based on the French model, which restores the old merchant class to its previous dominance. But the assembly of the Batavian Republic reject the new constitution.

September 14 A conservative coup, supported by French troops, announces meetings of primary assemblies to vote on a new constitution which reverts to a federalist system of government.

October 1 The primary assemblies reject the constitution by 52,219 votes to 16,771; the conservative directors announce that the constitution is accepted as the 350,000 abstentions were 'tacit affirmations'.

William V, Prince of Orange, in exile, authorises his supporters to hold office in the reorganised regime.

Peace with Britain (treaties of London and Amiens) restores economic prosperity.

1803 May Renewal of Anglo–French war. Napoleon demands military and naval support from the Batavian Republic for his projected invasion of England. But the federal system established in 1801 fails to produce the desired results, and the continual arrival of British goods in the republic infuriates Napoleon.

1804 November French coastguards and customs men, assisted by French troops, are ordered to supervise Dutch ports. Protest by the Dutch government leads to revocation of the order.

1805 April 29 Schimmelpenninck is appointed Grand Pensionary of the new administration (formally installed in The Hague, 10 May). The new regime embarks on a series of reforms creating the basis for the first national public administration in the Netherlands, and also reforming education and local government.

July 14 Gogel presents his plan for a reform of the financial system based on a national, centralised structure, rather than a provincial, federal one.

1806 January–March Rumours that Napoleon intends to change the government once again.

April 9 Death of William V.

June 4 Schimmelpenninck refuses to accept Napoleon's new proposals and resigns.

5 Louis Bonaparte accepts the invitation of Dutch representatives (under pressure from Napoleon) to become King of Holland.

18 Louis enters The Hague. His regime pushes through several cultural proposals begun in the early years of the Batavian Republic but shelved since 1801 (National Archives, National Art Collection, new Legal Code) and continues the centralising reforms begun under Schimmelpenninck.

1807 January 12 A gunpowder barge explodes by accident in the middle of Leiden, more than 500 houses are destroyed. Louis takes personal control of the emergency work and establishes a national Disaster Fund. This and similar actions win him popularity with the Dutch, but little sympathy from Napoleon.

1808 January 14–15 Violent storms break dykes and lead to serious flooding, especially in Zeeland.

30 Law to abolish guilds and end restrictions on trade introduced, but its implementation is ignored in many areas. Against Louis's wishes the Dutch are compelled to close all their ports to the British.

September 16 Angry that British goods still appear to be getting through the blockade, Napoleon prohibits Dutch goods from entering France.

1809 January Swollen rivers break their banks and cause serious flooding, especially between the Lower Rhine and the Waal.

July–September The British expedition to Walcheren. Napoleon is highly critical of the Dutch response and appoints Bernadotte military commander over Louis's head.

1810 January French troops are ordered into the southern provinces of the Netherlands.

February 4 French troops are ordered to occupy towns south of the Maas and the Waal.

16 French troops cross the Maas.

March 16 Louis is forced to accept a treaty ceding his southern provinces to France. But French troops continue occupying the country.

July 1 Louis abdicates.

13 The Netherlands are annexed to France. Lebrun becomes governor general.

1811 February 3 Conscription is introduced. This leads to disorders over the next two years.

1812 December News of the retreat from Moscow and of the very heavy losses sustained by the Dutch contingent in Napoleon's army, sparks off unrest which continues into the new year.

1813 March 8 The official birthday of William VI, Prince of Orange, witnesses pro-Orange and anti-French demonstrations.

April 19–21 Anti-French disorders in Leiden – the *drie schoften Oranje boven* (three marauders for Orange).

November 8–9 Russian and Prussian cavalry cross Dutch frontier.

15 Rising in Amsterdam.

17 Rising in The Hague.

30 William VI of Orange lands at Scheveningen after 18 years of exile.

December 2 William is proclaimed Prince Sovereign of the Netherlands, assuming name and title William I.

1814 March 28 William accepts the newly drafted constitution with a central, rather than a federal, structure for the country.

June 21 The allies at the Congress of Vienna agree to make Belgium part of the new Kingdom of the Netherlands.

7. Poland

Poland had ceased to exist as an independent state following the three partitions of her territory (1772, 1793 and 1795) by Austria, Prussia and Russia. In Lombardy in 1797 veterans of an insurrection against the last partition were organised as a Polish Legion to fight Austria on the side of the French. The Legion's hopes of a restored Poland were shattered by the Peace of Lunéville. The remnants of the Legion were suspect in Napoleon's eyes because of their republicanism; they were part of the French force sent to San Domingo (1803) and here they were decimated by disease.

1806 October Napoleon requests the original organiser of the Legion, General Dabrowski, to call upon Poles to take up arms against Prussia. French troops entering Polish territory during the war against Prussia are welcomed by townspeople and peasants, though less so by the nobility.

1807 January 14 Napoleon establishes a seven man Committee of Government led by Stanislaw Malachowski and made up of Poles to run the Polish territories seized from Prussia.

July At Tilsit Napoleon and Alexander agree to the creation of the Grand Duchy of Warsaw out of these territories.

22 Napoleon, at Dresden, grants a constitution for the duchy on the French model. Serfdom is abolished, but many feudal privileges are left with the landowners. The Napoleonic Code is introduced. Frederick Augustus, King of Saxony, is appointed duke, and takes the initiative in legislation; the administration is run by Poles, but under the direction of the French Resident, appointed by Napoleon.

1809 October Following the Austrian defeat in the Wagram campaign the duchy is enlarged by the addition of Polish territory acquired by Austria in the third partition.

1809–11 Polish support for Napoleon cools, particularly over his marriage to Marie Louise of Austria and his accompanying guarantee to Francis I of the integrity of Austria's remaining Polish lands. Napoleon firmly opposes the appointment of Hugo Kollataj, a radical leader, to the government of the duchy. Some radicals look to Tsar Alexander to re-establish Poland. But...

1812 June A large Polish contingent joins the *Grande Armée* in the invasion of Russia.

1813 February Russian troops enter Warsaw effectively ending the duchy's existence.

1814–15 The Congress of Vienna hands most of the territory of the duchy to Russia as 'Congress Poland'. Cracow, with its surrounding territory, is established as an independent free city.

8. Portugal

1799 Having ruled in place of his insane mother, Maria I, since 1792, John, Prince of Brazil, takes the formal title of Prince Regent.

1801 January France and Spain demand that Portugal abandon its alliance with Britain. The Portuguese failure to respond leads to
    May Spanish invasion and beginning of the 'War of the Oranges'.
    June 7 Treaty of Badajoz ends the war. Spain acquires Olivenza; Portugal is compelled to pay an indemnity and close her ports to British ships.

1803 June Following the rupture of the Peace of Amiens Portugal again declares her neutrality.
    December Portugal is compelled to pay an indemnity to France.

1804 October Spain enters the war against Britain on Napoleon's side and seeks Portuguese territory in return.

1805 April General Junot arrives in Lisbon as French ambassador. He attempts to persuade Portugal to side with France. The Prince Regent insists on maintaining neutrality.

1807 July The French demand that Portugal close her ports to British shipping by 1 September.
    August An ultimatum is received from Spain and France requiring a declaration of war on Britain, the confiscation of British goods, and the arrest of British men on Portuguese territory.
    October 1 Spanish and French representatives leave Lisbon.
    18 Junot's army begins to enter Spain; the first units crossing into Portugal in mid-November.
    27 The Prince Regent, the royal family and court embark on board ship in Lisbon for Brazil; bad weather prevents their departure until 29 November.
    30 Junot occupies Lisbon.

1808 February 1 Junot declares that the House of Braganza has ceased to rule and that the government of Portugal has passed to Napoleon represented in his (Junot's) person.

May Spanish uprising against Murat forces Junot to send troops to Spain, but encouraged by the Spanish example

June 6 there is an uprising in Oporto, the French governor is arrested and a provisional junta, declaring for the Prince Regent, is established under the bishop. Similar risings follow in Braga, Braganza, Guimarais and Viana. When the news reaches the Prince Regent in Brazil he issues a formal declaration of war against France.

July 25 French troops massacre the population of Evora after a rising, but this serves to strengthen Portuguese hostility rather than subdue it.

August 1 First British troops land to assist against the French.

17 Battle of Roliça.

21 Battle of Vimeiro.

31 Convention of Cintra. Junot evacuates Portugal.

1809 February An Englishman, Lt. Gen. William Carr Beresford is created marshal and commander-in-chief of the Portuguese army, and charged with its reorganisation.

Portugal itself is administered by a Council of Regency, though the Prince Regent and the court remain in Brazil.

March The French under Soult re-invade Portugal and occupy Oporto.

April Sir Arthur Wellesley returns to Lisbon as commander-in-chief of the British and Portuguese armies in the peninsula.

1810 June Masséna launches an attack against Portugal and Wellesley withdraws before him. The invasion brings terrible devastation to central Portugal and famine conditions in Lisbon during the winter.

1811 March His army hungry and demoralised, Masséna begins to withdraw from Portugal.

1814 May 30 Peace is signed with France, but the Prince Regent and the court remain in Brazil.

1816 Death of Maria I. The Prince Regent becomes John VI (20 March). The regime in Lisbon becomes increasingly reactionary under Antonio de Araújo, Count of Barca. Liberal agitation begins, centred in Masonic lodges and notably in Oporto.

1817 May A liberal plot is unearthed in Lisbon led by General Gomes Freire, a masonic leader who had commanded Portuguese troops fighting for Napoleon in Russia. Freire and 12 others are executed. The liberal opposition blames Beresford for the repression.

1820 August 24 Following the example of Spain the military in Oporto begin a bloodless revolution. The military want to remove Beresford and compel John VI to return from Brazil; their civilian allies, led by a magistrate, Fernandes Tomás, want an end to absolutism and the creation of a constitutional system.

1821 January–February Similar disorders in Brazil lead John VI to return to Portugal leaving his son, Pedro, in Brazil. John returns to find a constitutional system established as a result of the revolution.

9. Prussia

1802 May 23 Treaty with France expands Prussian territories west-
wards and in central Germany in compensation for the cession of
territory to France on the left bank of the Rhine.

1804 April Hardenberg begins substituting for Haugwitz regularly
as Foreign Minister; this division is given a more formal basis in
July.

June 1 Treaty with France confirms the neutrality of northern
Germany and its closure to Napoleon's enemies.

December 3 Stein is appointed Trade Minister.

1805 October 1 The Prussian army is mobilised following French
incursions.

November 3 Treaty of Potsdam between Austria, Russia and
Prussia. The latter offers to mediate with France on behalf of the
others.

December 13 Haugwitz meets Napoleon at Schönbrunn, where
the latter offers Prussia the electorate of Hanover in return for
small parcels of territory for Bavaria and France.

15 Haugwitz signs the Treaty of Schönbrunn.

1806 February Hardenberg, still pursuing an anti-French policy,
retires to his estates and begins secret negotiations with the Russians. Haugwitz, with his pro-French policy, becomes dominant in
Berlin.

April 1 Prussia begins the final annexation of Hanover.

July 12 Prussian rapprochement with Russia; Hardenberg's
foreign policy becomes dominant.

22 Having established the Confederation of the Rhine, Napoleon invites Frederick William to form a confederation of Northern
States 'to give imperial dignity to the House of Brandenburg'.

August 9 Prussian army mobilises.

September 26 Prussian ultimatum to Napoleon requiring him to
take his troops back across the Rhine by 8 October.

October 14 Battles of Jena and Auerstädt.

27 Napoleon enters Berlin.

November 16 Prussian envoys sign the Convention of Charlottenburg with Napoleon.

21 Frederick William refuses to ratify the terms of the Convention.

1807 January 3 Conflict between Stein and Frederick William over the former's refusal of the position of foreign minister, his support for Hardenberg, and his outspokenness. Stein is dismissed.

June 25 Franco–Prussian armistice.

30 Meeting between Frederick William and Napoleon; the latter urges Hardenberg's dismissal and his replacement with Stein.

July 3 Hardenberg dismissed.

9 Treaty of Tilsit between France and Prussia; the latter is greatly reduced in size losing all territory west of the Elbe and most of her Polish lands.

12 Treaty of Königsberg requires a war contribution be paid by Prussia to France. France requires also that the Prussian army be reduced to a maximum of 42,000 men.

October 3 Stein is nominated principal minister with wide powers.

9 Emancipation Edict, to take effect from 8 October 1810. The edict frees the serfs, abolishes distinctions affecting land tenure thus creating a free market in land, and abrogates all class distinctions in occupations or callings. Supplementary edicts suppress trade monopolies in food and textiles, and later (1810) in building, clothing and furnishing.

December (to March 1808) Fichte's 14 Sunday evening lectures in Berlin urging German self-assertion against Napoleon.

1808 January The court and government move from Memel to Königsberg.

April Publication of Fichte's lectures *Reden an die deutsche Nation* (Addresses to the German Nation).

League of Virtue (*Tugendbund*) founded as a focus for anti-French feeling.

June 30 Frederick William licenses the public statutes of the *Tugendbund* which conceal its anti-French intent.

July 27 Stein proposes an Austro–Prussian alliance to drive the French from Germany. A letter from Stein to this effect is captured by French troops.

August 31 Scharnhorst presents a proposal for creating a reserve army by means of the *Krümpersystem* of short service training.

November 19 Law on Municipal Government creates a degree of self-government in the towns with property owners electing aldermen and executive councillors.

24 Under pressure from Napoleon, and as a result of the revelations of Stein's seized letters, Frederick William is forced to dismiss Stein.

1809 February 20 Wilhelm von Humboldt is made responsible for Prussian education.

May Major von Schill leads his hussar regiment out of Berlin on the pretext of manoeuvres. He attempts to organise a national uprising. The attempt is unsuccessful and in the ensuing fighting (against Danish and Dutch troops) Schill's force is overwhelmed and he is killed (31 May).

December 23 Prussian court returns to Berlin.

31 The *Tugendbund* is dissolved by royal decree.

1810 June 4 Hardenberg appointed head of the government and continues the kinds of reform begun by Stein.

July 19 Death of Queen Louise.

September 14 Hardenberg meets Stein in secret at Hermsdorf.

October 27 Hardenberg is given title of Chancellor; the system of government with a Chancellor as head replaces Stein's plan for a collegiate system of ministers. All remaining guild restrictions are abolished completing the creation of industrial freedom. This is followed by a series of edicts abolishing tax exemptions and introducing new taxes in an attempt to solve the financial problems resulting from the payments due to France.

1811 September 14 New edict relating to land tenure makes peasants free proprietors of two-thirds of their holdings, the other third being given to their former landlords in compensation. Those peasants with the smallest holdings, however, become landless labourers. Both this and the edict of 1807 are subsequently limited by an edict of 26 May 1816 confining full emancipation to the better-off peasants.

1812 February 24 Prussia promises Napoleon 20,000 men for war against Russia.

March 11 Emancipation of the Jews in Prussia.

December 30 Convention of Tauroggen, signed between General Yorck and the Russians, makes Prussian troops with Napoleon's army neutrals.

1813 January 22 Frederick William leaves Berlin, which is occupied by French troops, for Breslau.

February 3 *Jäger* scheme introduced enabling men who could afford to purchase their own uniforms and equipment to volunteer ahead of conscription.

5–7 Summoned by Stein, now in service of the Tsar, the provincial estates of East Prussia (*Landtag*) meet in Königsberg and agree to raise 20,000 men.

9 *Landwehr* (militia) established; all men aged between 17 and 40 and not in the regular army or serving as *Jäger* were invited to volunteer.

26 Prussia signs treaty of Kalisch with Russia.

March 17 Prussia declares war on France. Frederick William issues patriotic appeals to his people (*An mein Volk*) and his army (*An mein Kriegsheer*) to prepare for sacrifices in their common cause.

April 21 *Landsturm* (home guard) established, though the law is not made public till June.

June 4 Armistice of Poischwitz with the French, but Prussia continues mobilising partly because of Napoleon's own efforts and also because she does not want to be overshadowed by Austria. The enormous size of the Prussian military commitment in the War of Liberation gives her authority at the peace settlement.

10. Russia

1800 February Tsar Paul expels the comte de Provence and the French *émigré* court from his territories.

December 16 Paul instigates the Armed Neutrality against Britain.

1801 January 20,000 Cossacks are ordered from Orenburg to invade British India. The Cossack army is destroyed by appalling weather and the invasion never takes place.

March 23 Paul is assassinated in a palace coup. His son Alexander becomes Tsar and reinstates some 12,000 army officers and civil servants dismissed by Paul.

April–June Alexander restores many of the governmental and administrative practices of Catherine the Great. He also begins a series of discussions with a group of young men – 'the Unofficial Committee' (Adam Czartoryski, Paul Stroganov, Victor Korchubey and Nicholas Novosiltsov). These continue throughout 1802 and 1803 and consider a constitutional charter, a bill of rights, and freeing the serfs.

1802 September 8 Eight specialised ministries are established replacing the old collegiate boards. In theory they are subject to the Senate, though this never becomes the case in practice. The ministers are to meet in committee; this never develops into a formal cabinet, but becomes an important assembly for considering matters of importance.

1803 February 20 The Free Labourers Law permits noble landowners to liberate their serfs and provides for small lots of land to be given to the latter. The law is not taken up by many landowners; less than 50,000 serfs are freed under its provisions.

1805 April Russia formally joins the coalition against Napoleon.
December 2 Battle of Austerlitz.

1806 July Russian alliance with Prussia.
October 16 Following the Turks' deposition of the rulers of Moldavia and Wallachia a Russian army crosses the Dniester.
December 24 Russian troops enter Bucharest.

27 Turkey declares war on Russia.

1807 February 8 Battle of Eylau.

June 14 Battle of Friedland.

25 Alexander and Napoleon meet at Tilsit.

July 7 Treaty of Tilsit between France and Russia.

August A shortlived armistice is arranged with Turks; both sides agree to withdraw from Moldavia and Wallachia, but the fighting is soon resumed.

1808 February Outbreak of Russo–Swedish war.

Mikhail Speranski increasingly becomes Alexander's principal advisor. He is made secretary of the commission for codifying the laws; he attempts a series of reforms, notably examinations for promotion in state service, which anger the nobility.

September 27–October 14 Alexander meets Napoleon at Erfurt, leading to the Convention of Erfurt (12 Oct). But relations between the two are cool: Alexander is disappointed by Napoleon's continuing demands on Prussia, by French garrisons on the Oder, and by the lack of assistance he has received against Turkey. Napoleon's proposal that he might marry a Russian princess (in place of Josephine) receives a non-committal response, but on his return to St. Petersburg Alexander announces the engagement of his only marriageable sister to the heir to the Duchy of Oldenburg.

November Armistice with Sweden.

1809 Speranski is directed to present proposals for improving the government and administration. He presents a draft Statute of State Laws which, drawing on the French Constitution of 1799, proposes an executive of ministers, a legislature of four tiers of elected assemblies (*duma*), and a judiciary headed by the Senate. There is also to be a Council of State composed of elder statesmen, advisors to the Tsar. Only the latter is established.

September 17 Peace of Fredrickshamm with Sweden. Russia gains Finland and Aaland

1810 January 1 The Council of State is formally opened with Speranski as the Imperial Secretary.

December 31 Alexander formally breaks with the Continental System.

1812 March 17 Speranski's enemies succeed in persuading the Tsar to dismiss him.

April 5 Russo–Swedish alliance to support the latter's conquest of Norway.

May 28 Peace of Bucharest with Turkey.

June 24 French troops cross the Niemen beginning the invasion of Russia.

September 7 Battle of Borodino.

14 French troops enter Moscow.

October 19 French troops evacuate Moscow.

December 16 The remnant of the French army recrosses the Niemen.

Alexander authorises the foundation of the Russian Bible Society intended to spread the Bible in the languages of the Empire. The first president is the Procurator of the Holy Synod, Prince A.N. Golitsin.

1813 February 28 Russo–Prussian alliance agreed at Kalisch.

March 14 Temporary Supreme Council set up in Poland. Alexander orders no reprisals against, and no victimisation of, the Poles for their support of Napoleon.

1815 The Congress of Vienna agrees to most Polish lands coming under Russian rule.

November 27 Alexander signs the Constitutional Charter establishing a parliamentary system for Poland. He regards this as an experiment for future developments in Russia proper.

December 24 A.A. Arakcheyev is appointed Deputy President of the Committee of Ministers with the task of supervising its deliberations. The ministries are reformed over the next decade; Arakcheyev becomes the focal point of government. This is to be a period of reaction, known as *arakcheyeshchina.*

1816–21 Arakcheyev develops the idea of, and establishes, military colonies. Troops are settled on the land as farmers and small manufacturers; the idea is to reduce the upkeep of the army and improve farming. The former is particularly pressing given the enormous expenditure incurred during the wars with France and Turkey.

1816 February Union of Salvation founded as a secret society by a group of Guards Officers (it becomes the Union of Welfare in 1817). The Union seeks constitutional government and the abolition of serfdom.

1817 February Alexander instructs Arakcheyev to prepare a plan for the emancipation of the serfs. The plan comes to nothing, but the serfs without land in the Baltic provinces are freed (Estland, 1811; Kurland, 1817; Livonia, 1819).

October Education and the Church are combined in the Ministry of Spiritual Affairs with Golitsin (Minister of Education since 1816) as Minister.

1818 March Alexander opens the *Sejm* (parliament) in Warsaw and instructs Novosiltsov to prepare a draft constitution for Russia. The draft is prepared, but never introduced.

1825 November 19 Death of Alexander.

December 14 Nicholas, Alexander's brother, proclaims himself Tsar; the secret societies in the army, already conspiring against Alexander, launch the unsuccessful Decembrist Revolt.

11. Scandinavia

There were two Scandinavian states at the beginning of the Napoleonic period, Sweden and the 'twin kingdoms' of Denmark and Norway. Their histories were closely intertwined, therefore they are considered together here.

1800 April 3 Gustavus IV crowned King of Sweden.

August The Danes had introduced a system of sending their merchant ships in convoy protected by warships; this enabled them to resist the British claims to the right of search. A British squadron is therefore ordered to Copenhagen to force the Danes to stop using convoys.

December The Armed Neutrality of Denmark, Russia and Sweden is organised against Britain.

1801 January Ships of the Armed Neutrality in British ports are seized. The British occupy the Danish West Indies.

April 2 Nelson wins the battle of Copenhagen. The British fleet prepares to sail against the Swedes, but the assassination of Tsar Paul and the defeat of the Danes bring about the collapse of the Armed Neutrality.

1805 January 14 Sweden agrees to admit Russian troops on to her territory for war against France.

October Following the battle of Trafalgar the Scandinavian states, both with large merchant marines, recognise that it is not in their interest to quarrel with Britain. Gustavus IV of Sweden, incensed by the execution of the duc d'Enghien, joins the coalition against Napoleon.

1806 September 9 The end of the Holy Roman Empire encourages Denmark to incorporate Holstein into its territory and to promote the Danish language there.

November 5 Bernadotte, in pursuit of Blücher's Prussian army after Jena, captures Lübeck, and with it a division of Swedish troops sent to aid the Prussians.

1807 July 9 Treaty of Tilsit between France and Russia makes the Danes fearful of a French attempt to force them to close their ports to British ships; a Danish army moves to Holstein to repel any French attack. At the same time the British are concerned about the French occupying Denmark and acquiring Danish warships and naval stores.

16 5000 British troops arrive off Rügen encouraging Gustavus IV to participate in a new offensive against France.

August 16 British troops land in Denmark.

20 With their British support withdrawn to assist in the attack on Denmark, the Swedes are forced to sue for an armistice with the French and they withdraw from Pomerania and Rügen.

September 2–7 British bombardment of Copenhagen, ends with Danish surrender and British carrying off or destroying Danish ships and stores. The Danes, now left with just one ship of the line, decide on a formal alliance with Napoleon and subsequently declare war on Britain; this creates particular problems for the Kingdom of Norway. Norwegian trade was closely linked to Britain; the end of this trade and the British blockade has a serious effect on the country. Contact is almost lost with Copenhagen, and the Danes create a Government Commission to supervise Norway (*Regjeringskommission*) under Prince Christian Augustus.

1808 February Without a declaration of war the Russians invade Finland (Swedish territory).

March Death of Christian VII of Denmark, and the succession of his son, Frederick VI (who has been acting as regent since 1784).

The Anglo–French conflict spreads to Scandinavia with the Dano–Swedish war. French troops under Bernadotte support the Danes.

May A British expedition under Sir John Moore, arrives off Gothenburg to aid the Swedes. Moore meets Gustavus, but quarrels with him over the use of the British troops. Moore is arrested, escapes to his troop transports, and takes his army back to Britain.

The Russians capture the key fortress of Sveaborg in Finland.

November A succession of defeats by the Russians results in the Swedes agreeing to abandon Finland.

December 7 Having checked a Swedish invasion of Norway, Christian Augustus concludes an armistice with the Swedes.

1809 March 13 Following the loss of Finland and the lack of success against the Danes, a group of army officers seize Gustavus IV and imprison him in the castle of Gripsholm. A provisional government is established under Gustavus's uncle, Duke Charles.

29 Gustavus voluntarily abdicates hoping to save the crown for his son.

May 1 The *Riksdag* is called by the provisional government. Plans are prepared for a new constitution and the election of a new king. The new constitution is based on the separation of powers between the executive (the King and his chosen ministers), the legislature (the *Riksdag*), and the judiciary; the *Riksdag* is confirmed as having the right to vote taxes.

Russian troops prepare to attack Stockholm; Britain advises the Swedes to make peace.

June 5 Duke Charles accepts the constitution and is proclaimed Charles XIII. The new king is old and childless therefore the *Riksdag* looks for a crown prince: King Frederick VI of Denmark is considered, partly because he would unite Scandinavia, but rejected because of his absolutist principles; Christian Augustus is chosen, partly in the hope that this might occasion the union of Sweden and Norway, but also because of his popularity.

September 17 Treaty of Fredrickshamm concludes the Russo–Swedish war; Sweden cedes Finland.

December 10 Peace of Jönköping between Denmark and Sweden with no territory changing hands.

1810 January Peace signed between France and Sweden; Christian Augustus enters Sweden as crown prince.

May Sudden death of Christian Augustus leads to rumours of poisoning which generate social and political unrest. The *Riksdag* is forced to seek a new crown prince.

August 21 French Marshal Bernadotte accepts the offer to be crown prince of Sweden. He was chosen in the belief that he would bring stability and might ensure the return of Finland; Bernadotte was singled out because of his good treatment of the Swedish prisoners at Lübeck.

October 20 Bernadotte arrives in Sweden; he adopts the Lutheran faith; he effectively becomes regent for the old king.

November Sweden declares war on Britain, but does not pursue the conflict with any vigour.

1811 February 25 Napoleon refuses the Swedish request that he acquiesce in their acquisition of Norway. He instructs the Swedes to enforce the continental system or else he will occupy Swedish Pomerania.

1812 January Angered by the Swedish reluctance to press the war against Britain Napoleon occupies Swedish Pomerania.

April Bernadotte meets the Tsar in Finland; negotiations between them result in the Russians agreeing to help the Swedes conquer Norway and Bernadotte promises, once this is achieved, to lead a Swedish army in support of the Russians against Napoleon.

1813 January Denmark, having vigorously pursued the war against Britain, is ruined economically; the country is formally declared bankrupt.

March 3 Britain agrees to the Russo–Swedish compact of the previous April by the Treaty of Stockholm.

April Prussia agrees to the Russo–Swedish compact.

May Frederick VI of Denmark sends his cousin and heir presumptive, Christian Frederick, to Norway as *Stattholder*.

18 Bernadotte lands troops at Stralsund, but does little with them, leading to friction between the allies.

July 12 Compact of Trachenberg settles the differences between the allies. Bernadotte's Swedes become fully engaged in the war against Napoleon.

1814 January 14 By the Treaty of Kiel Denmark renounces sovereignty over Norway in favour of Sweden; but the Norwegians reject the agreement insisting that it violates international law and that they have the right to determine their own sovereignty.

May 17 A Norwegian representative assembly meets at Eidsvoll. It agrees a liberal constitution and elects the *Stattholder* Christian Frederick as king. This action leads to a Swedish invasion but, almost simultaneously, to negotiations.

August 14 The Convention of Moss is agreed whereby Norway is to keep her new, independent constitution but recognising the King of Sweden as her king.

October Meeting of a Special *Storting* (legislature) in Oslo receives Christian Frederick's abdication and ratifies the Convention of Moss.

November 4 Charles XIII of Sweden is elected King of Norway.

12. Spain

1800 October 7 Convention of San Ildefonso signed with France, confirmed by the Treaty of Aranjuez, 21 March 1801.

Godoy is returned to power as generalissimo.

1801 May–June War of the Oranges against Portugal, concluded by the Treaty of Badajoz. Spain acquires the small frontier district of Olivenza.

1803 October Threatened by Napoleon, Spain promises him a monthly payment of 6m. francs and agrees to enforce Portuguese neutrality.

1804 October 5 Four British frigates stop four Spanish frigates carrying Peruvian treasure to Cadiz.

December 12 Spain declares war on Britain. Plans are begun for the combined French and Spanish fleets to draw off the British channel fleet thus enabling Napoleon to mount an invasion.

1805 October 21 Franco–Spanish fleet defeated at Trafalgar.

1806 February Godoy proposes the dismemberment of Portugal to Napoleon.

1807 October 27 Convention of Fontainebleau signed with France authorising French troops to march through Spain to attack Portugal.

29 Godoy persuades Charles IV to arrest his son and heir, Ferdinand, insisting that Ferdinand is plotting the death of his parents. In the resulting confusion Napoleon pours additional troops into Spain.

1808 February Recognising that Napoleon has designs on Spain Godoy is prepared to fight.

March 17 Charles IV in Aranjuez is faced with a popular uprising – the *Motín de Aranjuez* – spearheaded by the Royal Guards. This is the first pronunciamento by soldiers in Spanish history. Charles abdicates, Godoy is arrested, Ferdinand VII becomes king.

23 Murat enters Madrid at the head of a French army.

April 10 Ferdinand VII leaves Madrid to meet Napoleon.

May 2 An uprising by the people of Madrid against Murat's troops – the *Dos de Mayo* – is brutally suppressed.

5 Charles IV and Ferdinand VII meet Napoleon at Bayonne. They both agree to renounce the Spanish throne: Charles retires to Rome; Ferdinand moves to Valençay where he spends the next six years under military guard.

The popular insurrection against the French, combined with a revolution against the old order, spreads across Spain with juntas declaring for Ferdinand in, e.g. Oviedo (24 May), Zaragoza (25 May), Galicia (30 May), Catalonia (7 June).

July 7 Joseph Bonaparte is crowned King of Spain and the Indies at Burgos.

20 Joseph enters Madrid.

21 A French army is defeated at Bailén by the army of the Seville Junta.

August 1 Joseph leaves Madrid to take refuge on the frontier.

September Representatives of the provincial juntas meet in Aranjuez as the Central Junta.

November Napoleon launches an attack against the Spanish armies on the line of the Ebro.

December 4 Madrid surrenders to the French.

1809 February 20 Zaragoza falls to the French after an appalling siege of three months in which perhaps 40,000 died. Its commander, Palafox, becomes a national hero.

May 22 The Central Junta proposes calling a reformed Cortes.

July 27–28 Battle of Talavera.

November 19 Junta's armies defeated at Ocaña and Alba de Tormes.

1810 January–February French armies conquer Andalucia. The Central Junta is overthrown by a coup.

February 5 The French begin the siege of Cadiz where a new regency has been formed following the fall of Seville.

8 Catalonia, Aragon, Navarre and Biscay are removed from Joseph's control and put under French military jurisdiction – this is later extended to Burgos and Valladolid-Palencia-Toro in May.

April–May Juntas in Spanish America declare their independence under the pretext of declaring for Ferdinand; their assumption being that Spain is about to fall to Napoleon.

September 16 Insurrection begins in Mexico.

24 The new Cortes, elected by a system of indirect household suffrage and including representatives from the colonies, meets on the Isla de Léon outside Cadiz. It later moves to the city.

1812 March 19 The Liberal Constitution of Cadiz is issued by the Cortes, assuring freedom of the press, but not of religion, and establishing a uniform legal code for the whole country.

July 22 Battle of Salamanca leading to Joseph's departure from Madrid.

August 12 Wellington enters Madrid.

24 The French siege of Cadiz is finally raised.

1813 February 22 The Cortes abolishes the Inquisition.

June 21 Battle of Vitoria leading to the French withdrawal from Spain.

1814 March 24 Ferdinand VII returns to Spain.

April 22 *Manifiesto de las Persas,* a manifesto signed by 69 deputies to the Cortes denouncing the liberals and the Constitution of 1812.

May 4 By a military coup Ferdinand VII repudiates the Constitution of 1812.

10 The liberal leaders in Madrid are arrested.

September Francisco Espoz y Mina attempts a military coup in Pamplona; the first of several such attempts involving officers, resentful of the way in which Ferdinand favoured young noblemen who had not served in the war, and other ranks, disaffected over pay and the prospect of being sent to the Americas to put down colonial independence movements.

1815 May Spanish troops refuse to march against Napoleon unless they are paid.

September Unsuccessful military coup in Corunna.

1817 April Unsuccessful military coup in Catalonia.

1819 July Military conspiracy led by Major Rafael Riego and the Conde del Abisbal in Cadiz collapses when the latter defects.

1820 January 1 Pronunciamento by Riego in Cadiz in favour of the Constitution of 1812.

February The military revolt spreads across Spain.

March 7 Ferdinand VII accepts the Constitution and appoints a new ministry.

July 9 The Cortes assembles.

August 31 Riego enters Madrid in triumph.

But political instability continues with a succession of short-lived governments and army rebellions, which eventually lead to

1823 April 7 Invasion of Spain by French troops to restore order and to restore Ferdinand to full power.

13. Switzerland

Since the Middle Ages Switzerland had been a federation of cantons with no strong central power. The French occupation in April 1798 led to the creation of the Helvetic Republic with a directory of five and a bicameral legislature elected by universal manhood suffrage. A military alliance with France led to an Austro–Russian invasion in 1799 and fighting which ravaged the country.

1801 May Napoleon grants a new constitution, but unrest and disorder continue.

1802 September 30 Napoleon decrees the Act of Mediation (amplified 19 Feb 1803) which revises the administrative structure and redefines the boundaries of the 19 cantons in the Helvetic Confederation. Each canton is allowed control of its own customs, education and money, but freedom before the law is guaranteed throughout the confederation. The six city cantons – Zürich, Berne, Solothurn, Fribourg, Basel and Lucerne – become directing cantons, each having seniority in turn with its chief magistrate for the year acting as *Landamann* for the confederation with custody of the seal of the republic and the presidency of the assembly. Napoleon is named protector of the confederation.

Over the next decade the confederation remains closely allied to France participating in the Blockade and sending troops to the *Grande Armée*. Napoleon periodically separates territories from the confederation:

1806 Neuchâtel is first occupied by French troops and then given as a principality to Marshal Berthier.

1810 July The Valais is incorporated into France as the department of the Simplon.

1811 January Ticino is occupied by Franco–Italian troops ostensibly to prevent smuggling.

1813 November 15 Following the battle of Leipzig, *Landamann* Hans von Reinhard calls the Diet. This declares Swiss neutrality, but does not recall Swiss troops from the French army. There is a rise of anti-French feeling, but little unity among the Swiss.

1814–15 The Congress of Vienna guarantees Swiss neutrality and provides for a loose union of 22 cantons along the lines of that in existence before the French Revolution.

14. Turkey (The Ottoman Empire)

Turkey was a power in Europe by virtue of its occupation of the Balkans which gave it frontiers with Austria and Russia. The hospodars (governors) of the frontier provinces of Moldavia and Wallachia were usually wealthy Greeks and while not authorised to conduct foreign affairs, they were becoming more and more involved with Austria and Russia.

Selim III had become Sultan in 1789. He admired French culture and, concerned by defeats at the hands of Austria and Russia at the beginning of his reign, he embarked on a series of reforms. These provoked hostility, especially his attempts to Europeanise the army which infuriated the janissaries, the traditional military force of the empire. Throughout the Napoleonic period the reforms begun by Selim, and the hostility of the janissaries, created conflict at the heart of the empire.

General Bonaparte's expedition to Egypt had brought France and Turkey into conflict.

1801 October 9 Preliminary peace agreement with France (finalised June 1802).

1804 February–March Kara George is elected leader of the Serbian insurgents against Ottoman rule.

1806 August The Serbs defeat two Turkish armies.

October Turkish action against the hospodars of Moldavia and Wallachia leads to a Russian army crossing the Dniester.

November The British order the Sultan to make peace with Russia; a British fleet sails off the coast of Constantinople, but is driven off.

1807 An uprising against Selim's reforms spreads to Constantinople and culminates on

May 29 Selim is deposed and replaced by his cousin, Mustapha IV, who proceeds to reverse the reforms.

July At Tilsit Napoleon seeks to mediate between Russia and Turkey, this leads to

August Armistice in the fighting in Moldavia and Wallachia, which is soon ignored by both sides.

Winter Reformers persuade Bairaktar Pasha to march on Constantinople.

1808 July 28 Bairaktar Pasha's army deposes Mustapha, but Selim has been murdered by the janissaries. Mahmud II (Mustapha's brother) becomes sultan, appoints Bairaktar Pasha as grand vizier, and reforms are reintroduced.

November Janissaries attack Bairaktar Pasha's house, where he is killed; but their attack on the Sultan is repulsed with heavy losses. Mahmud temporarily halts the reform programme.

December 26 The National Council of Serbia recognise Kara George and his descendants as hereditary rulers.

1809 June 5 Treaty of friendship between Britain and Turkey signed at Charnack.

1812 May 28 Helped by British mediation a peace treaty is concluded at Bucharest between Russia and Turkey. Russia annexes Bessarabia (part of Wallachia); Turkey is now free to turn against Kara George.

1813 September Kara George is forced to flee to Austria (moving to Russia in 1814).

October Turkish troops occupy Belgrade.

1815 August The Serbian revolt, renewed under Milosh Obrenovich, results in a degree of Serbian autonomy (extended in December) with Milosh being recognised by the Sultan as governor.

15. The United States

1800 November 17 Congress meets in Washington for the first time.

December 3 Election for president with Aaron Burr and Thomas Jefferson running as Democratic-Republican nominees, and John Adams and Charles C. Pinckney the Federalist candidates.

1801 February 11 The ballots for the election are counted, Burr and Jefferson win, but tie with 73 votes each.

17 After much manoeuvring, mainly the work of Alexander Hamilton, Jefferson is chosen as president with Burr as vice-president.

March 4 Jefferson inaugurated.

May 14 The Pasha of Tripoli (a centre for the Barbary Pirates) declares war on the US dissatisfied with American tribute payments.

October 16 Robert R. Livingston sails for France as American minister.

1802 October 16 Louisiana has been French territory since October 1800, but the Spanish governor has been left in post. He abolishes the right of American citizens to deposit goods, brought down the Mississippi, in New Orleans before being loaded on ocean-going ships. The move determines Jefferson to seek to purchase New Orleans.

1803 January 12 Jefferson appoints James Monroe Envoy Extraordinary to France to attempt to buy New Orleans and, if possible, Florida.

March 1 Ohio becomes the 17th state.

April 11 Talleyrand informs Livingston that France is prepared to sell the whole of Louisiana.

12 Monroe arrives in France.

May 2 Monroe and Livingston sign a treaty and two conventions with France purchasing Louisiana for $15m., and thus doubling the size of the United States.

October 20 The Senate ratifies the Louisiana Purchase.

31 A frigate, the USS Philadelphia, runs aground off Tripoli and is captured.

December 20 The US takes possession of the southern part of Louisiana in a ceremony at New Orleans.

1804 February 16 American seamen sail into Tripoli harbour and sink the USS Philadelphia.

March 9 The US takes possession of the northern part of Louisiana in a ceremony at St. Louis.

Federalist extremists in New England, concerned that the Louisiana Purchase will lead to them being in a permanent minority in the US, contemplate secession from the union. Burr runs for the governorship of New York as part of this separatist movement.

April 25 Burr is heavily defeated in the New York election, and blames his defeat on Hamilton.

July 11 Duel between Burr and Hamilton; the latter is mortally wounded.

August–September Tripoli is bombarded by US ships.

September 25 The 12th Amendment to the Constitution is adopted providing for separate elections for president and vice-president so as to prevent any repetition of the problem created in February 1801.

December 5 Jefferson is re-elected president; George Clinton, vice-president.

1805 April 26 US Marines capture the port of Derna near Tripoli.

June 4 End of war against Barbary Pirates. The US agrees to pay $60,000 ransom for the crew of USS Philadelphia, but the annual tribute to Tripoli is discontinued.

1806 February 12 The Senate condemns British seizures of American cargoes and seamen.

April 18 Congress adopts the Non-Importation Act forbidding the importation of British goods; this is to take effect from November 15.

December 19 Jefferson suspends the Non-Importation Act.

31 Treaty negotiated in London by James Monroe and William Pinkney to protect American ships. But Jefferson does not believe that the Senate will ratify it and does not submit it for such (March 1807).

1807 February 19 Burr is arrested and charged with conspiring to lead an expedition against Spanish territory (there remains doubt about his actual intentions). He is subsequently (24 June) indicted for treason.

June 22 HMS Leopard fires on USS Chesapeake and seizes four seamen.

July 2 Jefferson orders British warships to leave American waters. They do not.

August 3–September 1 Trial and acquittal of Burr. He goes into voluntary exile in Europe until 1812.

December 22 Jefferson signs the Embargo Act forbidding American citizens from participation in maritime trade. The act provokes discontent particularly among New England merchants.

1808 January 9 A new Embargo Act seeks to strengthen the first (a third act is passed 12 March).

December 7 James Madison is elected president; George Clinton is vice-president.

1809 January 9 The Enforcement Act provides for the seizure of any goods suspected of being intended for shipment in violation of the Embargo Act.

February 23 Jonathan Trumbull, Governor of Connecticut, condemns the Embargo Acts as unconstitutional.

March 1 The Non-Intercourse Act repeals the Embargo Acts. American citizens are allowed to engage in maritime trade once again, but not with either Britain or France. The president is empowered to restore trade relations with either combatant providing it rescinds its orders and decrees affecting neutral commerce.

4 Madison inaugurated.

April 19 Following an agreement with David Erskine, the British minister in Washington, that Britain can exempt US ships from the Orders in Council, Madison proclaims the restoration of trade with Britain. But Britain repudiates Erskine's proposal and Madison reinstates the Non-Intercourse Act against her (9 August).

1810 May 1 The Non-Intercourse Act is replaced by Macon's Bill No. 2 (proposed by Nathaniel Macon of North Carolina). This restores trade with Britain and France but orders that, if one of the two ceases its restrictions on neutral shipping by 3 March 1811, then the president may prohibit trade with the other power unless it also ceases its restrictions within the following three months.

November 2 In the belief that the French have abolished their restrictions on neutral shipping Madison issues a proclamation prohibiting trade with Britain from 2 March 1811, unless the Orders in Council are rescinded.

1811 May 16 The frigate, USS President, fires on the corvette,

HMS Little Belt in the belief that it has impressed American seamen. Nine British seamen are killed.

1812 April 10 Britain informs the US that since the French have not rescinded their decrees against neutral shipping then the Orders in Council will remain in force.

June 4 Louisiana becomes the 18th state.

18 US declares war on Britain. The elite of New England are opposed to the war; Massachusetts declares a fast against the war and, with Connecticut, refuses the federal government's request for militia.

November The British blockade Delaware and Chesapeake Bays seriously disrupting American coastal traffic.

December 2 Madison is re-elected president; Elbridge Gerry is vice-president.

1813 May 27 The British blockade is extended from the Gulf Coast to New York.

November 19 The British blockade is extended to cover Long Island Sound.

1814 January Madison accepts a proposal from Castlereagh to start peace negotiations.

April 25 The British blockade is extended to New England.

August 8 Peace negotiations open at Ghent.

24–25 British troops enter Washington and burn the public buildings (including the White House).

December 15 Representatives from the New England states, angry at the war and concerned about the rise of slaveholder power within the US, meet at the Hartford Convention.

24 Treaty of Ghent ends the war.

1815 January 5 The Hartford Convention ends agreeing resolutions designed to limit the power of the federal government, but the peace makes these redundant.

8 Unaware of the peace British and American troops fight the battle of New Orleans.

February 11 News of the treaty reaches the US.

15 The Senate ratifies the treaty.

July 3 Commercial convention negotiated between Britain and the US; each abolishes duties discriminating against the other and the US is permitted to trade with the East Indies.

Chronologies: cultural and scientific landmarks

1800 *De la littérature* (Mme de Staël)
La Maja nue (Goya)

1801 *Die Jungfrau von Orleans* (Friedrich Schiller)
William Wordsworth and S.T. Coleridge publish the second edition of *Lyrical Ballads* with the Preface (the first edition had appeared in 1798).
Richard Trevithick's road steam-engine carries passengers.
Elgin Marbles brought to London (purchased by British Museum in 1816).

1802 *Delphine* (Mme de Staël)
La génie du Christianisme (Chateaubriand)
Joseph Gay-Lussac discovers his law on the expansion of gases (his key text on the subject is published in 1809).

1803 Canova begins work on the Tomb for Vittorio Alfieri in Florence (finished 1810)
Traité d'economie politique (J.B. Say)
Second edition, enlarged and amended of *An Essay on the Principle of Population* (Thomas Malthus) (first edition, 1798)
Robert Fulton's steamboat Clermont sails on the Seine.

1804 *René* (Chateaubriand)
Wilhelm Tell (Schiller)
Eroica (Beethoven) (The symphony was originally planned as a celebration of Napoleon, but disillusion with the emperor led Beethoven to declare on the version published in Vienna in 1806 that it 'celebrates the memory of a great man'.)
Les pestiférés de Jaffa (Gros)

1805 *Fidelio* (Beethoven) (First staged in Vienna, it was cut for performances in 1806, and the final version appeared in 1814.)
Wordsworth completes a major revision of *The Prelude* (final version appears 1819).

1806 *Adolphe* (Benjamin Constant)
La bataille d'Aboukir (Gros)
Memoir on Electrochemistry (Humphrey Davy)
The Vendôme Column is begun in Paris (finished 1810), as are the Arc du Carrousel (finished 1808) and the Arc de Triomphe (finished 1836).

1807 *Sun rising through vapour* (J.M.W. Turner)
The church of La Madeleine in Paris is redesigned, initially as

Napoleon's Temple of Glory (then handed back to the Catholic Church; the rebuilding is finished in 1842).

The first gas lamps are used for street lighting in London.

1808 *Pastoral Symphony* (Beethoven)
Reden an die deutsche Nation (Fichte)
Faust (Goethe)
Dos de Mayo (Goya)
La bataille d'Eylau (Gros)
Marmion (Walter Scott)

1809 *Philosophie zoologique* (Lamarck)
Quarterly Review founded

1810 *Los Desastres de la Guerra* (Goya)
First edition of *Annales de mathématiques.*

1811 *Sense and Sensibility* (Jane Austen) published (written 1797–98)
Dedham Vale (John Constable)
Garden of the Hesperides (J.M.W. Turner)

1812 First and second cantos published of *Childe Harold* (Lord Byron) (third and fourth published 1816 and 1818 respectively).
Officier de chasseurs à cheval (Géricault)
Kinder- und Hausmärchen (Jakob and Wilhelm Grimm's collected fairytales begin publication)
Nash submits design for Regent's Park, London.
Gesellschaft der Musikfreunde established in Vienna.

1813 *Pride and Prejudice* (Jane Austen) published (written 1796–97)
Cuirassier blessé quittant le feu (Géricault)
A New View of Society (Robert Owen)
Tancredi (Rossini)
Queen Mab (Percy Bysshe Shelley)
Parliament sanctions the plan for Regent's Street.
Royal Philharmonic Society established in London.
First edition of *Journal für die reine und angewandte Mathematik*

1814 *Mansfield Park* (Jane Austen)
The Corsair (Byron)
Waverley (Scott)
The Excursion (Wordsworth)
George Stephenson's locomotive 'Blücher' makes a successful trial.

1815 *On First Looking into Chapman's Homer* (John Keats)

1816 *Emma* (Jane Austen)
    Il Barbiere di Siviglia (Rossini)

Rulers and governments

1. Europe's principal ruling families

See genealogical tables for the Bourbon monarchs on page 314, for the Bonapartes on page 315, and for the Habsburg monarchs on page 316.

2. Monarchs and principal ministers of the leading powers

Austria

While an experiment was made with a form of cabinet 1801–7 the monarch exercised direct personal rule seeking the advice of trusted ministers. The monarch's wishes could be obstructed by delegates to the different estates of the Empire, but only the nobility of Hungary, sitting in the Hungarian Diet, gave any serious trouble notably over the question of taxes and military recruitment.

Monarch
Francis II Holy Roman Emperor until 6 Aug 1806, after that Francis I, Emperor of Austria. While both Holy Roman Emperor and Emperor of Austria, Francis was also King of Hungary.

Principal ministers

1800–1801	Ferdinand, Count Trauttmansdorff (Minister of Foreign Affairs)
1801–Dec 1805	Ludwig, Count Cobenzl (Lord Chamberlain, Chancellor, and Minister of Foreign Affairs)
Dec 1805–Oct 1809	Johann, Count Stadion (Lord Chamberlain and Chancellor)
Oct 1809–Mar 1848	Klemens Metternich (Lord Chamberlain and Minister of State, Minister of Foreign Affairs, later Lord Chamberlain and Chancellor)

Britain

Executive power was nominally in the hands of the sovereign, but was, in reality exercised by a cabinet of ministers chosen by the monarch from the two houses of parliament. The upper house consisted of peers and bishops who held their seats by appointment, hereditary right or, in the case of Irish and Scottish peers, by election. Members of the lower house were elected directly from the counties and boroughs on a widely differing franchise.

Monarch

George III, from 1811 George, Prince of Wales, acted as regent because of his father's illness.

Principal ministers

William Pitt's administration (ends March 1801)

First Lord of the Treasury and Chancellor of the Exchequer	William Pitt
Foreign Secretary	Lord Grenville
Home Secretary	Duke of Portland
Secretary of War	Henry Dundas
Secretary at War	William Windham

Addington's administration (March 1801–May 1804)

First Lord of the Treasury and Chancellor of the Exchequer	Henry Addington
Foreign Secretary	Lord Hawkesbury
Home Secretary	Portland
	(from Aug 1804) Charles Philip Yorke
Secretary of War (with responsibility for the colonies)	Lord Hobart

Pitt's second administration (May 1804–Jan 1806)

First Lord of the Treasury and Chancellor of the Exchequer	Pitt
Foreign Secretary	Lord Harrowby
	(from Jan 1805) Lord Mulgrave
Home Secretary	Hawkesbury
Secretary for War and the Colonies	Earl Camden
	(from July 1805) Viscount Castlereagh

Ministry of All the Talents (Feb 1806–March 1807)

First Lord of the Treasury	Lord Grenville
Chancellor of the Exchequer	Lord Henry Petty
Foreign Secretary	Charles James Fox
	(from Sep 1806) Charles Grey, Viscount Howick

| Home Secretary | Earl Spencer |
| Secretary for War and the Colonies | Windham |

Portland's administration (March 1808–Sep 1809)

First Lord of the Treasury	Portland
Chancellor of the Exchequer and Chancellor of the Duchy of Lancaster	Spencer Perceval
Foreign Secretary	George Canning
Home Secretary	Hawkesbury (became the Earl of Liverpool in 1808)
Secretary for War and the Colonies	Castlereagh

Perceval's administration (Oct 1809–May 1812)

First Lord of the Treasury and Chancellor of the Duchy of Lancaster	Perceval
Foreign Secretary	Earl Bathurst (from Dec 1809) Marquis of Wellesley (from Apr 1812) Castlereagh
Home Secretary	Richard Ryder
Secretary for War and the Colonies	Liverpool

Liverpool's administration (from June 1812)

First Lord of the Treasury	Liverpool
Chancellor of the Exchequer	Nicholas Vansittart
Foreign Secretary	Castlereagh
Home Secretary	Viscount Sidmouth (formerly Henry Addington)
Secretary for War and the Colonies	Bathurst

France

Napoleon sought to maintain executive power in his own hands. A Council of State (40 members) chosen by Napoleon was treated as part of the executive, but drafted bills. The Constitution of the Year VIII (1799) provided for a three chamber legislature: Senate, Tribunate, and *Corps législative*. Napoleon himself chose the members of the Senate, but there was an elective element in the appointment of the other chambers. Universal manhood suffrage was established to the extent that every man was allowed to vote in his cantonal assembly for a communal list made up of one tenth of the number of voters; the men on this list selected one tenth of their number for the departmental list; the men on the departmental list then selected one tenth of their number for the national list. These indirect elections provided the Senate with a list of some 5000 men from whom they selected deputies to the Tribunate (100 members, abolished in 1807) and the *Corps législative* (legislative body, 300 members). The system was revised in 1802 and departmental electoral colleges were established; men were now appointed electors for life and were chosen from among the largest tax payers in a department. No lasting changes occurred under the first restoration, however during the Hundred Days the electoral college was revised and a Chamber of Deputies was established. This latter was maintained under the second restoration when a bicameral system similar to that in Britain was established with the creation of a chamber of peers alongside the chamber of deputies. The franchise, and the ability to stand for election, again depended on tax qualifications.

Monarchs, etc.

Napoleon Bonaparte, Consul for Life, 4 Aug 1802, Emperor, 18 May 1804, abdicated 6 Apr 1814.
Louis XVIII, King of France (first restoration, Apr 1814–Mar 1815)
Napoleon Bonaparte, Emperor (the Hundred Days, Mar–June 1815)
Louis XVIII, King of France (second restoration, from July 1815)

Principal ministers

Consulate and Empire (1800–14)
Napoleon's ministers were given departmental responsibilities but these sometimes overlapped, and the Emperor's increasing use of the Council of State also cut across departmental specialisms.

Secretary of State	Hughes Bernard Maret (Dec 1799–Apr 1811)
	Pierre Daru (Apr 1811–Nov 1813)
	Maret (Nov 1813–Apr 1814)
Finance	Charles Gaudin (Nov 1799–Apr 1814)

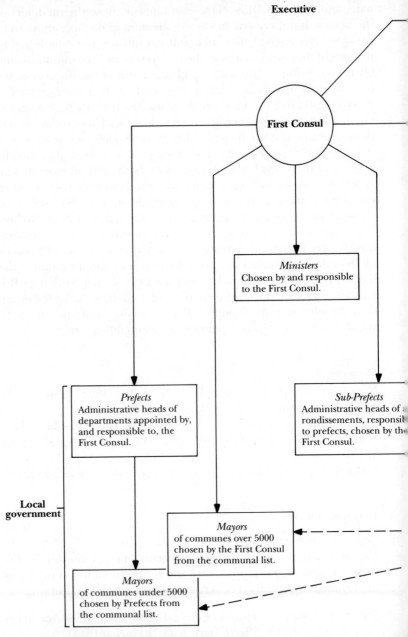

Executive

First Consul

Ministers
Chosen by and responsible
to the First Consul.

Sub-Prefects
Administrative heads of :
rondissements, responsib
to prefects, chosen by th
First Consul.

Prefects
Administrative heads of
departments appointed by,
and responsible to, the
First Consul.

**Local
government**

Mayors
of communes over 5000
chosen by the First Consul
from the communal list.

Mayors
of communes under 5000
chosen by Prefects from
the communal list.

The structure of civil government in Napoleonic France. (This system was basic
life Consulship (Constitution of the Year X/2 and 4 Aug 1802) and the empire

Legislature

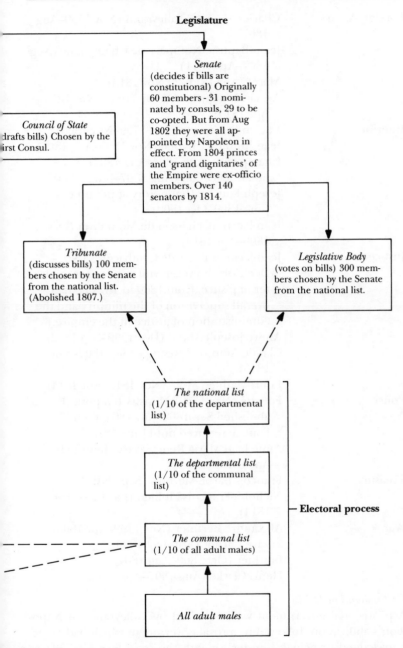

Senate
(decides if bills are constitutional) Originally 60 members - 31 nominated by consuls, 29 to be co-opted. But from Aug 1802 they were all appointed by Napoleon in effect. From 1804 princes and 'grand dignitaries' of the Empire were ex-officio members. Over 140 senators by 1814.

Council of State
(drafts bills) Chosen by the First Consul.

Tribunate
(discusses bills) 100 members chosen by the Senate from the national list. (Abolished 1807.)

Legislative Body
(votes on bills) 300 members chosen by the Senate from the national list.

The national list
(1/10 of the departmental list)

The departmental list
(1/10 of the communal list)

The communal list
(1/10 of all adult males)

All adult males

Electoral process

Established under the Constitution of the Year VIII (13 Dec 1799) and modified by the Constitution of the Year XII/18 May 1804)

101

Foreign Affairs	Charles Maurice Talleyrand (Nov 1799–Aug 1807)
	Jean–Baptiste Nompère de Champagny (Aug 1807–Apr 1811)
	Maret (Apr 1811–20 Nov 1813)
	Armand Augustin Caulaincourt (Nov 1813–Apr 1814)
Interior	Lucien Bonaparte (Dec 1799–Nov 1800)
	Jean-Antoine Chaptal (Nov 1800–Aug 1804)
	Champagny (Aug 1804–Aug 1807)
	Emmanuel Crétet (Aug 1807–June 1809)
	Joseph Fouché (temporary appointment June 1809–Oct 1809)
	Jean-Pierre Bachasson de Montalivet (Oct 1809–Apr 1814)
Justice	Jean-Jacques Régis de Cambacérès (Nov –Dec 1799; however while no longer minister of justice, from 1800 to 1814 he had overall supervision of the ministry and the administration of justice in the empire.)
	André Joseph Abrial (Dec 1799–Sep 1802)
	Claude-Ambroise Regnier (Sep 1802–Nov 1813)
	Louis-Mathieu Molé (Nov 1813–Apr 1814)
Police	Fouché (Nov 1799) Ministry temporarily abolished Sep 1802–July 1804, then Fouché restored until June 1810.
	Anne Jean Marie René Savary (June 1810–Apr 1814)
Treasury	François Barbé-Marbois (Sep 1801–Jan 1806)
	Nicholas-François Mollien (Jan 1806–Apr 1814)
War	Alexandre Berthier (Nov 1799–Apr 1800)
	Lazare Carnot (Apr–Oct 1800)
	Berthier (Oct 1800–Aug 1807)
	Henri Clarke (Aug 1807–Apr 1814)

First restoration 1814

A provisional government was organised by Talleyrand on Napoleon's abdication, followed by a royal government which had no acknowledged principal minister, though the royal favourite, Blacas d'Aulps, was sometimes seen as such.

Finance	Joseph Dominique, Baron Louis
Foreign Affairs	Talleyrand
Interior	Abbé de Montesquiou
Justice	Dambray, Charles
King's Household	Pierre Louis, duc de Blacas d'Aulps
Police	Jacques-Claude Beugnot
War	General Pierre Dupont

The Hundred Days

Finance	Gaudin
Foreign Affairs	Caulaincourt
Interior	Carnot
Justice	Cambacérès
Police	Fouché
Treasury	Mollien
War	Marshal Louis Davout

Second restoration

After Waterloo a provisional government was formed under the direction of Talleyrand and Fouché. This was replaced in Sep 1815 by a government under the direction of a former *émigré*, the duc de Richelieu.

Finance	Louis, comte de Corvetto
Foreign Affairs	Armand du Plessis, duc de Richelieu
Interior	Vincent, comte de Vaublanc
Justice	Barbé-Marbois, comte François de
War	Clarke

Prussia

The monarch ruled through his ministers who were responsible solely to him. A series of reforms were carried out following the defeat of 1806, notably, in 1808, the creation of a Council of State consisting of the King, princes of the royal house, the King's ministers and privy councillors appointed for their expertise in particular areas. Representative bodies were briefly established in 1811 and again in 1812–15 to administer new taxation.

Monarch
Frederick William III

Principal ministers

(From 1808 there were departmental ministers rather than simply a principal minister)

Foreign Affairs	Christian Heinrich Kurt, Count von Haugwitz (1792–Nov 1806)
	Karl August von Hardenberg (Apr 1804–Feb 1806, working in tandem with Haugwitz)
	Karl Friedrich von Beyme (Nov 1806–Apr 1807)
	Hardenberg (Apr–July 1807)
	Heinrich Friedrich Karl, Baron von und zum Stein (Sep 1807– Nov 1808)
	August Friedrich Ferdinand, Count Goltz (Nov 1808–June 1814)
	Hardenberg (June 1814–Sep 1818)
Interior	Alexander, Count Dohna-Schlobitten (Nov 1808–June 1810)
	Hardenberg (June 1810–June 1814)
Finance	Karl, Baron Stein zum Altenstein (Nov 1808–June 1810)
	Hardenberg (June 1810–Dec 1813)
	Ludwig von Bülow (Dec 1813–Nov 1817)
War	Gerhard Johann David von Scharnhorst (1808–1810)
	Herman Ludwig von Boyen (June 1814–1819)

Russia

The Tsar had no formal cabinet or council of ministers, but a committee of ministers with a permanent secretary evolved from 1802. There was no parliament or any other form of representative body.

Monarch

Paul I (assassinated March 1801) succeeded by his son Alexander I

Principal ministers

Finance	Count Alexei Vassiliev (1802–6)
	Fyodor Golubzov (1807–10)

	Count Dimitri Guriev (1810–23)
Foreign Affairs	Peter, Count von der Phalen (1800–2)
	Count Alexander Voronzov (1802–4)
	Prince Czartoryski (1804–7)
	Count Nicolai Rumyanzev (1807–14)
	Ivan Andreyevich Weidermeyer (1815–16)
Interior	Count Victor Kochubey (1803–7)
	Alexei Kurakin (1807–11)
	Opsi Kozodavlev (1811–19)
War	Sergei Vyazminitinov (1802–8)
	Alexei Andreyevich Arakcheyev (1808–10)
	Mikhail Andreas Barclay de Tolly (1810–12)
	Andrei Gorchakov (1812–15)
Chairman of the Council of Ministers	Count Nikolai Saltykov (1812–16)

3. Rulers of other/secondary powers

Baden

Charles Frederick, Margrave since 1738, established as Grand Duke 13 August 1806, succeeded by his grandson.
Charles Ludwig Frederick 10 June 1811.

Bavaria

Maximilian I Joseph, Elector since 1799, established as king, 1 January 1806.

Denmark

Frederick VI (Regent since 1784) succeeded his father (Christian VII) 13 March 1808. Died 8 December 1839.

The Netherlands

As the Batavian Republic it was governed by councils until 1805.
Rutger Jan Schimmelpenninck appointed Grand Pensionary, 29 April 1805.
Louis Bonaparte created King of Holland, 5 June 1806, abdicated 1 July 1810.
The Netherlands were annexed to France July 13 1810.
William I proclaimed Prince Sovereign of the Netherlands, 2 December 1813; crowned King of the United Netherlands 16 March 1815.

Portugal

Maria I succeeded as joint ruler with her husband Peter III (died 1786) 24 February 1777.
Prince John acted as regent for Maria (his mother) from 1792.
Following the French occupation (November 1807) the royal family moved to Brazil.
John VI succeeded on Maria's death, 20 March 1816.

Saxony

Frederick Augustus III succeeded his father as Elector, 17 December 1763, created King Frederick Augustus I, 11 December 1806.
The kingdom was ruled by Prussia then Russia, October 1813–January 1815, when Frederick Augustus was returned.

Spain

Charles IV succeeded his father, 14 December 1788, abdicated 20 March 1808.
Ferdinand VII succeeded his father 20 March 1808, abdicated 2 May 1808.
Joseph Bonaparte created king 6 June 1808.
Ferdinand restored 11 December 1813.

Sweden

Gustavus IV succeeded his father, 29 March 1792, abdicated, 6 June 1809.
Charles XII succeeded his brother, 6 June 1809.

Turkey

Selim III succeeded his uncle 28 April 1789, deposed 29 May 1807.

Mustapha IV succeeded his cousin, 29 May 1807, deposed 28 July 1808.

Mahmud II succeeded his brother, 28 July 1808.

The United States

John Adams, President 1797–1801.
Thomas Jefferson, President 1801–9.
James Madison, President 1809–16.

Württemberg

Frederick II succeeded his father as Duke 23 December 1797, created Elector 27 April 1803, created king 1 January 1806.

4. Principal honours and ranks bestowed by Napoleon

On the creation of the Empire in 1804 Napoleon established a new, imperial nobility which continued to expand until his fall. In round numbers he gave some 3600 titles: 42 were made princes and dukes (29 of these were military men); 500 were made counts (135 military men); 1500 were made barons (920 military men); 1500 chevaliers (almost 1200 military men). Of these, 290 individuals received two titles. The majority of the recipients were French, or were from territories newly annexed to, or associated with, France. About 1000 of the recipients were drawn from the nobility of the old regime, of these 680 were French, 170 Italian, and 60 Poles.

In addition to the new nobility Napoleon also re-established the military rank of Marshal and created an imperial court with a series of honorific and semi-honorific posts.

Dates and full names are given for those individuals not included in the biographies in Section VII.

The imperial family

Napoleon I, Emperor of the French (1804), King of Italy (1805)
Napoleon, King of Rome (1811)

Bonaparte, Jerome, Prince of France (1804), King of Westphalia (1807)
Bonaparte, Joseph, First Prince of the Blood (1804), King of Naples (1806), King of Spain (1808). Grand Elector of the Empire
Bonaparte, Louis, King of Holland (1806). High Constable of the Empire
Bonaparte, Lucien, Prince of Canino (1807)
Bacciochi, Pasquale, Prince of Piombino (1805), Prince of Lucca (1806), Grand Duke of Tuscany (1809)
Beauharnais, Eugène de, Prince (1805), Viceroy of Italy (1805). Arch-Chancellor of State
Borghese, Camillo, Italian Prince, Duke of Guastalla (1806)

Murat, Joachim, Grand Duke of Cleves (1806), King of Naples (1808). Grand Admiral of the Empire
Marshal (1804)

Beauharnais, Josephine de, Empress (1804)
Marie-Louise of Austria, Empress (1810)

Bonaparte, Caroline, Grand Duchess of Berg (1806), Queen of Naples (1808)
Bonaparte, Elisa, Princess of Piombino (1805), Princess of Lucca (1806), Grand Duchess of Tuscany (1809)
Bonaparte, Letizia, *Madame mère*, Dowager Empress (1804)
Bonaparte, Pauline, Duchess of Guastalla (1806)

Beauharnais, Hortense de, Queen of Holland (1806)

Princes of the Empire

Bernadotte, Jean, Prince of Ponte-Corvo (1806)
Marshal (1804)
Berthier, Louis-Alexandre, Prince of Neuchâtel (1806), and of Wagram (1809). Vice-Constable of the Empire, Master of the Hunt.
Marshal (1804)
Davout, Louis-Nicolas, Duke of Auerstädt (1808), Prince of Eckmül (1809)
Marshal (1804)
Masséna, André, Duke of Rivoli (1808), Prince of Essling (1810)
Marshal (1804)
Ney, Michel, Duke of Elchingen (1808), Prince of the Moskwa (1813)
Marshal(1804)
Poniatowski, Josef Anton, Polish Prince
Marshal (1813)
Talleyrand, Charles-Maurice, Prince of Benavente (1806), Vice-Grand Elector of the Empire

Dukes

Arrighi de Casanova, Jean-Toussaint (1778–1853), Duke of Padua (1808)

Augereau, Charles, Duke of Castiglione (1808)
Marshal (1804)

Bessières, Jean-Baptiste (1768–1813), Duke of Istria (1809)
Marshal (1804), Commander of the Imperial Guard

Cambacérès, Jean-Jacques, Duke of Parma (1808), Arch-Chancellor of the Empire

Caulaincourt, Armand, Duke of Vicenza (1808), Grand Master of the Horse

Clarke, Henri, Duke of Feltre (1809)

Dalberg, Emmerich-Joseph-Wolfgang-Héribert (1773–1833), Duke of Dalberg (1810)

Duroc, Gerard-Christophe-Michel (1772–1813), Duke of Friuli (1808), Grand Marshal of the Palace

Fouché, Joseph, Duke of Otranto (1809)

Gaudin, Charles, Duke of Gaëta (1809)

Junot, Andoche, Duke of Abrantès (1809), Colonel-General of Hussars

Kellermann, François-Etienne-Christophe (1735–1820), Duke of Valmy (1808)
Honorary Marshal (1804)

Lannes, Jean, Duke of Montebello (1808)
Marshal (1804)

Lebrun, Charles-François, Duke of Piacenza (1808), Arch-Treasurer of the Empire

Lefebvre, François-Joseph (1755–1820), Duke of Danzig (1807)
Honorary Marshal (1804)

MacDonald, Etienne-Jacques-Joseph-Alexandre (1765–1840), Duke of Taranto (1808)
Marshal (1809)

Maret, Hughes-Bernard, Duke of Bassano (1809)

Marmont, Auguste-Frédéric-Louis-Viesse de, Duke of Ragusa (1808)
Marshal (1809)

Melzi d'Eril, Francesco, Duke of Lodi (1807), Chancellor of the Kingdom of Italy

Moncey, (Jeannot de Moncy) Bon-Adrien (1754–1842), Duke of Conegliano (1808)
Marshal (1804)

Mortier, Adolphe-Edouard-Casimir-Joseph (1768–1835), Duke of Treviso (1808)
Marshal (1804)

Nompère de Champagny, Jean-Baptiste, Duke of Cadore (1809), Intendant-General of the Crown

Oudinot, Nicolas-Charles (1767–1847), Duke of Reggio (1810)
  Marshal (1809)
Régnier, Claude-Ambroise, Duke of Massa (1809), Grand Judge
Savary, Anne-Jean-Marie-René, Duke of Rovigo (1808)
Soult, Nicolas, Duke of Dalmatia (1808)
  Marshal (1804)
Suchet, Louis-Gabriel, Duke of Albufera da Valencia (1813)
  Marshal (1811)
Victor, Claude-Victor (1764–1841), Duke of Belluno (1808)
  Marshal (1807)

The remaining marshals

Brune, Guillaume-Marie-Anne (1763–1815),
  Marshal (1804)
Gouvion-St-Cyr, Laurent (1764–1830), Count (1808),
  Marshal (1812)
Grouchy, Emmanuel de (1766–1847), Count (1809),
  Marshal (1815)
Jourdan, Jean-Baptiste,
  Marshal (1804)
Pérignon, Catherine-Dominique de (1754–1818), Count (1811),
  Honorary Marshal (1804)
Sérurier, Jean-Mathieu-Philibert (1742–1819), Count (1809),
  Honorary Marshal (1804)

Other dignitaries of the imperial court

Boyer, Alexis, Baron (1757–1833), First Surgeon
Corvisart, Jean-Nicolas, Baron (1755–1821), First Physician
Daru, Pierre-Antoine-Nol-Bruno, Count, Intendant-General of the
  Private Domain
David, Jacques-Louis, Chevalier, First Painter
Fesch, Joseph, Cardinal and Archbishop of Lyon, Grand Almoner
La Bouillerie, François-Marie-Pierre-Roullet, Baron (1764–1833),
  Treasurer-General of the Crown and the Extraordinary Domain
Legendre de Luçay, Jean-Baptiste-Charles, Count (1754–1836),
  First Prefect of the Palace

de Montesquiou-Fezensac, Elizabeth-Pierre, Count (1764–1834), Grand Chamberlain

de Nansouty, Etienne-Marie-Antoine Champion, Count (1768–1815), First Master of the Horse

de Rémusat, Augustin-Laurent, Count (1762–1823), First Chamberlain

de Ségur, Louis-Philippe, Count (1753–1839), Grand Master of Ceremonies

The departments of Napoleon's Empire

The department (*département*) was the principal administrative unit of the French Empire. *Départements* were created initially in 1790 in the attempt to establish administrative divisions of roughly the same size in France. Given the annexations of the Revolutionary wars there were, by 1800, 98 *départements;* at its peak Napoleon's empire had 130. Each was supervised by a prefect (*préfet*), and was sub-divided into four or five *arrondissements* supervised by subprefects.

1. The French departments, and their principal town (*chef-lieu*), the seat of the departmental prefects

Ain. Bourg.
Aisne. Laon.
Allier. Moulins.
Basses-Alpes. Digne.
Hautes-Alps. Gap.
Alpes-Maritimes (established 1793). Nice.
Ardèche. Privas.
Ardennes. Charleville.
Ariège. Foix.
Aube. Troyes.
Aude. Carcassonne.
Aveyron. Rodez.
Bouches-du-Rhône. Marseille.
Calvados. Caen.
Cantal. Aurillac.
Charente. Angoulême.
Charente-Inférieure. Saintes (from 1810, La Rochelle).
Cher. Bourges.
Corrèze. Tulle.
Corse. Bastia.
 (From Aug 1793 until Aug 1811 Corsica was divided into two departments:
 Golo. Bastia; **Liamone.** Ajaccio.)
Côte-d'Or. Dijon.
Côtes-du-Nord. Saint-Brieuc.
Creuse. Guéret.
Dordogne. Périgueux.

Doubs. Besançon.

Drôme. Valence.

Eure. Evreux.

Eure-et-Loir. Chartres.

Finistère. Quimper.

Gard. Nîmes.

Haute-Garonne. Toulouse.

Gers. Auch.

Gironde. Bordeaux.

Golo, see **Corse.**

Hérault. Montpellier.

Ille-et-Vilaine. Rennes.

Indre. Châteauroux.

Indre-et-Loire. Tours.

Isère. Grenoble.

Jura. Lons-le-Saunier.

Landes. Mont-de-Marsan.

Liamone, see Corse.

Loire (established 1793 out of **Rhône-et-Loire**). Montbrison.

Haute-Loire. Le Puy.

Loire-Inférieure. Nantes.

Loiret. Orléans.

Lot. Cahors.

Lot-et-Garonne. Agen.

Lozère. Mende.

Maine-et-Loire. Angers.

Manche. Coutances (from 1801, St. Lô).

Marne. Châlons-sur-Marne.

Haute-Marne. Chaumont.

Mayenne. Laval.

Meurthe. Nancy.

Meuse. Bar-le-Duc.

Mont-Blanc (established 1792). Chambéry.

Morbihan. Vannes.

Moselle. Metz.

Nièvre. Nevers.

Nord. Douai (from 1802, Lille).

Oise. Beauvais.

Orne. Alençon.

Pas-de-Calais. Arras.

Puy-de-Dôme. Clermont-Ferrand.

Basses-Pyrénées. Pau.

Hautes-Pyrénées. Tarbes.

Pyrénées-Orientales. Perpignan.

Bas-Rhin. Strasbourg.

Haut-Rhin (this incorporated the short-lived *département* of **Mont-Terrible** established 1798–1800, with its *chef-lieu* at Porrentruy, out of recently annexed territories). Colmar.

Rhône (established 1793 out of **Rhône-et-Loire**). Lyon.

Haute-Saône. Vesoul.

Saône-et-Loire. Mâcon.

Sarthe. Le Mans.

Seine (established 1795 out of **Paris**). Paris.

Seine-et-Marne. Melun.

Seine-et-Oise. Versailles.

Seine-Inférieure. Rouen

Deux-Sèvres. Niort.

Somme. Amiens.

Tarn. Albi.

Tarn-et-Garonne (established 1808 from parts of the **Lot-et-Garonne, Lot, Aveyron, Gers** and **Haute-Garonne**). Montaubon.

Var. Draguignan.

Vaucluse (established 1793). Avignon.

Vendée. Fontenay-le-Comte (from 1811, La Roche-sur-Yon).

Vienne. Poitiers.

Haute-Vienne. Limoges.

Vosges. Epinal.

Yonne. Auxerre.

2. Departments annexed during the Revolutionary wars

Dyle (1795). Brussels.
Escaut (1795). Ghent.
Forêts (1795). Luxembourg.
Jemappes (1793–5). Tournai.
Léman (1798). Geneva.
Lys (1795). Bruges.
Meuse-Inférieure (1795). Maastricht.
Mont-Tonnerre (1797). Mainz.
Deux-Nèthes (1795). Antwerp.
Ourthe (1795). Liège.
Rhin-et-Moselle (1797). Coblenz.
Roer (1797). Aix-la-Chapelle.
Sambre-et-Meuse (1797). Namur.
Saar (1797). Trier.

3. Departments annexed in Italian and Swiss lands

Apennins (1805). Chiavari.
Arno (1808). Florence.
Doire (1802). Ivrea.
Gênes (1805). Genoa.
Marengo (1802). Alessandria.
Méditerranée (1808). Livorno.
Montenotte (1805). Savona.
Ombrone (1808). Siena.
Pô (1802). Turin.
Sesia (1802). Vercelli.
Simplon (1810). Sion.
Stura (1802). Cuneo.
Taro (1808). Parma.
Tibre (1810). Rome.
Trasimène (1810). Spoleto.

4. Departments annexed in Dutch and German lands

Bouches-de-l'Elbe (1810). Hamburg.
Ems-Occidental (1810). Groningen.
Ems-Oriental (1810). Aurich.
Ems-Supérieur (1810). Osnabrück.
Bouches-de-l'Escault (1810). Middelburg.
Frise (1810). Leeuwarden.
Lippe (1810). Münster.
Bouches-de-la-Meuse (1810). The Hague.
Bouches-du-Rhin (1810). Bois-le-Duc.
Bouches-du-Weser (1810). Bremen.
Bouches-de-l'Yssel (1810). Zwolle.
Yssel-Supérieur (1810). Arnhem.
Zuider-Zee (1810). Amsterdam.

Similar administrative divisions were created in the satellite states of the Empire. Thus the Kingdom of Italy was divided into 24 *dipartimenti* supervised by *prefetti* and their subordinate *vice-prefetti*; Westphalia was divided into eight departments; see 5 and 6 on pp. 123–4.

5. Departments of the Kingdom of Italy

Adda. Sondrio.
Adige. Verona.
Adriatico. Venice.
Agogna. Novara.
Alto Adige. Trent.
Alto Po. Cremona. Lodi.
Bacchiglione. Vicenza.
Basso Po. Ferrara. Rovigo.
Brenta. Padua.
Crostolo. Reggio.
Lario. Como.
Mella. Brescia.
Metauro. Ancona.
Mincio. Mantua.
Musone. Macerata.
Panaro. Modena.
Passariano. Udine.
Piave. Belluno.
Olona. Milan.
Reno. Bologna.
Rubicone. Forli.
Serio. Bergamo.
Tagliamento. Treviso.
Tronto. Fermo.

6. Departments of the Kingdom of Westphalia

Elbe. Magdeburg.
Fulda. Cassel.
Hartz. Heiligenstadt.
Leine. Göttingen.
Ocker. Brunswick.
Saale. Halberstadt.
Werra. Marburg.
Weser. Osnabrück.

The maps illustrating the various departments of the Empire listed above can be found between pages 306 and 311.

Economic and military potential of the leading powers

Austria; Britain; France; Prussia; Russia

1. The economic and military potential of Austria

Population

Probably around 27 million of whom 5 million were in the Kingdom of Hungary.

In 1800 only about 6 percent of the population lived in cities of 20,000 or more.

Vienna was the largest city with about 247,000 inhabitants; Prague had about 75,000 and Budapest about 54,000.

Economy

The population was mainly rural, with about a third gaining its livelihood from the primary sector (agriculture, fisheries, forestry). Agricultural production varied from relatively modern and productive (in some of the Habsburg hereditary lands and Bohemia), to backward (in the Alpine lands which had difficulties because of problems with transport), to primitive (eastern Galicia and eastern Hungary).

The Habsburgs pursued a rigorous Mercantilist policy which aimed to keep out foreign goods and create a self-sufficient empire. There was a common customs boundary to the Empire, but also some internal barriers.

The Revolutionary and Napoleonic wars had a deleterious effect on the economy, particularly illustrated by the inflation which hit the paper money (*Bankozettel*) issued to meet the wars' needs.

Table 1 **Bankozettel** *in circulation 1795–1810*

1795	35.5	million
1796	46.8	million
1800	200	million
1806	450	million
1808	650	million
1809	729	million [1]
	846	million
1810	1060	million

[1] This increase was primarily the result of the War of 1809.

The notes were called in by the *Finanzpatent* (20 Feb 1811) and exchanged for new bonds at the rate of five to one. But inflation, and new issues of paper money, continued.

Army

The strength of the army varied between 250,000 and 425,000 men during the Napoleonic period. The officers were drawn from the nobility and gentry; the rank and file were long-service volunteers and pressed men. There was a short-lived experiment in the creation of a militia in 1809.

Navy

A small force was based in the Adriatic, but it contained no line of battle ships, and even this ceased to exist when the Adriatic provinces were lost (1809–14).

2. The economic and military potential of Britain

Population

Table 2 Population (in 000s)

	1801	1811	1821
England:	8,479	9,673	11,405
Wales:	541	611	718
Scotland:	1,610	1,804	2,090
Ireland:	5,216	5,956	6,764
Total:	15,846	18,044	20,977

The majority of the population still lived close to the land, but London with 1,117,000 inhabitants at the beginning of the century, was the largest city in Europe.

Several other British cities were among the largest in Europe:

Birmingham	71,000
Dublin	165,000
Edinburgh	83,000
Glasgow	77,000
Liverpool	82,000
Manchester	75,000

Overall the British Isles had one of the largest urban populations in Europe during the Napoleonic period.

Table 3 Percentage of population living in cities and towns of over 20,000 inhabitants c.1800

	Percentage in towns of 100,000 or more	Percentage in towns of 20,000 or more
Austria	2.63	3.56
Bavaria	–	3.7
Denmark	10.9	10.9
England and Wales	9.73	16.94
France	2.8	6.7
Hungary	–	2.31
Ireland	3.1	6.6
Italy	4.45	–
The Netherlands	11.5	24.5
Portugal	9.5	10.3
Prussia	1.8	6
Russia	1.4	9.75
Saxony	–	7.7
Scotland	–	13.9
Spain	1.4	9.75
Sweden	–	3
Switzerland	–	1.3

After: A.F. Weber, *The Growth of Cities in the Nineteenth Century: A Study in Statistics* (first published 1899, reprinted Cornell University Press, New York,1963, pp. 144–45).

Economy

About a third of the population gained its livelihood from the primary sector, and just under a third from manufacturing, mining and industry. British manufacturing industry began pulling ahead of the rest of Europe, particularly in textile manufacture. At the beginning of the French Revolution there had been little significant difference between the British and French economies, but as the wars progressed the differences grew.

Table 4 British and French economic statistics (annual averages c.1780–1815)

	Britain	(period)	France	(period)
Output of grain crops (in million quintals)	35	(c.1790)	98.1	(1781–90)
	43	(c.1810)	94.5	(1803–12)
Output of coal and lignite (in million metric tons)	11.2	(1800)	0.8	(1811)
	16.2	(c.1815)	0.9	(c.1815)
Output of pig iron (in thousand metric tons)	69	(1788)	141	(1781–90)
	127	(1796)		
	248	(average 1800–13)	200	(average 1803–12)
Raw cotton consumption (in thousand metric tons)	8.1	(1781–90)	4	(1781–90)
	13.9	(1791–1800)		
	31.8	(1801–14)	8	(1803–12)

(After: Carlo M. Cipolla ed. *The Fontana Economic History of Europe: The Emergence of Industrial Societies – 2,* Collins/Fontana, London, 1973)

Table 5 *Official values of total British Exports (1802–12) (by country and zone, in £ thousands)*

	1802	1803	1804	1805	1806	1807	1808	1809	1810	1811	1812
Russia	1,282	1,260	1,200	1,508	1,692	1,700	395	879	877	731	1,807
Sweden	91	82	125	124	175	653	2,358	3,524	4,871	523	2,308
Denmark & Norway	427	1,684	3,776	4,360	1,438	4,898	21	258	236	726	757
Prussia	818	1,544	3,941	5,071	462	153	70	595	2,597	57	84
German states	8,005	5,111	1,335	1,652	5,608	351	1,532	5,953	2,153	61	199
Holland & Belgium	4,393	1,692	2,338	365	1,157	1,657	358	2,458	487	261	306
France	2,390	1,184	20	1	–	–	2	1	732	420	1,010
Total North & West Europe	*17,406*	*12,556*	*12,735*	*13,027*	*10,533*	*9,412*	*4,736*	*13,666*	*11,952*	*2,778*	*6,470*
Portugal	1,171	452	806	1,167	1,194	756	431	841	1,492	4,729	3,461
Madeira & Azores	113	109	103	228	242	264	643	589	483	380	303
Spain	1,227	741	961	105	41	91	778	2,276	1,207	1,032	951
Canaries & Balearics	81	65	37	6	34	15	111	147	186	148	109
Gibraltar	530	487	560	184	512	844	1,372	3,605	?	?	3,450
Italy, Sicily, Sardinia	1,950	642	351	490	271	534	282	343	165	266	408

Austria & Malta	21	134	114	127	261	750	2,914	2,152	?	?	5,272
Ottoman Empire	163	154	82	132	130	25	14	102	96	266	564
Total South Europe	*5,256*	*2,784*	*3,015*	*2,439*	*2,684*	*3,278*	*6,545*	*10,054*	*7,656*	*12,186*	*14,518*
Total Europe	*22,662*	*15,337*	*15,746*	*15,465*	*13,216*	*12,690*	*11,281*	*23,721*	*19,606*	*14,956*	*20,987*
United States	5,320	5,273	6,398	7,147	8,613	7,921	3,992	5,188	7,813	1,432	4,136
Ireland, Isle of Man Channel Islands	3,772	3,617	3,713	4,018	3,845	4,307	4,931	4,920	3,645	4,940	5,591
Asia	2,930	2,733	1,766	1,669	1,937	1,884	1,933	1,648	1,717	1,665	1,769
Africa	1,162	819	1,175	992	1,433	798	533	706	484	317	444
Canada	1,583	1,082	1,057	865	951	1,061	1,125	1,748	1,845	1,910	1,419
British West Indies	3,472	2,237	3,828	3,444	4,212	4,087	5,453	} 8,352	7,284	?	4,397
West Indies under British occupation	344	108	486	487	816	702	1,493				1,772
American Colonies of other powers	162	124	212	185	1,473	1,174	3,735	?	?	?	2,687
Total	*41,412*	*31,439*	*34,451*	*34,309*	*36,527*	*34,567*	*34,554*	*50,287*	*45,870*	*32,410*	*43,242*

Source: François Crouzet *L'économie britannique et le blocus continental*, 2nd edn. Economica, Paris, 1987.

Table 6 Subsidy payments by Britain 1793–1816

(The strength of the British economy, and the flexibility of its fiscal system, enabled enormous subsidy payments to be paid to Britain's allies. While there are difficulties in estimating the exact size of these payments, not the least of which is the confused manner in which some of the accounts were kept, the following is the most accurate and up-to-date assessment.)

1793	Hanover	452,551
	Hesse-Cassel	190,622
	Sardinia	15,000
1794	Baden	20,196
	Brunswick	17,659
	Hanover	601,476
	Hesse-Cassel	418,132
	Hesse-Darmstadt	91,372
	Prussia	1,200,000
	Sardinia	200,000
1795	Austrian Loan	4,600,000
	Baden	6,794
	Brunswick	46,778
	Hanover	340,192
	Hesse-Cassel	317,492
	Hesse-Darmstadt	85,224
	Sardinia	150,000
	Brunswick	53,645
	Hanover	3,736
	Hesse-Darmstadt	62,651
1797	Austrian Loan	1,620,000
	Brunswick	15,565
	Hesse-Darmstadt	19,249
	Portugal[1]	10,000
1798	Brunswick[2]	7,000
	Portugal[1]	103,000
1799	Hesse-Darmstadt	none
	Portugal[1]	87,675
	Russia	1,386,070

Table 6 cont.

1800	Austria	816,666
	German Princes	1,066,667
	Portugal[1]	10,000
	Russia	537,126
1801	Austria	none
	German Princes	200,000
	Hesse-Cassel[2]	100,000
	Portugal	200,000
1802	Hesse-Cassel[2]	33,451
	Russia[2]	200,000
1803	Hanover2	110,155
	Russia[2]	63,000
	Portugal	none
1804	Hesse-Cassel2	83,303
1805	Austria	1,000,000
	Hanover	26,190
	Russia	300,000
	Sweden	132,500
1806	Austria[2]	500,000
	Hanover	76,865
	Hesse-Cassel[2]	18,982
	Russia[2]	50,000
	Sweden	311,400
1807	Hanover	19,899
	Hesse-Cassel	45,000
	Prussia	187,613
	Russia[3]	614,183
	Sicily[4]	1,094,002
	Sweden	248,128
1808	Portugal	140,156
	Sicily	353,438
	Spain	2,325,668
	Sweden[5]	1,094,023
1809	Austria	1,187,500
	Portugal	539,369
	Portuguese Loan	600,000
	Sicily	313,836
	Spain	473,919
	Sweden	300,000

Table 6 cont.

1810	Portugal	1,986,069
	Sicily	425,000
	Spain	557,952
1811	Portugal	1,832,168
	Sicily	275,000
	Spain	539,554
1812	Portugal	2,276,833
	Sicily[6]	628,532
	Spain	1,036,598
	Sweden[7]	500,000
1813	Austria	700,000
	Prussia	650,039
	Portugal	2,486,012
	Russia[8]	1,058,436
	Sicily	440,000
	Spain	877,200
	Sweden	1,334,992
1814	Austria	939,523
	Denmark	121,917
	Hanover	535,000
	Portugal	1,345,082
	Prussia[9]	1,438,643
	Russia[10]	2,708,834
	Sicily	316,666
	Spain	1,820,932
	Sweden	800,000
1815	Austria	1,654,921
	Hanover	270,940
	Portugal	54,915
	Prussia[11]	2,156,513
	Russia[12]	2,000,033
	Sicily	33,333
	Spain	147,295
	Sweden	608,048
	Minor Powers[13]	1,723,727
1816	Austria	416,667
	Russia	972,222
	Sicily	117,748
	Sweden	422,766

1 Paid to agents in London for purchase of supplies.
2 Payments for claims arising out of past service.
3 £500,000 of this sum was due Russia from her 1805 treaty, while the balance was the value of arms sent her in 1807.
4 This is the total of all subsidies to Sicily between 1804 and 1807.
5 Of this amount, £94,023 is the value of arms sent that year.
6 Includes arms valued at £40,060.
7 Includes arms and credit in London, totalling £300,000.
8 Includes arms valued at £400,936.
9 Includes approximately £401,371 paid in 'federative paper'.
10 Includes approximately £783,000 paid in 'federative paper'.
11 Includes approximately £469,728 paid in 'federative paper'.
12 Includes approximately £888,922 paid in 'federative paper'.
13 These payments were completed in February 1816.

After: John M. Sherwig, *Guineas and Gunpowder: British Foreign Aid in the Wars with France*, Harvard University Press, Cambridge, Mass. 1969.

Army

The British army was maintained at some 132,000 men during the Peace of Amiens; it had reached about 150,600 by the beginning of 1804, following which it rose steadily to a peak of about 260,800 at the beginning of 1813. The officers were drawn from the nobility and gentry; the men were volunteers, though sometimes recruited by trickery or coercion. Roughly one-fifth of the army were foreign and colonial troops, the most significant of these corps being the 8000 men of the King's German Legion and the 8000 men in the West Indian regiments.

The Portuguese army, which on paper consisted of 56,000 men and had over 350 British officers and NCOs, was employed alongside the British army throughout the Peninsular War.

For home defence Britain had a militia recruited by ballot in the counties of able-bodied men aged between 18 and 45; many of the men, however, were substitutes paid for by the ballotted men. The regiments were county based and while they were moved out of their county of origin, they could not be moved out of the kingdom. The militia stood at about 85,500 men at the beginning of 1804 and gradually declined to about 69,700 at the beginning of 1813. The militia was successfully used as a recruiting pool for the regular army.

There were also volunteer corps of part-time soldiers coming forward to defend their locality in case of invasion or internal disorder. They were especially prominent during the invasion scare following the rupture of the Peace of Amiens. The government received offers from over 300,000 volunteers in England, Wales and Scotland, and 70,000 in Ireland. Their effectiveness was probably questionable, and from 1809 there were attempts by the government to get them to transfer into a newly organised, and better supervised Local Militia.

Navy

There were about 135,000 men in the Royal Navy at the beginning of 1804 rising to a peak of about 150,000 nine years later. Probably about three-quarters of the men had been pressed into service, but precise assessments are difficult as many pressed men were allowed to declare as volunteers and thus collect the recruiting bounty.

There were many foreign seamen serving in the fleet, particularly Americans who were often pressed from the crews of merchantmen on the high seas.

The British battle fleet was the largest in the world: in 1799 there were 146 ships of the line (i.e. battleships usually carrying a minimum of 74 guns) with another 46 under repair or construction. In addition there were 25 ships carrying about 50 guns each, 176 frigates (with about another 50 under construction or repair), and scores of smaller craft. However, in any one year Britain was never able to man and equip all her ships of the line; the maximum achieved was 113 in 1808–9.

3. The economic and military potential of France

Population

Table 7 Population (in 000s)

1800	29,100
1805	29,500
1810	30,000
1815	30,300

Probably about three-quarters of the population were rural dwellers. Paris was the largest city with a population of about 547,000 in 1800; the three other cities of any significant size were Bordeaux (91,000), Lyon (110,000) and Marseilles (111,000).

But Napoleon's Empire stretched way beyond the boundaries of France. At its peak the 130 departments included Belgium, The Netherlands, and parts of Italy and Switzerland; there were also his satellites and his allies.

The Empire contained many of Europe's other largest cities: Amsterdam 201,000, Genoa 100,000, Milan 170,000, Rome (the Empire's second city) 153,000, Turin 78,000 and Warsaw 100,000 (population estimates for c.1800).

Table 8 The populations of the states of the 'Grand Empire' 1813

130 imperial departments ....42,406,142 ⎤	43,937,142
Illyrian provinces..1,531,000 ⎦	
Kingdom of Spain (1797).. 10,541,221	
Kingdom of Italy 6,508,931	
Kingdom of Naples 4,590,000	
Grand Duchy of Warsaw... 3,800,262	
Kingdom of Bavaria (1811)... 3,339,828	
Kingdom of Westphalia (1811) 2,065,973	
Kingdom of Saxony (1811) 1,993,588	
States forming the 2nd College	
of the Rhenish Confederation 1,632,297	
Swiss Confederation... 1,439,273	
Kingdom of Württemberg (1811) 1,301,958	
Grand Duchy of Baden (1811) 949,639	
Grand Duchy of Hesse (1811) 565,922	
Grand Duchy of Frankfurt (1811) 290,445	
Grand Duchy of Würzburg.. 273,000	
Principalities of Lucca and Piombino 179,030	

Total: *83,408,509*

Source: Geoffrey Ellis, *Napoleon's Continental Blockade: The Case of Alsace*, Clarendon Press, Oxford, 1981.

Economy

The loss of France's West Indian colonies, British naval supremacy, and Napoleon's military dominance of Europe led to a shift in French trade from the Atlantic coast (with catastrophic results for Bordeaux) to Europe. France was envisaged as the focus for European trade, and the most favoured partner in the Empire. This shift gave a powerful boost to the textile trade in Alsace which, although it lagged behind British developments, was protected by the continental system. But there were a variety of problems within the project to create a European-wide market of the Empire, not the least of which was the continuing disruption of Napoleon's wars (see Tables 9 and 10).

Army

From 1805 Napoleon sought to maintain a standing army of 500,000 to 600,000 men. However, when he took to the field he usually had only some 200,000 Frenchmen with him supplemented by contingents from the Empire and his allies (see Table 11).

The French army was recruited by conscription; promotion to all ranks was largely through merit. The Jourdan Law passed in Fructidor Year VI (September 1799) required all males aged 18–25 to register. But there were exceptions and it was possible for a man chosen by lot to purchase a replacement; this clearly favoured the wealthy and provoked much discontent. Between 1800 and 1810 it was rare for more than 73,000 of the men eligible in any one year to be called up. The Russian campaign of 1812 and the emergency of 1813–14, however, both saw an enormous call up. Evasion of the law, and desertion were widespread in both France (especially in the more remote and backward areas) and where conscription was established in the Empire; few imperial requirements were as unpopular and evoked such hostility.

The National Guard could be called upon for internal defence and for assisting with the maintenance of internal order, but it was rarely used; the notable exceptions being in 1809, when on the occasion of the British expedition to Walcheren the guards of the 15 northern departments were mobilised, and during the invasion of 1813–14.

Navy

The imperial navy was also recruited by conscription. On the rupture of the Peace of Amiens Napoleon had only 13 ships of the line ready for sea; two years later, with the addition of ten Dutch ships, he had about 50. Following the defeat of Trafalgar he could only muster 34 ships in 1807; but six years later he had more than 80 with another 35 under construction. His publicly declared target was 150 ships of the line.

Table 9 *Official values of French foreign trade 1786–1824*

Year	Imports	Exports	Total Trade
1787	551	440	991
1788	517	466	983
1789	576	441	1,017
1792[1]	929	802	1,731
1797[2]	353	211	564
Yr. V	369	226	595
1798	298	253	551
Yr. VI	309	254	563
1799	253	300	553
Yr. VII	290	301	591
1800	323	271	594
Yr. VIII	351	272	623
1801	415	304	719
Yr. IX	434	305	739
1802	465	325	790
Yr. X	493	339	832
1803	430	346	776
Yr. XI	500	373	873
1804	440	380	820
Yr. XII	511	411	922
1805	492	375	867
Yr. XIII	548	401	949
1806	477	455	932
Yr. XIV	532	465	997
−1806			
1807[3]	393	376	769
	418	385	803
1808	320	331	651
	401	341	742
1809	288	332	620
	358	341	699
1810	339	365	704
	385	377	762
1811[4]	299	328	627
1812	308	419	727
1813	251	354	605
1814	239	346	585
1815[5]	199	422	621
1816	242	547	789
1817	332	464	796

Table 9 cont.

Year	Imports	Exports	Total Trade
1818	335	502	837
1819	294	460	754
1820	335	543	878
1821	355	450	805
1822	368	427	795
1823	317	427	744
1824	401	505	906

1 The figures for 1792 are so much higher than those for any other year in the series that they may well be distrusted.
2 Two sets of figures are given for each year from 1797 to 1806 inclusive. They show the discrepancies between totals based on the Gregorian calendar and those on the Republican. The upper set in each case is from the figures of the 'Statistique générale' of 1838. The lower sets are from the ministerial tables in A.N. F^{12} 251.
3 The upper sets of figures for each year in the period 1807–10 are from the 'Statistique générale' of 1838. The lower sets are from the tables in A.N. F. ^{12} 251
4 Only one set of figures is given for each of the years 1811–15 inclusive, as the details in the above sources all concur.
5 Figures for the years 1816–24 are from the 'Statistique générale' of 1838.

After: Ellis, *op.cit.*

Table 10 Principal destination of French exports 1806–17 (official values in millions of francs)

Year	United States	United Kingdom[2]	Kingdom of Holland	Hanse towns	Kingdom of Denmark	'Etats d'Allemagne'[3]	Kingdom of Prussia	Russian Empire	Republic of Switzerland	Austrian Empire	Kingdom of Italy	Other Italian states[1]	Kingdom of Spain	Kingdom of Portugal	Ottoman Empire & 'Barbary'
Year XIV & 1806	45.923	–	56.546	24.119	30.806	126.132	10.718	1.558	26.673	1.436	40.059	20.172[c]	65.311	9.280	5.826
1807	43.159	–	45.123	3.376	35.556	99.465	1.207	0.383	23.577	0.505	40.607	17.121[d]	65.614	6.946	2.445
1808	1.825	–	80.217	5.797	2.652	131.838	1.122	0.802	23.331	0.591	44.310	11.648[e]	33.202	0.091	3.954
1809	1.384	–	66.667	3.717	28.435	115.618	2.005	4.030	18.815	0.785	43.840	14.721[f]	33.907	–	6.633
1810	4.411	38.918	44.574	1.967	0.779	143.391	0.728	0.817	21.217	3.441	51.646	20.505[g]	38.343	–	5.367
1811	14.655	29.987	16.432	3.128	9.401	110.544	1.130	0.207	20.706	1.894	52.563	20.388[h]	40.427	–	6.055
1812	24.799	76.973	included in figure for Hanse towns	24.534	30.145	111.034	2.125	0.145	16.877	1.146	56.906	31.263[i]	38.163	–	3.928
1813	31.622	114.632		9.564	9.349	72.514	0.859	–	22.829	0.281	47.944	16.262[j]	22.168	–	5.624
1814	4.498	53.369	53.549	4.972	1.466	65.303	2.028	4.674	27.122	1.805	30.622[b]	16.001[k]	61.774	10.541	3.132
1815	56.113	38.624	64.664[a]	3.195	3.380	81.178	10.565	4.152	26.871	0.667	20.427[b]	35.280[l]	54.337	10.805	4.488
1816	43.145	26.563	72.891	2.912	4.909	73.037	10.677	4.677	24.927	1.453	18.827	18.027[m]	56.642	13.532	2.587
1817	41.783	41.562	48.295	2.423	3.729	56.211	10.027	5.790	19.158	0.544	15.103	17.958[n]	50.094	6.789	2.934

[a] As from 1815 the reconstructed Kingdom of Holland included Belgium; [b] Entry cited as 'Italy' as from 1815; [c] of which 14.566 to Kingdom of Etruria; [d] 12.907 to K. of Etr.; [e] 8.149 to K. of Etr.; [f] 6.817 to K. of Etr. and 4.042 to States of Rome; [g] of which 12.014 to Kingdom of Naples and 7.213 to port of Leghorn; [h] 19.011 to K. of Nap.; [i] 28.627 to K. of Nap.; [j] K. of Nap. only entry for 1813; [k] of which 11.607 to Kingdom of Sardinia and 4.042 to K. of Nap.; [l] 32.279 to K. of Sard.; [m] 16.287 to K. of Sard.; [n] 14.729 to K. of Sard.

[1] i.e. Kingdom of Etruria (till 1809), Kingdom of Naples (and Sicily after 1815), Kingdom of Sardinia, States of Rome, and some others; [2] By special licence in 1810–13; [3] 'Etats d'Allemagne' = the states of the Rhenish Confederation as formed on 12 July 1806, with its later signatories

After: Ellis, *op.cit.*

Table 11 Contributions to the Imperial Army

State	Before 1808		Spain 1808–14		Austria 1809		Russia 1812		1813–14		Total	
	(a)[1]	(b)[2]	(a)[1]	(b)[2]	(a)[1]	(b)[2]	(a)[1]	(b)[2]	(a)[1]	(b)[2]	(a)[1]	(b)[2]
Italy	14,000	2,000	30,000	21,000	19,000	2,500	30,000	20,000	28,000	21,000	121,000	60,500
Naples	–	–	9,000	1,300	–	–	8,000	6,000	13,000	2,000	30,000	9,300
Bavaria	46,000	1,000	–	–	30,000	8,000	25,000	22,000	9,000	5,500	110,000	36,500
Saxony	6,000	1,000	–	–	18,300	3,400	26,000	23,400	15,000	2,500	66,100	30,400
Württemberg	11,000	1,000	–	–	13,600	3,000	13,600	13,000	10,500	2,000	48,700	19,000
Baden	4,600	500	3,000	2,500	6,800	1,000	7,600	7,000	7,000	1,500	29,000	12,000
Smaller German States	9,600	500	14,600	11,000	14,500	2,500	12,500	9,000	9,300	3,500	60,500	26,500
Berg	1,200	50	4,300	2,500	1,900	500	5,000	4,700	800	750	13,200	8,500
Westphalia	–	–	8,200	7,000	8,000	500	27,800	25,500	8,000	1,000	52,000	34,000
Poland	–	–	–	–	12,500	1,500	57,000	30,000	15,000	9,000	84,800	40,500
Spain	15,000	–	–	–	–	–	–	–	–	–	15,000	–
Holland[3]	15,000	500	2,000	900	–	–	–	–	–	–	17,000	1,400
Denmark	–	–	–	–	–	–	12,000	–	12,000	–	24,000	–
Austria	–	–	–	–	–	–	30,000	10,000	–	–	30,000	10,000
Prussia	–	–	–	–	–	–	17,000	500	–	–	17,000	500
Total	*122,000*	*6,550*	*71,100*	*46,200*	*124,600*	*23,000*	*271,500*	*170,700*	*127,900*	*48,750*	*718,300*	*289,100*

1 Round number of contingent sent to Imperial Army.
2 Round number of certified losses.
3 From 1810 The Netherlands was incorporated into the French Empire and conscription on the French model was introduced; 14,000 Dutch troops were part of the army which invaded Russia in 1812.

After: Jean Tulard ed. *Dictionnaire Napoléon*, Fayard, Paris, 1987.

4. The economic and military potential of Prussia

Population

Table 12 Population

c. 1795 (on Third Partition of Poland)	c.8.7 million (including c.2.5 million Poles)
1807 (following Treaty of Tilsit)	c.5 million
1816 (following Congress of Vienna)	c.10.3 million

The population was overwhelmingly rural; Berlin was the capital and principal city with about 172,000 inhabitants in 1800.

Economy

The economy was agrarian-based with perhaps as much as three-quarters of the population being peasants. The war had a profound effect on the economy. On the negative side it produced an enormous debt aggravated by the indemnity demanded by the French.

However, on the positive side the defeat of 1806 prompted considerable economic reforms: notably the emancipation of the peasantry and the abolition of restrictive guild practices. Moreover the Vienna settlement gave Prussia new territories in the Rhineland, which were among the most economically advanced and prosperous in Germany and were well endowed with natural resources.

Table 13 Prussian national debt

1806 (before Jena)	55 million Thalers
1810	100
1812	112
1816	206

Army

The army of Frederick the Great, which was defeated in the war of 1806, was recruited by a system linking regiments to specific areas and thus linking all males with the country's defence. The Treaty of Tilsit limited the army to 42,000 men, but the *Krümpersystem* developed by military reformers allowed for the creation of a reserve. When Prussia took the field against Napoleon in 1813 she produced the largest army, proportionate to population, of any of the allies, about 279,000 men. Of these perhaps 28 percent were men of the existing army (42,000) and the *Krümper* (36,000 though this may only in fact have raised about a third of this number); 59 percent were the product of conscription; and 10 percent were volunteers (including 8000 *Jägers*). The reforms following Jena swept away much of the old officer corps; they encouraged promotion by merit, opening the senior ranks to capable non-nobles, and pioneered the development of a powerful general staff. At the same time the rigid discipline and linear formations of the old army were relaxed, producing more flexible and more independent battlefield formations.

Navy

None.

5. The economic and military potential of Russia

Population

About 37.5 million in European Russia in 1800. These were overwhelmingly rural dwellers. The two principal cities were St. Petersburg (220,000 inhabitants) and Moscow (250,000).

Economy

Largely agriculturally based; the land was worked by serfs on the private estates, and by state peasants where the government was the landowner. The state peasants had more personal autonomy than the serfs, but the Tsar could give them and their land to private persons, in which case they became the serfs of the new owner. There had been some industrial development under Peter the Great (Tsar 1700–25) particularly in industries supporting the military, notably iron; until the late eighteenth century, when she was overtaken by Britain, Russia had been the largest producer of iron in the world. As with the other powers the effects of war and the economic blockade had a deleterious effect on the economy particularly noticeable in the depreciation of paper money as a result of wartime inflation.

Army

The officers were drawn from the nobility and the gentry; the rank and file were recruited by an annual levy and served for 25 years. In an emergency there could be additional levies; there were three in 1812 bringing in 420,000 men. Overall the strength of the army increased from about 430,000 in 1805 to 600,000 in 1812, but given the threat from the Turkish Empire and the needs of internal security, only about a third of this number was available for fighting

Napoleon. Discipline was harsh, the supply of arms and ammunition inadequate, medical provision and general administration were poor. In addition to the regular army there were irregular troops, notably the Don Cossacks who were organised into 60 cavalry regiments in 1812. A militia of about 200,000 men was raised in 1806–7 and again in 1812. This participated in the fighting both on Russian soil and abroad.

Table 14 Depreciation of Russian paper money 1790–1814

Year	Amount of paper money issued in year	Amount in circulation on 31 December of year	Value in silver of one ruble of paper money
1774	2,207,075	20,051,800	100
1790	11,000,000	111,000,000	87
1794	21,550,000	145,550,000	68.5
1798	31,356,765	194,931,605	62.5
1801	8,799,000	221,488,335	71.66
1805	31,540,560	292,199,110	73
1809	55,832,720	533,201,300	43.33
1810	46,172,580	579,373,880	25.4
1811	2,020,520	581,394,400	26.4
1812	64,500,000	645,894,400	25.2
1813	48,791,500	798,125,900	20

(Source: Marc Raeff, *Michael Speransky: Statesman of Imperial Russia, 1772–1839,* Martinus Nijhoff, The Hague, 1957, p.84 n.1)

Navy

In 1805 there was a Baltic fleet of 32 ships of the line and 12 frigates, and a Black Sea fleet of 12 ships of the line and four frigates.

Biographies

Abrial, André-Joseph, comte (1750–1828) French statesman. An advocate in the Parlement of Paris he objected to Chancellor Maupeou's legal reforms in the early 1770s and moved temporarily to Senegal where, for a short period, he ran a government office. From 1791–9 he served as a commissioner in the tribunal of cassation. As Minister of Justice (1799–1802) he was involved in the reorganisation of the judicial system. He lost office when Napoleon combined, briefly (1802–4), the ministries of justice and police; he was recompensed with the position of senator and the Legion of Honour.

Addington, Henry, Viscount Sidmouth (1757–1844) British statesman. The son of a society physician, he was educated at Winchester and Oxford and entered parliament in 1784. A close friend and supporter of Pitt (q.v.) he became Speaker of the Commons in 1789 and held the position until 1801. On Pitt's resignation he was invited to form a ministry, and it was this which negotiated the Peace of Amiens. Addington was a poor war leader and yielded the premiership to Pitt in 1804 serving as Lord President of the Council until July 1805, and accepting the title Viscount Sidmouth. He was Lord Privy Seal in the 'Talents' ministry, but broke with them over their attempt to allow military commissions to Catholics and dissenters. He became Home Secretary in Lord Liverpool's administration in 1812, and as such was closely associated with the repressive policies against the Luddites and the post-war radicals. He stood down from the Home Office in December 1821, but continued as a member of the cabinet until 1824 when he resigned over the government's recognition of the independence of the Spanish American colonies. He took little part in public affairs in his last twenty years, but he remained a staunch supporter of old style Church and King politics voting against Catholic emancipation (1829) and the First Reform Bill (1832).

Alexander I (1777–1825) Tsar of Russia. Alexander was educated in the court of his grandmother Catherine the Great and, while steeped in the tradition of the Russian autocracy, he absorbed much Enlightenment thinking through his Swiss tutor, César Laharpe. When, following his father's assassination in March 1801, he became Tsar, he aspired to introducing administrative, educational and social reforms. He met with a group of four like-minded young nobles – the 'unofficial committee' – regularly throughout 1802–3, and between 1808 and 1812 his principal advisor was the reforming Speranski (q.v.). But little was achieved. In foreign affairs Alexander reversed his father's policies, coming to terms with Britain and forming alliances with Austria and Prussia. He waged war against Napoleon from 1805–7 when the defeat at Friedland forced Russia to make peace and led to the historic meeting of the two emperors at Tilsit. Alexander was greatly impressed with Napoleon but strains rapidly developed in the alliance agreed at Tilsit culminating in the French invasion of Russia in 1812. Alexander played a key role in the final coalitions against Napoleon and in redrawing the map of Europe at the Congress of Vienna. He increasingly came under the influence of evangelical revivalists and became possessed with a fanatical pietism; these contributed to his ideas for the Holy Alliance. The last decade of his reign saw the eclipse of his earlier Enlightenment aspirations and he relied more on the ruthless Arakcheyev (q.v.) for his internal policies.

d'Angoulême, Louis-Antoine de Bourbon, duc (1775–1844) The eldest son of the comte d'Artois (q.v.) he became an *émigré* with his father in July 1789. He fought in the *émigré* armies against the Revolution, following which he spent many years in exile in England. Early in 1814 he joined Wellington's (q.v.) army in southern France and, on 12 March in Bordeaux, he proclaimed the restoration of the Bourbons. Entrusted with organising the royalist resistance during the Hundred Days, he acquitted himself well but was eventually forced to sign the Convention of La Palud. He travelled to Spain where he took command of other royalist exiles, and he led these into southern France following Waterloo, re-establishing Bourbon control in the Midi. In 1823 he commanded the French army sent to Spain to re-establish Ferdinand VII (q.v.). On his father's accession to the throne in 1824 he became Dauphin, but he was forced into exile again following the Revolution of 1830. When his father died he took the title 'Louis XIX', though most legitimists recognised his nephew, 'Henry V', as heir.

Arakcheyev, Alexei Andreyevich (1769–1834) Russian soldier and statesman. The son of a small landowner in Tula province. As a young artillery officer he was recommended to the Tsarevitch Paul and was charged with reorganising the Gatchina army corps. He met the task with ruthless efficiency and, on becoming Tsar, Paul promoted him and put him in charge of reorganising the imperial army. But Arakcheyev's ruthlessness and the far-reaching nature of his reforms made him enemies and led to his eclipse. Tsar Alexander (q.v.) brought him back from obscurity to be inspector general of artillery in 1803, minister of war in 1808, and senator and member of the council of ministers in 1810. Again his enemies brought about his temporary fall from favour. After 1815 he became Alexander's chief counsellor and friend, giving his name to this period of reaction in Russian history (*Arakcheyevshchina*). He withdrew from public life on Alexander's death and retired to his estates where he died.

Arndt, Ernst Moritz (1769–1860) German man of letters and patriot. Began his adult career as a Lutheran pastor but renounced this at the age of 28. In 1800 he commenced teaching History at the University in Greifswald from where he published a series of books and pamphlets critical of French aggression, most notably the first part of *Geist der Zeit* (Spirit of the Times) (1806). German excitement, and Napoleon's anger, forced him to take refuge in Sweden but in pamphlets, songs and poems he continued to urge the German people to rise up against the French. He insisted that 'to be one people is the religion of the day.' In 1809 he returned to Germany in disguise, and three years later he became private secretary to Stein (q.v.). Following the defeat of Napoleon he accepted the chair of History at the University of Bonn (1818) but his continuing demands for reform brought him into conflict with the Prussian government. In 1820 he was banned from teaching; the ban was to remain in force for twenty years. During the Revolutions of 1848 he became a deputy to the Frankfurt parliament.

Artois, Charles Philippe de Bourbon, comte d' (1757–1836) The youngest brother of Louis XVI he was violently opposed to reform both before, and in the early years of, the Revolution. He became one of the first *émigrés* leaving France immediately after the fall of the Bastille and not returning until 1814. He succeeded as King Charles X in 1824. Throughout the restoration he was the focus for unreconstructed royalism and the clerical party. He was forced to abdicate in the Revolution of 1830 and died in exile.

Augereau, Pierre-François-Charles (1757–1816) French soldier. The son of a poor Parisian stone-mason he enlisted in the army in 1774. He developed a reputation for duelling and was forced to desert after fighting an officer. He subsequently served in the Russian army against the Turks, deserting to join first the Prussian and then the Neapolitan army. In 1792 he volunteered for the French Revolutionary army, and was a general before the end of the following year. He fought with distinction throughout the wars, notably in Bonaparte's Army of Italy at Lodi and Castiglione. He played a central role in the Fructidor coup (1796) and, though developing political ambitions himself, he threw in his lot with Bonaparte after Brumaire. Created marshal (1804). Severely wounded at Eylau, after which he fell from favour though made Duke of Castiglione in 1808. He served in Spain, where he acquired a reputation for brutality and cruelty, and in the Russian campaign. In 1814 he broke with Napoleon and publicly reviled him; his attempt to rally to the Emperor during the Hundred Days was rebuffed. He retired to his estate at La Houssaye, and continued there until his death as the Bourbons refused to have anything to do with him. He was noted for his great height, his coarseness, and his attraction for booty.

Bacciochi, Pasquale (Felix) (1762–1841) A Corsican of Genoese extraction remembered principally for marrying Elisa Bonaparte (q.v.) in 1797. He had an undistinguished career in the Royal Regiment of Corsica before the Revolution; he resumed his military life after his marriage rising to the rank of colonel in 1802. In 1804 he was made a senator with a salary of 25,000 francs and he left the army. The following year, by virtue of being Elisa's husband, he became Prince of Piombino; in 1809 he became Grand Duke of Tuscany for the same reason. Here he took the name Felix (fortunate or happy). He separated from his wife on the fall of Napoleon, but was reconciled with her shortly before her death.

Bagration, Peter, Prince (1767–1812) Russian soldier. Born into a noble Georgian family he joined the Russian army in 1782. He served with distinction in wars against the Poles and the Turks, and then in the Austerlitz campaign. In 1808 he led a daring march over the frozen Gulf of Finland and captured the Aaland Islands. He was killed at Borodino.

Barbé-Marbois, François, marquis de (1745–1837) French statesman. Born into a family of lawyers in Metz he began government service as a diplomat under the old regime. In 1780 he was French consul general to the United States Congress. In 1785 he was made intendant of San Domingo where his able and honest administration reorganised the colony's finances. He served as a diplomat again in the early years of the Revolution, was elected to the Council of Ancients under the Directory, but exiled to Guiana in 1797 for alleged royalist sympathies. He returned to France after Brumaire and was appointed a Councillor of State and Treasury Minister (1801). His term of office at the Treasury was noted for its honesty and improved administration, but in January 1806 he was made the scapegoat for an economic crisis brought about primarily by new wars and the speculative ventures of Ouvrard (q.v.) and the *Négociants réunis* to bring Spanish-American silver through the British blockade. The following year he was restored to favour and made President of the Court of Accounts which audited the Treasury. He was appointed a senator in 1813 but rallied to the Bourbons in 1814. With the exception of the Hundred Days he continued to serve in the Court of Accounts until retiring in 1834.

Barclay de Tolly, Mikhail Andreas (1761–1818) Also known in Russia as Mikhail, Prince Bogdanovich. Russian soldier of Scottish descent. He fought against the French in the battles of 1806–7 and commanded the Russian army against the Swedes in 1808–9. Russian Minister of War 1810–12. Heavily criticised for withdrawing before Napoleon at Smolensk, he went on to serve under Kutusov at Borodino. Appointed commander-in-chief after Bautzen, and made a count after Leipzig. He led the Russian army in the invasion of France in 1814, for which he was promoted to field marshal; he also commanded the Russians in the 1815 invasion, after which he was made a prince.

Beauharnais, Eugène de (1781–1824) Stepson to Napoleon. Born in Paris he was the son of General Alexandre de Beauharnais (guillotined June 1794) and Josephine (q.v.), the future wife of Napoleon. Initially he resented his mother's marriage to General Bonaparte, but he served under Bonaparte as aide-de-camp in the Italian campaign of 1796–7. Thereafter he served competently and faithfully and, while never asking for advancement or place (unlike most of the Bonaparte family) he was well rewarded. He was made a prince when the Empire was established in 1804 and viceroy of Italy in 1805. Early in 1806 he married Princess Augusta Amelia, daughter of Max Joseph (q.v.) of Bavaria, and while the marriage was designed to cement Napoleon's alliance with the new Kingdom of Bavaria, the couple became deeply attached to each other. Eugène was an able administrator and a courageous, if not especially gifted soldier. He served in the Russian campaign commanding a large Italian contingent, and remained loyal to Napoleon until the first abdication. He retired to Munich in 1814 where he was created Duke of Leuchtenberg and then prince of Eichstädt. He took no part in the Hundred Days, and continued to live in Munich until his death.

Beauharnais, Hortense Eugénie de (1783–1837) Step-daughter of Napoleon and wife of Louis Bonaparte. Born in the French West

Indies she returned to Europe with her mother in the early stages of the Revolution. Like her brother Eugène (q.v.) she initially opposed her mother's marriage to General Bonaparte. In 1802 she married Louis; it was not a happy match, rumours abounded of her infidelities, but she bore Louis three sons, the youngest of whom, Charles Louis Napoleon (1808–73) was to become the Emperor Napoleon III. As Louis's wife she became Queen of Holland (1806–10). She remained loyal to her step-father when he forced her husband's abdication, and this loyalty continued through the Hundred Days. After Waterloo she was exiled to Arenberg in Germany with Charles Louis Napoleon; her eldest surviving son remained in his father's care. She enthusiastically encouraged her youngest son's political ambitions.

Bellegarde, Heinrich von (1756–1845) Austrian soldier. The son of the Saxon minister of war, he joined the Austrian army in 1778. He distinguished himself in the war against Turkey (1788–9) and the campaigns against Revolutionary France, serving notably as chief of staff to Archduke Charles (q.v.) in 1796. From 1806 to 1808 he was governor of Galicia. He fought at Aspern-Essling and Wagram, following which he was appointed president of the Imperial War Council where he supervised the reorganisation of the army and the raising of recruits. In 1813 he was appointed commander of the Austrian armies in Italy where he negotiated the surrender of the viceroy, Eugène de Beauharnais (q.v.). In 1814 he was made governor of Lombardy and Venetia, and commanded the troops which defeated Murat's (q.v.) Neapolitan army. In 1816 he returned to Vienna as the Seneschal to Crown Prince Ferdinand. He subsequently served as both a minister and, again, as president of the Imperial War Council (1820–25). In 1825 blindness forced him to retire from public life.

Benningsen, Levin August (1745–1826) Russian soldier. Born in Hanover he first served in the Hanoverian army. He joined the Russian army in 1773 and fought in the wars against the Turks and the Poles. In 1801 he was involved in the conspiracy which brought about the death of Tsar Paul. In 1806–7 he commanded the Russian army against Napoleon at Pultusk, Eylau and Friedland. A quarrel with Kutusov (q.v.) led him to resign in 1812, but he returned to active service on Kutusov's death, leading part of the Russian army at Leipzig. He retired to his Hanoverian estates in 1818.

Bentinck, Lord William (1774–1839) British soldier and statesman. The second son of the 3rd Duke of Portland (q.v.) he joined the Foot Guards as an ensign in 1791. He served in the campaign in the Netherlands in 1794–5 and in 1799 he was attached to the Russian army during the war of the Second Coalition. From 1803 to 1807 he served as Governor of Madras until recalled by the directors of the East India Company following a Sepoy mutiny. At the beginning of the British involvement in the Peninsular War he was sent on a diplomatic mission to Madrid later joining Moore's army to fight at Corunna; he then served briefly under Wellington (q.v.). In 1811 he was sent as ambassador to the Neapolitan Court and appointed commander of British forces in the Mediterranean. In Sicily he instigated a series of reforms which brought the hostility of Queen Maria Caroline. In 1813 he had the Queen removed from the island and in the following year issued a proclamation calling upon Italians across the peninsula to rise in defence of their liberties. He had no official appointment for the next decade then, in 1827, he was made Governor General of Bengal. From 1833–5 he was Governor General of India where he was noted for his reforms including the abolition of *Suttee* (wives committing suicide on their husband's funeral pyre) and the *Thugee* bandits. He left India because of failing health. He died in Paris.

Beresford, William Carr (1768–1854) British soldier and Portuguese Marshal. The illegitimate son of the Marquis of Waterford he joined the army in 1785. He lost an eye in a shooting accident in the following year. Served with distinction in several theatres during the Revolutionary wars. He was given a command in South Africa in 1805, crossed the Atlantic to South America where he captured Buenos Aires (1807) but was, almost immediately, forced to surrender his entire force. He escaped back to Britain and was posted to the Peninsular. Early in 1809 he was given the task of reorganising the Portuguese army, which he achieved with considerable success. Wounded at Salamanca. At the end of the Peninsular War he was given a pension and the title Baron. Made a viscount in 1823 he was appointed Master General of the Ordnance in Wellington's cabinet five years later. He is generally recognised as having been a better military organiser and administrator than field commander.

Bernadotte, Jean Baptiste Jules (1763–1844) French soldier, subsequently Charles XIV, King of Sweden and Norway. The son of a Gascon *avocat* he enlisted in the army shortly after his father's death in 1780. He rose to non-commissioned rank before the Revolution, was elected an officer and served with distinction during the Revolutionary wars achieving the rank of general. In August 1798 he married Désirée Clary, sister-in-law of Joseph Bonaparte. Regarded by many as an alternative national leader to the then General Bonaparte, he nevertheless remained aloof during the Brumaire coup subsequently becoming reconciled to the Bonapartist regime. He was created marshal in 1804 and Prince of Ponte Corvo in 1806. During the early years of the Empire he showed ability as an administrator, notably as governor of Hanover (1804), as well as a soldier, but he was not always in favour with Napoleon. In August 1810 he was elected as Crown Prince of Sweden and heir to the childless Charles XIII (q.v.); from the close of that year he assumed the leadership of that country acting as regent during the King's prolonged illnesses. In 1812 he began a rapprochement with Russia, and subsequently with Britain and Prussia; all three powers agreed to the Swedish acquisition of Norway. He led a Swedish army against Napoleon during the German War of Liberation. After the battle of Leipzig he switched his attention to a rapid campaign against Denmark for the possession of Norway. Briefly he hoped to become ruler of France after Napoleon's first abdication, but settled for the Swedish throne to which he succeeded as Charles XIV in 1818. He ruled the country competently, if autocratically, until his death, aged 81, in 1844.

Bernstorff, Christian Günter, Count von (1769–1835) Danish and Prussian statesman. Son of a Danish foreign minister, he began his diplomatic career for Denmark in 1787. On his father's death in 1797 he became foreign minister, and served as principal minister in Denmark 1800–10. He returned to his diplomatic career in 1811 and represented Denmark at the Congress of Vienna. In 1817 he became Danish ambassador to Berlin where Hardenberg (q.v.) suggested that he transfer to Prussian service; this he did in the following year. He represented Prussia at the Congress of Aix-la-Chapelle (1818) thereafter becoming Prussian foreign minister. He generally supported the reactionary policies of Metternich (q.v.) in Restoration Europe. He played a key role in establishing the Customs Union (*Zollverein*) which contributed to the Prussian domination of Germany. Poor health forced his retirement in 1832.

Berthier, Louis Alexandre (1753–1815) French soldier. Born in Versailles, the son of an officer of the engineers, he enlisted in the army at the age of 17 serving in the engineers, the dragoons and on the staff. He fought with the French army in America during the War of Independence, returning as a colonel. He sided with the Revolution and in 1796 became Bonaparte's chief of staff in Italy.

He excelled at military organisation rather than field command and served as chief of staff for most of Napoleon's campaigns. Minister of War 1800–06, he was promoted to marshal in 1804 and subsequently made Prince of Neuchâtel (1806) and Wagram (1809). In 1814 he switched his allegiance to the restored monarchy though he maintained links with Napoleon on Elba. During the Hundred Days he withdrew to Bamberg, where he died after falling from a balcony (possibly suicide) on 1 June 1815.

Beugnot, Jacques-Claude (1761–1835) French administrator. Like his father he served in the administration of the old regime as an *avocat* in the Paris Parlement. In 1791 he was elected to the Legislative Assembly where he made a name for himself as an orator. Arrested in October 1792 he remained in prison until the fall of Robespierre (1794). He came to prominence after Brumaire as an advisor to Lucien Bonaparte (q.v.) and was instrumental in establishing the prefectures, serving himself as Prefect of Seine–Inférieure (1800–1806). His abilities as a prefect led Napoleon to appoint him to the council of state, and subsequently to direct him to organise first the Kingdom of Westphalia and then the Grand Duchy of Berg and Cleves. He was created a count of the empire in February 1810. In the turbulent period 1813–15 he held a succession of administrative and political posts under both Napoleon and Louis XVIII, including serving as the latter's minister of police. He retired from public life in 1824, but was appointed to the Chamber of Peers six years later.

Beyme, Karl Friedrich von (1765–1838) Prussian statesman. Born in Königsberg he became a close confidant of the Crown Prince Frederick William (q.v.) and when the latter became king (1797) Beyme was given the official title 'privy councillor of the cabinet'; his critics labelled him the 'invisible prime minister'. While he had some liberal leanings, helped to draft the Legal Code of 1794, and campaigned for the abolition of some forms of serfdom, he sided with the peace party before the disaster of 1806 and was opposed to the radical proposals of the reformers around Stein (q.v.) thereafter. In spite of Beyme's differences with the reformers the King appointed him as *Grosskanzler* (supreme judicial administrator) during Stein's ministry and he kept the ear of the monarch while not having any formal role in the administration. From his position he conspired against Stein. He served as Justice Minister 1808–10 and again 1817–19. He died on his estates at Steglitz.

Blücher, Gebhard Leberecht, Prince von (1742–1819) Prussian soldier. Born in Rostock he entered the Swedish army at the age of 14. In 1760, during the Pomeranian campaign, he was captured by the Prussians and was persuaded to enter their service. He became a successful cavalry officer, noted for courage, outspokenness, and a hot temper. He fought with distinction in both the Revolutionary wars and the disastrous campaign of 1805–6, after which he became recognised as a leader of the Prussian patriot party. His public statements about France led to him being recalled from the post of military governor of Pomerania in 1812 and virtually banished from the court. The following year, thanks to Scharnhorst (q.v.), he was put in command of the Prussian army in Silesia and conducted a successful campaign against the French culminating in the invasion of France and the march on Paris of 1814. In June 1814, as a reward for his service, he was created Prince of Wahlstadt. The following year he led the Prussian army in the Waterloo campaign.

Bonaparte, Caroline (Maria Annunziata) (1782–1839) Youngest sister of Napoleon; wife of Joachim Murat (q.v.). Christened Maria Annunziata, she was given the name Caroline by Napoleon. In 1800 she married Murat, and from then on proceeded to pressure her brother for honours for both her husband and herself; in 1806 they were given the Grand Duchy of Berg and Cleves, and two years later the Kingdom of Naples. During her husband's absences with the imperial army she acted in his place as an absolute ruler; nor was she averse to intriguing against both him and her brother. Following the Russian campaign both she and Murat approached Napoleon's enemies in the hopes of securing their kingdom. After Napoleon's final defeat, and Murat's death, she lost Naples but took the title the Countess of Lipona (an anagram of Napoli). Granted a pension by the French government she retired to Florence where she died.

Bonaparte, (Maria Anna) Elisa (1777–1820) Eldest sister of Napoleon. Born in Ajaccio she was admitted to the seminary of St. Cyr for the education of young noblewomen, but returned to her family when the Revolution forced its closure. In May 1797 she married the Corsican Bacciochi (q.v.); the couple moved to Paris where she established a literary salon. Like her sister Caroline (q.v.) she bickered with Napoleon's wife Josephine (q.v.) and was greedy for honours. In 1805 she and her husband were given the small principality of Piombino, and subsequently Lucca, then Tuscany. She was an enthusiastic reformer and reorganiser of her new territories;

Bacciochi was given little say in these matters. As the marriage cooled she took a succession of lovers. She was not averse to conspiring against her brother, but on Napoleon's fall she offered to join him on St. Helena if it would be permitted. Taking the title Countess of Compignano she finally settled in Trieste where, briefly reconciled with Bacciochi, she died.

Bonaparte, Jerome (1784–1860) The youngest brother of Napoleon he first served in the Consular Guard and was then transferred to the navy. Leaving his ship in the West Indies he travelled in the United States where he met and married an American woman, Elizabeth Patterson, by whom he had a son. Napoleon did not approve of the marriage and eventually annulled it by imperial decree requiring Jerome to marry a German princess, Catherine of Württemberg. In 1807 Napoleon made him King of Westphalia, and as such he held a junior command in the Russian campaign. Jerome rallied to his brother during the Hundred Days and fought at Waterloo. Following the defeat he was forced to separate from his wife; he spent the next thirty years mainly in Germany and Switzerland, finally settling in Trieste. He returned to France in 1847 and subsequently held largely honorific posts under Napoleon III.

Bonaparte, Joseph (1768–1844) The elder brother of Napoleon he studied law at Pisa. His rise as a diplomat began with the growing importance of his brother as an army commander; he was involved in the discussions leading to the Treaties of Lunéville and Amiens. Though he did not always agree with his brother, Napoleon made him first King of Naples (1806) and then King of Spain (1808); in both countries Joseph introduced reforming legislation and sought to shield his subjects from his brother's exactions. Driven from Spain by Wellington he served as Lieutenant-General of France early in 1814 while Napoleon conducted the military campaign on the north-eastern frontier. He retired from public life on the first restoration; after 1815 he resided for a while in the United States, but then returned to Europe dying in Florence in 1844.

Bonaparte, Louis (1778–1846) A brother of Napoleon he was educated for a military career and served with General Bonaparte as an aide in the Italian and Egyptian campaigns. He was made a general in 1804 and, the following year, was appointed governor of Paris taking on a variety of administrative and military tasks. In 1806 Napoleon made him King of Holland but a series of differences emerged between the brothers, particularly over Louis's liberal treatment of his subjects and the breakdown of his marriage (to Napoleon's step-daughter Hortense de Beauharnais (q.v.)). In 1810 these differences reached their nadir; Louis abdicated and the Netherlands were annexed to the French Empire. Louis spent most of the rest of his life in Rome, principally concerned with literary pursuits. His third son, Charles Louis Napoleon (1808–73) was to revive the French Empire as Napoleon III (1852–70).

Bonaparte, Lucien (1775–1840) A brother of Napoleon he attended a seminary in Aix and, during the early years of the Revolution, was an active Jacobin. Under the Directory he served in the Council of 500 and, as president of this body, he played an important role in the coup of Brumaire. During the Consular period serious political differences emerged between the two brothers: Lucien had the more liberal ideas; Napoleon considered that Lucien's wife did not come from a good enough pedigree. Lucien retired from politics to lands in the Papal States where he took the title Prince of Canino. On the French annexation of the Papal States he took ship for the United States (1809) but was captured by the British and spent some time under surveillance in England. He stood by Napoleon during the Hundred Days, and, after 1815, spent the remainder of his life in Italy.

Bonaparte, Maria Letizia (c.1750–1836) Napoleon's mother. Born Maria Letizia Ramolino into an old Corsican family of Florentine origin. Her father, a petty official on the island, died when she was five. In 1764 she married Carlo Buonaparte, a young Corsican patriot, by whom she had 12 children (four of whom died in infancy). She brought her family up in relative frugality, the more so following Carlo's death in 1785. In spite of her son's triumphs and the wealth and honours heaped upon her, she continued to live frugally and out of the limelight. In March 1805 she was given the title *Madame mère*, which had been reserved for dowager queens during the old regime. She joined Napoleon on Elba in 1814, and followed him to Paris during the Hundred Days. After Waterloo she retired to Rome where she lived under the protection of Pius VII (q.v.).

Bonaparte, Napoleon, see Napoleon I.

Bonaparte, Pauline (Paola Maria) (1780–1825) Napoleon's second sister, noted for her great beauty, and her succession of lovers. In 1797 she married General Victor-Emmanuel Leclerc. She travelled with her husband when he commanded the military expedition to

San Domingo where he died of cholera (1801). Returning to France she married Prince Borghese (q.v.) in November 1803. The marriage was not successful, both partners taking lovers. In 1806 she and her husband were given the principality of Guastalla; but she was not noted for intrigue against her brother to the extent of her sisters. After Waterloo she retired to Rome with her mother, and was reconciled with Borghese. She sought permission to join Napoleon on St. Helena, but he died before she could set out. She died in Florence.

Borghese, Camillo Filippo Ludovico, Prince (1775–1832) Italian nobleman, second husband of Pauline Bonaparte (q.v.). The scion of a patrician Roman family he was one of the richest men in Italy, nevertheless he fought on the French side in the Revolutionary wars in Italy. In 1803 he married Pauline, and this brought him new, imperial honours, notably he was made Duke of Guastalla and Governor General of the departments beyond the Alps (i.e. the Genoese provinces and Piedmont). The marriage to Pauline was not happy, but the couple were reconciled after Napoleon's fall.

Bourrienne, Louis-Antoine Fauvelet de (1769–1834) Napoleon's secretary and memorialist. Born in Sens he became a friend of the young Bonaparte when they were together at Brienne Military Academy. He accompanied Bonaparte on the Italian and Egyptian campaigns becoming his secretary in 1797 – a post for which his intelligence and speed at dictation ably suited him. In 1802 he was dismissed for dishonest financial dealings. Napoleon gave him another official post in 1805 as Minister Plenipotentiary to Hamburg, but again he was dismissed, on this occasion for selling exemptions to the blockade. He sided with the Bourbons during the restoration, served as a minister, but again his financial dealings brought disgrace and he retired to Caen where he died in a lunatic asylum. His memoirs were published in 1829 and were largely ghost-written from the notes which he gave to his publisher. The memoirs were a great success though they are now generally regarded as unreliable.

Boyen, Herman Ludwig von (1771–1848) Prussian soldier. He entered the army in 1787, but also attended the University of Königsberg where he was greatly influenced by Kant. He became convinced of the need to remould society on the basis of justice, honour and morality, and he believed that the army, recruited on the basis of universal conscription, could be central in this. His ideas appealed to Scharnhorst (q.v.), and when he had recovered from wounds received at Auerstädt, he became deeply involved in the Prussian military reforms. When Frederick William (q.v.) refused to turn against Napoleon in 1811 he resigned as a colonel in the Prussian army and joined the Russians. He returned to Prussia in 1813 and the following year was made Minister of War. He drafted the Military Law of 3 September 1814 which established conscription in peace-time and formulated the regulations for the *Landwehr*. Disillusioned with the reactionary policies of the post-war period he resigned in 1819 over the extent to which the army and the *Landwehr* should be combined. He served as Minister of War for a second time between 1841 and 1847.

Brunswick (Braunschweig), Charles William Ferdinand, Duke of (1735–1806) German soldier. Began his military career in the Seven Years War and distinguished himself in several battles under both British and Prussian command. Towards the end of the war he married the sister of George III. He subsequently travelled widely in Europe, succeeding his father as Duke of Brunswick in 1780. He ruled as an enlightened despot, but maintained his links with Prussia (Frederick the Great was his uncle) frequently acting for her on diplomatic missions and holding the rank of field marshal in the Prussian army. In 1792 he was appointed to command the allied armies marching on Paris and he put his name to the notorious manifesto (actually written by an *émigré*) threatening the revolutionaries with vengeance if the French royal family was harmed. Forced to retreat after the battle of Valmy he continued to command the allied forces in the following year, but, feeling that he could not make a military move without the interference of the Prussian King, he returned to govern his duchy. In 1806, at the personal request of the Prussian queen, he agreed to command the Prussian army against Napoleon. He was mortally wounded at Auerstädt.

Brunswick (sometimes **Brunswick-Oels**), **Frederick William, Duke of** (1771–1815) German soldier. The fourth son of Charles William Ferdinand, Duke of Brunswick (q.v.) he became one of Napoleon's most inveterate enemies. During the Wagram campaign (1809) he formed a *Freikorps*, 'the Black Legion of Vengance', also known as the Black Hussars, which invaded Saxony capturing Dresden (11 June) and Leipzig (19 June). After the Austrian armistice Brunswick and his Hussars fought their way across Germany to the mouth of the Weser where they were evacuated by a British squadron. He stayed in London, hailed as a hero, until 1813, when he re-entered Prussian service. Serving under Wellington during the Waterloo campaign, he was killed at Quatre Bras.

Bülow, Dietrich Heinrich (1757–1807) Prussian soldier and military analyst. He served in the Prussian army from 1773–89 after which he published a series of works on military affairs beginning, in 1799, with *Geist des neuen Kriegssystems* (Spirit of the new system of war). These works analysed French military success and the new kind of war inaugurated by the French Revolution; they were often confused and contradictory, but have also been considered of sufficient merit to permit Bülow being described as the father of modern military science. He argued for a national, conscript army and was highly critical of the system left over from Frederick the Great. This infuriated the Prussian old guard who believed Bülow insane and had him imprisoned in 1807; he passed from Prussian captivity into Russian hands, and died in prison in Riga.

Bülow, Friedrich Wilhelm (1755–1816) Prussian soldier and elder brother of the military theorist D.H. Bülow (q.v.). He entered the Prussian army in 1768 and served in the campaigns against Revolutionary France, in the disastrous war of 1806, and in the Wars of Liberation. As a reward for his role in the latter he was created Count von Dennewitz in 1814. The following year he commanded the IV Corps which bore the brunt of the fighting on the Prussian side at Waterloo.

Burdett, Sir Francis (1770–1844) English radical politician. Educated at Westminster School and Oxford, followed by a tour in France and Switzerland. He was in Paris during the early months of the Revolution. In 1793 he returned to England where he married Sophia Coutts, the daughter of a wealthy banker. He entered parliament in 1796 as member for Boroughbridge, and began to associate with the radical Whigs. In 1802 he was elected MP for Middlesex; this was followed by long legal proceedings which resulted, in 1806, in the nullification of his election. In 1807 he was elected MP for Westminster. He raised a series of reform issues in parliament, notably flogging in the army and the question of parliamentary reform itself. In April 1810 he was imprisoned in the Tower for a breach of parliamentary privilege in publishing a speech calling for the release from custody of John Gale Jones, a well-known radical. Burdett's imprisonment provoked riots in London. On his release he avoided the crowds which had gathered to give him a triumphal procession and returned quietly to his home; some radicals never forgave him for this. In 1820 he was fined £2000 and imprisoned for three months for criticisms of the authorities over Peterloo. He was involved in the campaigns which led to Catholic emancipation (1828) and the First Reform Act (1832), but thereafter he became increasingly conservative in outlook.

Cadoudal, Georges (1771–1804) A leader of the *chouans* during the Revolution and Consulate. Born near Auray in the Morbihan. He was involved in the Vendéan insurrection against the Revolution from its beginning in 1793, thereafter he organised royalist *chouan* guerrillas in Brittany. He hoped that Napoleon might restore the monarchy and had an interview with him in 1800. Napoleon himself tried to win his allegiance with the offer of a general's commission and 100,000 francs a year if he would give up his royalist activities. Continuing to conspire on behalf of the monarchy Cadoudal fled to England, returning to Brittany in the summer of 1803 armed with British money to finance an insurrection in Paris. He was arrested in Paris in March 1804 and executed the following June.

Cambacérès, Jean-Jacques Régis de (1753–1824) French statesman. Born into a noble family in Montpellier, like his father he studied law. Elected to the National Convention in 1792 he interested himself in legal reform and stayed out of contentious politics during the Terror. He served in political and administrative posts under both the Thermidorians and the Directory. His capacity for hard work, his ability, intelligence and knowledge of the law appealed to Bonaparte, and contributed to his appointment as consul after Brumaire. He acted briefly as Minister of Justice at the close of 1799, but throughout the Consulate and Empire he supervised the administration of justice and played a key role in the preparation of the Civil Code. Appointed Arch-Chancellor of the Empire, during Napoleon's absences he also supervised the imperial administration presiding over the senate and most of the meetings of the council of state. In 1808 he was created Duke of Parma. Loyal to Napoleon, he was still prepared to speak his mind and counselled against the abduction of d'Enghien (q.v.), and against the invasions of both Spain and Russia. He served reluctantly during the Hundred Days, and was exiled as a regicide during the second restoration. In 1818 he was restored to his French citizenship and returned to France where he spent the last six years of his life in retirement; shrewd investments during his time in public life had made him a very wealthy man.

Canning, George (1770–1827) British statesman. Canning's father had been disowned by his gentry family and lived a penurious existence as a barrister, wine merchant and writer. He died a year after his son was born. The family was persuaded to acknowledge the young Canning, giving him a small estate of £200 a year, and sending him to Eton and Oxford. He entered parliament in 1793 becoming a staunch supporter of Pitt (q.v.) and winning a reputation for his brilliant oratory. Under-Secretary of State for Foreign Affairs from 1796 to 1799 and Joint Paymaster of the Forces in 1800, he resigned with Pitt in 1801. He used his merciless wit in journals like the *Anti-Jacobin* as well as against political opponents; in 1801 this included Pitt's successor, Addington (q.v.). On Pitt's return to office he became Treasurer of the Navy (1804–6). He was Foreign Secretary from 1807 to 1809. In this post he quarrelled with Castlereagh (q.v.) and was wounded in the resulting duel (1810). He held no cabinet post for the next twelve years, but his abilities brought him considerable administrative and committee work, notably as president of the Board of Control (1816–20) where he was influential in organising the affairs of British India. On Castlereagh's suicide (1822) he became Foreign Secretary where he recognised the independence of the American colonies in revolt against Spain and backed the Greeks in their struggle for independence against Turkey. When Liverpool had a stroke in February 1827, Canning became Prime Minister. He died the following August.

Canova, Antonio (1757–1822) Italian sculptor. Born near Treviso into a family of stonemasons. He worked in his grandfather's shop until he was 12 when his talent caught the eye of a patron who sent him to study in Venice. A successful sculptor by his early twenties, he moved to Rome where he executed several celebrated pieces for the Church. In 1802, following an invitation from Napoleon, he made the first of two trips to Paris. He executed several busts of the imperial family as well as statues, most notably a nude Venus (for which the model was Pauline Bonaparte (q.v.)). Napoleon was offended by a classical statue of himself modelled on the Belvedere Apollo (and subsequently acquired by the Duke of Wellington). Canova refused to accept both a position at the imperial court and the Legion of Honour and was critical of Napoleon for taking so many Italian works of art to France. In 1815, under the terms of the Second Treaty of Paris, he supervised the return of many of these. His tomb for Vittorio Alfieri (1803–10) in Florence is regarded as one of the first representations of Italy as a nation state; it was seen by contemporaries as a political statement, and inspired later nationalists.

Biographies

Carnot, Lazare-Nicolas-Marguerite (1753–1823) French soldier and administrator. The son of a Burgundian advocate he joined the army engineers at the age of 20 and was promoted captain in 1783. He made a name for himself as a writer on military matters, particularly fortifications. Sympathetic to the ideas of the Revolution he was elected to the Legislative Assembly (1791) then to the Convention (1792). Appointed to the Committee of Public Safety in August 1793 he took control of the war effort and bears much of the credit for the success of the Revolutionary armies. His achievements as the 'organiser of victory' helped save him after Thermidor; he was chosen as one of the five Directors in November 1795. He went into exile to escape arrest during the coup of Fructidor, but returned after that of Brumaire. Serving briefly as Minister of War (1800–1801) he went into retirement disliking Napoleon's penchant for personal rule. Appointed senator in 1802 and given a pension in 1809 he continued to oppose Napoleon and devoted much of his time to scientific pursuits and to writing on military matters. When France was invaded in 1814 he offered his services to Napoleon and he was made a general and governor of Antwerp, which he defended brilliantly. He again joined Napoleon during the Hundred Days and served as Minister of the Interior. Exiled as a regicide, on the second restoration he travelled in eastern Europe before settling in Magdeburg where he died.

Castaños, Francisco Xavier (1756–1852) Spanish soldier. He fought in a series of campaigns before the French Revolution, notably in the siege of Gibraltar (1779–82) and in expeditions against the Barbary pirates. As Captain General of the Campo del Gibraltar he led his army in revolt against the French, 30 May 1808. It was his army in Andalucia which defeated Dupont at Bailén, though he himself was not present on the field. The only partisan of Godoy (q.v.) to have remained in a position of high command he was hated by the Palafox (q.v.) faction, while several of his subordinates were jealous that he had stolen the credit for Bailén. In 1809 his enemies had him disgraced, but the following year he came back to head the Regency. He assisted Wellington in the campaigns of Salamanca and Vitoria, and his dismissal by the Spanish government in June 1813 prompted a serious dispute between that government and Wellington. After 1815 he served as a member of the Council of State, tutor to Isabella II, and President of the Council of Castile.

Castlereagh, Robert Stewart, Viscount (1769–1822) British statesman. The eldest son of an Ulster landowner he entered the Irish parliament in 1790 and the British parliament four years later. When his father became an earl (1796) he accepted the courtesy title of Viscount Castlereagh. Between 1797 and 1800 he held a succession of administrative posts in the Irish government, notably Lord Privy Seal (1798). He urged the union of Britain and Ireland and the emancipation of the Catholics; when George III (q.v.) refused to agree to the latter in 1801, like Pitt (q.v.), he resigned. In 1805 Pitt made him Secretary for War and the Colonies. Out of office under the 'Talents' he returned to the War Office in 1807 where he became a firm supporter of Wellesley in the Peninsular. Serious friction with Canning (q.v.) at the Foreign Office resulted in a duel and temporary eclipse. In March 1812 he was appointed Foreign Secretary and, on the assassination of Perceval (q.v.), he became leader of the Commons; he continued to hold both posts until his death. He played a key role in organising the final coalitions against Napoleon and represented Britain at the Congress of Vienna. It was Castlereagh who proposed St. Helena for Napoleon's exile. In the post-war world he opposed many of the reactionary policies pursued by the European monarchs, but as leader of the Commons he was strongly associated with the reactionary policies pursued at home. On the death of his father (1821) he became 2nd Marquess Londonderry. Afflicted by ill-health and mental disorder, in the following year he committed suicide by cutting his throat.

Caulaincourt, Armand-Augustin-Louis (1773–1827) French statesman. Born into a noble family in Picardy he enlisted in the royal cavalry when only 14. Refusing to emigrate he served throughout the Revolutionary wars. In 1801, probably on Talleyrand's (q.v.) advice, he was sent to St. Petersburg to negotiate an understanding between France and Russia. He was involved with the kidnapping of d'Enghien (q.v.) and was ordered to justify it to the Baden government. Appointed grand master of the horse (1804) and Duke of Vicenza (1808). He served as ambassador to St. Petersburg (1807–11) from where he was recalled at his own request given the growing friction between France and Russia. He counselled against the invasion of Russia, but went on the expedition and was chosen by Napoleon as his personal companion when he left the army to return to Paris. During 1813 and 1814, as Minister of Foreign Affairs, he attempted to negotiate a settlement with the allies. Talleyrand wanted him in the provisional government of 1814, but Caulaincourt remained loyal to Napoleon. Reluctantly he was Minister of Foreign Affairs again during the Hundred Days; he considered diplomatic efforts at that time to be futile. On the second restoration he retired to his estates where he died.

Champagny, Jean-Baptiste Nompère de (1756–1834) French statesman. Born into the nobility, he served as a naval officer during the old regime. A deputy for the nobility to the Estates General he concerned himself with naval matters, but retired to private life in 1791. In 1799 Bonaparte made him councillor of state for the department of the navy, and later sent him as ambassador to Vienna. Alleged to have profited from his appointment as Minister of the Interior (1804–7) he nevertheless replaced Talleyrand (q.v.) as Foreign Minister (1807–11). In 1808 he was created Duke of Cadore. He sided with the first restoration and was made a peer, but joined Napoleon during the Hundred Days and lost the new honours following Waterloo. His peerage was restored in 1819. He died in Paris.

Chaptal, Jean-Antoine (1756–1832) French chemist and statesman. The son of well-to-do peasants in the Lozère his abilities were encouraged by a wealthy uncle who was a physician in Montpellier. He studied medicine at Montpellier and chemistry in Paris returning to teach the former at the University of Montpellier and establishing a new chemical factory in the city employing the latest methods. A supporter of the early phase of the Revolution he was opposed to the policies of the dominant Jacobins in Paris and led the opposition to them in Montpellier. This action nearly cost him his life, but his services as a chemist and administrator were needed to improve the production of ammunition for the Revolutionary armies. Recognising his ability Bonaparte made him first a member of the Council of State and then Minister of the Interior (1800–1804). Chaptal played a key role in establishing the new administrative structure for France, in developing public works, technical education, and in collecting statistical information. He retired in 1804 to supervise his chemical factories and to develop farming techniques on his own property. From here he continued to give advice to successive governments. In 1818 he was appointed to the Chamber of Peers. His books on chemistry and industry were popular and made new knowledge widely available; his memoirs are considered to be among the most reliable of Napoleon's subordinates.

Charles (Carlos) IV (1748–1819) King of Spain. The second son of Charles III of Spain who succeeded his father in 1788 since his elder brother was epileptic and insane. Of mediocre intelligence and mentally unstable he is generally supposed to have played little part in government preferring to leave matters to his wife, Maria Luisa of Parma and the royal favourite Godoy (q.v.). Charles joined the first coalition against Revolutionary France, but agreed to make peace in 1795, and became a French ally in 1796. Between 1801 and 1808 he generally supported Napoleon's policies. Forced to abdicate by his son, Ferdinand (q.v.) in 1808, he hoped that Napoleon would restore him; instead Napoleon compelled both Charles and Ferdinand to renounce the throne. Charles eventually retired to Rome where he died.

Charles XIII (1748–1818) King of Sweden. The second son of King Adolphus Frederick of Sweden and his queen (the sister of Frederick the Great) he worked with his brother, Gustavus III on reform projects in their country, and served as admiral in the Swedish fleet during the Russo-Swedish War (1788). On the assassination of his brother (1792) he was regent until his nephew's majority in 1796. On the latter's accession as Gustavus IV (q.v.) he largely retired from public life, but was again appointed regent after the coup of March 1809. The following summer he was elected king. His health and abilities were failing fast and when Bernadotte (q.v.) was chosen as his heir he yielded all authority to him. He became King of Norway as well as Sweden in 1814.

Charles (Karl Ludwig) of Habsburg (1771–1847) Archduke of Austria and brother of Francis II (q.v.). Even though he was epileptic and of a sensitive nature he was determined to be a soldier and joined the Austrian army in 1790. He served during the Revolutionary wars becoming commander of the Austrian armies on the Rhine in 1796. Promoted to Field Marshal in 1801 he tried to introduce reforms into the army but was thwarted by the bureaucracy and the court; he lost his position in 1805 after criticising the new war against Napoleon. Recalled in 1806 as commander-in-chief he began, at last, to implement his reforms. He considered the Austrian army not yet ready when war was again declared on France in 1809, but, under his leadership, it defeated the French at Aspern-Essling, and performed well at Wagram. He retired from the army and public life after 1809 to concentrate on his family and on his military writings. He is regarded as second only to Wellington as a military commander against the French. In 1822 he succeeded to the Duchy of Saxe-Teschen.

Charles Frederick (Karl Friedrich) (1728–1811) Grand Duke of Baden. Born in Karlsruhe he became Margrave of the Protestant principality of Baden in 1738. In 1771 he succeeded also as ruler of the catholic principality of Baden-Baden thus uniting the territories divided during the Reformation. Inspired by the ideas of the Enlightenment he chose reformist ministers and this led to the abolition of torture (1767) and the freeing of many serfs (1783). He supported the reorganisation of Germany by the *Reichsdeputationshauptschluss* and by Napoleon, not the least since these enlarged his territories. In 1803 he was made elector, and three years later grand duke. His son was killed in an accident in 1801 and as a result his grandson, Charles Ludwig Frederick (q.v.), became his heir. His final years saw the introduction of some French style reforms, such as the Code Napoleon.

Charles Ludwig Frederick (Karl Ludwig Friedrich) (1786–1818) Grand Duke of Baden. The grandson of Charles Frederick of Baden (q.v.), he became heir to the duchy on the death of his father in 1801. In 1806 he married Stephanie de Beauharnais, the cousin of the Empress Josephine (q.v.); it was a political marriage to cement the alliance with Napoleon. In 1809 he became co-regent with his grandfather, and succeeded him as Grand Duke in 1811. His rule was characterised by liberal reforms; he gave Baden both a constitution and a parliament. His own son died in infancy, after which he arranged for the succession to go to his grandfather's children by his second, morganatic marriage.

Chateaubriand, François-René de (1768–1848) French statesman and man of letters. Born into a noble family at Saint Malo, the youngest of 10 children. Initially sympathetic to the Revolution, he travelled briefly in America in 1791, returning to serve in the *émigré* army in which he was wounded in 1793. During his exile in England (1793–1800) he began to develop his writing skills. In 1800 he returned to France; his name was removed from the list of proscribed *émigrés*, and he began to make a name for himself through his writing. *Le génie du Christianisme*, initially conceived as a defence of Christianity, appeared at the same time as the Concordat and earned him both public acclaim and official approval. In 1803 he was sent to Rome as first secretary to the embassy, but he did not get on with Cardinal Fesch (q.v.) and was recalled to be French minister to the Valais. Before he could leave for Switzerland the news of the execution of d'Enghien (q.v.) prompted him to resign in disgust. From then on he became an open, but cautious critic of Napoleon. In 1807 he was banished from Paris for writing an essay comparing Napoleon to Nero published in a journal of which he was part owner, *Le Mercure de France*. In 1814 he declared for the Bourbons with a pamphlet *De Bonaparte, des Bourbons, et de la nécessité de se rallier à nos princes légitimes*. A minister during the second restoration, he was dismissed in 1816 for a pamphlet critical of Louis XVIII; the following year he began a celebrated liaison with Mme Récamier (q.v.) which was to continue until his death. French ambassador to Berlin (1821), and to London (1822), he represented France at the Congress of Verona (1822) organising the French intervention in Spain. He served briefly as Minister of Foreign Affairs (1823–4). Minister to Rome in 1827, he resigned in 1829. He spent most of the 1830s completing and revising his memoirs, which are now the best known of his works, and which began to be published a few months after his death.

Chauvin, Nicolas Mythical French soldier and super-patriot. Allegedly born in Rochefort c.1780, he enlisted in the army at 18, fought in numerous campaigns, was wounded 17 times, and was rewarded with a sword of honour and a pension of 200 francs. But Chauvin's first ever appearance appears to have been in the Cogniard brothers' play *La Cocade Tricoleure* (1831). The character was then developed by Arago in searching for the etymology of *chauvinisme* for the *Dictionnaire de la conversation* (1834).

Christian Augustus, Prince (1768–1810) Crown Prince of Sweden. The third son of Duke Frederick I of Schleswig-Holstein, he was educated at the University of Leipzig before joining the Danish army. He served as an officer in the Austrian army 1799–1801; on his return, in 1803, he was appointed military commander of southern Norway. At the beginning of the Anglo-Danish war (1807) he was made president of the *Regjeringskommission* in Norway; here he checked a Swedish invasion and negotiated an armistice (Dec 1808). Following the Swedish coup of March 1809 he played a very complex role in Scandinavian politics attempting to mediate peace between Denmark and Sweden and unite the two countries under Frederick VI (q.v.). His own politics were more liberal than those of Frederick and made him more preferable to the Swedes who chose him as their Crown Prince in August 1809. Having changed his name to Charles Augustus, he entered Sweden on 6 January 1810. The following May he died of a stroke while reviewing troops. Rumours that his death was the result of poisoning prompted serious disorder.

Clarke, Henri-Jacques-Guillaume (1765–1818) French soldier and administrator. Of Irish extraction he entered the *Ecole Militaire* in

1781 and was promoted captain three years later. Briefly dismissed as politically unreliable during the early stages of the Revolutionary wars he reached the rank of general in 1793. Under the Directory he became head of the war ministry's topographical department. Sent to Italy in 1796 he came under Bonaparte's influence. He served in a variety of capacities under the Consulate and in the early stages of the Empire; Napoleon made him governor of Vienna after Austerlitz (1805) and governor of Berlin after Jena (1806). In 1807 he was created Duke of Feltre and Minister of War; he brought order to the latter office but he had little to do with policy and was largely required to facilitate Napoleon's war plans. In 1814 he rallied to the Bourbons and went into exile with Louis XVIII during the Hundred Days. In the second restoration he was again Minister of War and was promoted to marshal when he left office in 1817.

Clausewitz, Karl von (1780–1831) Prussian soldier and military thinker. Joined the army in 1792 and saw action in the Revolutionary wars. Entered the Berlin military academy in 1801 and became the protégé of its director, Scharnhorst (q.v.). Captured during the Jena campaign (1806) he finally returned to Prussia in 1809 where he assisted Scharnhorst in the reorganisation of the Prussian army. Fought as a Russian officer in the campaigns of 1812–14. He re-entered Prussian service in 1814 and fought in the Waterloo campaign. In 1818 he was promoted to major-general and appointed as director of the Military Academy (*Allgemeine Kriegsschule*) where he remained until 1830. He died of cholera in 1831. He is chiefly remembered for his study *Vom Kriege* (On War) published after his death, an analysis of the philosophy of war.

Cobenzl, Ludwig von (1753–1809) Austrian statesman. Born into a noble family which had provided diplomats for the Habsburgs since the sixteenth century he became a protégé of Chancellor Kaunitz and served in a variety of diplomatic posts: Copenhagen (1774); Berlin (1777); St. Petersburg (1779). He negotiated the Third Partition of Poland (1795) and the Treaty of Campo Formio (1797) on Austria's behalf. In September 1800 he was put in charge of Austrian foreign affairs, and a year later was appointed chancellor. While a good diplomatist he was not a particularly able politician; moreover in spite of his rank he never had full control of affairs as the Emperor Francis (q.v.) took an active interest and listened to the advice of Colloredo (q.v.). Made the scapegoat for the Austrian defeat at Austerlitz, he was dismissed in December 1805.

Colloredo, Franz von, Count (1731–1807) Austrian statesman. Hostile to the Enlightenment, a conservative and loyal to the Church, he was appointed by the Emperor Joseph II as tutor to his eldest nephew, Francis (q.v.). When Francis became emperor he made Colloredo head of his private secretariat and created a special rank for him of *Kabinettsminister.* He remained a powerful influence at court until the disastrous Austerlitz campaign during which he was dismissed in November 1805.

Consalvi, Ercole (1757–1824) Cleric and Papal statesman. Born in Rome where he entered the Church. He was accused by the French government of being instrumental in the killing of General Duphot during a riot in Rome in December 1797; for this he was imprisoned on the creation of the Roman Republic (January 1798). Secretary to the Conclave which elected Pius VII (q.v.) (November 1799), the new Pope made him Cardinal Secretary of State. He negotiated the final draft of the Concordat but was furious when, without consultation, Napoleon added the Organic Articles to it; he also developed an antipathy to Napoleon's uncle, Cardinal Fesch (q.v.). He showed his hostility to Napoleon over the arrest of Pius VII; his refusal to attend the Emperor's marriage to Marie Louise led to his being exiled to Rheims. Permitted to see Pius VII in 1813, he urged him to resist Napoleon, and was consequently imprisoned at Béziers until the end of the Empire. While the Papacy had no formal representation at the Congress of Vienna, Consalvi was present, spoke on the Pope's behalf, and persuaded the delegates that the Papal States should remain intact. As Secretary of State in the Papal States during the restoration he introduced a variety of reforms, but was regarded as too liberal by many of the clerics and was dismissed on Pius VII's death.

Constant (de Rebecque), Henri Benjamin (1767–1830) French man of letters and politician, usually referred to simply as Benjamin Constant. Born in Lausanne, the son of an army officer of French Huguenot descent, he was educated in Germany and in Britain where he met several prominent Whigs. He briefly served in the court of the Duke of Brunswick (q.v.), moving to Paris after the fall of Robespierre. He became the lover of Madame de Staël (q.v.) and, with her, a key figure in moderate republican circles which had an influence on the Directory. The two became important liberal critics of the Bonapartist regime and went into exile in 1803. Principally spending the next ten years in Germany, he returned to Paris during the first restoration where he wrote several pamphlets urging, in particular, constitutional monarchy and freedom of the press. He met, and switched his allegiance to, Napoleon during the Hundred Days and drafted the *acte additionel*. He served as a liberal deputy for most of the restoration and continued to be a strong advocate of press freedom. Following the Revolution of 1830, and shortly before his death, he briefly held office under Louis Philippe.

Crétet, Emmanuel (1747–1809) French statesman. The son of a merchant in the Isère he went to work for a Bordeaux shipowner, made a fortune in trade with America, and became director of a fire insurance company in Paris. He increased his fortune during the Revolution by purchasing monastic lands near Dijon. Elected to the Council of Ancients under the Directory he was active in tax legislation. He rallied to Bonaparte after Brumaire and was made a councillor of state, a senator, and director general of bridges and highways in the Ministry of the Interior. In the latter post he carried through a number of reforms and improvements. In 1806 he was appointed governor of the Bank of France, which he reorganised within a year. In 1807 he was appointed Minister of the Interior, but a serious illness forced his early retirement before he could have much impact.

Cuesta, Gregorio García de la (1740–1812) Spanish soldier. Having gained some success in the war against Revolutionary France he was made President of the Council of Castile in 1798. Three years later his opposition to Godoy (q.v.) led to his disgrace. Ferdinand VII (q.v.) made him Captain General of Castile in March 1808 and here, against his will, he was forced to join the rising against the French. In September the Central Junta had him arrested for defying its authority, but it subsequently appointed him to command the Army of Extremadura. He co-operated reluctantly with Wellington (q.v.) in the Talavera campaign, and was incapacitated by a stroke, 12 August 1809. He retired to Majorca, eventually becoming its governor. He died in 1812 after further quarrels with the British.

Czartoryski, Adam Jerzy, Prince (1770–1861) Polish statesman. Czartoryski fought for his native Poland during the Second Partition of the country (1793); his family estates were confiscated during the Third Partition (1795) when he entered Russian service and had some of his lands restored. He became a close friend and confidant of Grand Duke Alexander and was appointed foreign minister when Alexander succeeded as Tsar. He organised the Russian alliance with Austria and Britain which led to the Austerlitz campaign. In 1805 he drafted a notable memorial for the reorganisation of Europe proposing that Germany be divided between Austria and Prussia, that the latter powers agree to an autonomous Poland under the protection of an enlarged Russia, and that the overall balance of power be maintained by Britain and Russia. He lost favour and ministerial rank in 1807, but retained close links with the Tsar and was with him at the Congress of Vienna. Czartoryski became a senator in Congress Poland, and served as president during the Polish Revolution of 1830. Following the Polish defeat he emigrated to Paris where he spent his last thirty years, and where his house became a centre for Polish politics and culture.

Dabrowski (sometimes **Dombrowski**), **Jan Henryk** (1755–1818) Polish soldier. Born near Cracow he served in the Saxon army between 1770 and 1784, and joined the Polish army in 1791. In 1795, following the Third Partition of Poland, he took refuge in France and raised a Polish Legion to fight alongside the French armies in Italy. Promoted general in 1800. In 1806 he returned to Poland and at Poznan he recruited a Polish division for service in the imperial army; this fought at Danzig and Friedland. He served with the Polish corps in the Russian campaign and was wounded at the Berezina. After Leipzig he succeeded Poniatowski (q.v.) as commander of the Polish corps. On the fall of Napoleon he returned to Poland (1814) where, reconciled with the Tsar, he was made a senator. He retired from public life in 1816. The hymn of the Polish Legion, *Mazurek Dabrowski*, became the Polish national anthem.

Dalberg, Karl Theodor von (1744–1817) German cleric. Before the Revolution he was a leader of the Catholic Enlightenment. He succeeded as civil governor of Erfurt in 1772, and was subsequently elected as coadjutor of Mainz and of Worms (1787) and of Constance (1800). In 1802 he succeeded as Archbishop-Elector of Mainz and as such was the only ecclesiastical prince in Germany to survive the secularisation of 1803. From Mainz he tried to reactivate the machinery of the Holy Roman Empire into a central government for Germany, but eventually threw in his lot with Napoleon. He participated in the coronation in Notre Dame and, in 1806 was created Prince-Primate of the Confederation of the Rhine. He attempted to turn the latter into a federal state but was thwarted by the reluctance of the German princes to give up their independence. Napoleon created him Grand Duke of Frankfurt in 1810. He went into exile in Zurich after the battle of Leipzig, and published a justification of his activities in 1815 saying that he had only ever been motivated by a desire for the unity and independence of Germany. He died in Ratisbon.

Daru, Pierre-Antoine-Noel-Bruno, comte (1767–1829) French military administrator. The son of an advocate who had become secretary general in the Intendant's office in Languedoc, his first position was as a clerk in that office until, in 1784, his father purchased him a position in the quartermaster corps of the royal army. Suspected, and briefly imprisoned during the Terror, he continued as a quartermaster during the Revolutionary wars. His capacity for hard work and his efficiency hastened promotion and in 1799 he was chief quartermaster for Masséna's (q.v.) Army of Switzerland. Napoleon put great confidence in him, notably charging him with the supply of the *Grande Armée* during the Austerlitz and Jena campaigns and then with levying contributions from the defeated enemies. He urged Napoleon to marry a French woman rather than an Austrian princess, and advised against the invasion of Russia, but he accompanied Napoleon during the latter as minister secretary of state. He served as minister for the administration of war in 1813–14 and again during the Hundred Days. Appointed a member of the Chamber of Peers during the second restoration he became best known for his literary output, publishing histories of Venice and Brittany, his own poetry, and translations of Horace.

David, Jacques-Louis (1748–1825) French painter. Born in Paris, by the Revolution he had developed a reputation for his large canvases depicting classical subjects. He became an enthusiast for the Revolution; he joined the Jacobin Club, was elected to the National Convention and voted for Louis XVI's execution. He planned the great republican festivals and painted republican martyrs, notably *Marat assassiné*. He was imprisoned after Thermidor, but began a long relationship with Bonaparte in 1797, subsequently producing several paintings of propaganda value to the imperial regime: *Bonaparte au mont Saint-Bernard* (1800); *Le sacre* (1807); *La distribution des aigles* (1810). He was appointed First Painter to the Emperor in 1804, and later created a senator and an officer of the Legion of Honour. Forced into exile as a regicide by the second restoration, he settled in Brussels where he returned to classical subjects.

Davout (sometimes Davoût or Davoust) Louis-Nicolas (1770–1823) French soldier. Born into the nobility at Annoux (Yonne) he entered the *Ecole Militaire* in 1785. He served with distinction in the early campaigns of the Revolution and was promoted general early in 1793. Suspected because of his noble birth, he was briefly removed from the active list, but subsequently fought in the Rhineland (1794–7), in the Egyptian campaign, and at Marengo. In 1801 he was made commander of the Consular Guard, and a marshal in 1804. One of the ablest of Napoleon's generals he was also noted for his strict discipline; these attributes ensured that his III Corps was often entrusted with key manoeuvres and with bearing the brunt of enemy attacks as, for example, at Austerlitz. His brilliant victory at Auerstädt (1806) was celebrated by his creation as Duke of Auerstädt (1808); in 1809 he was made Prince of Eckmühl. He retired from public life during the first restoration, but rejoined Napoleon on his return from Elba and was appointed Minister of War. He remained in Paris during the Waterloo campaign, and took charge of the city's defence in its aftermath. On the second restoration he was deprived of his rank and titles, but these were returned when he became reconciled to the Bourbons in 1817 and two years later he was made a member of the Chamber of Peers.

Despard, Edward Marcus (1751–1803) British soldier and revolutionary. The youngest son of an Irish landed family he joined the army in 1760 serving mainly in the West Indies. He showed particular ability as an engineer, rising to the rank of colonel and becoming Military Superintendent of Yucatan. His unpopularity with local officials led to his recall in 1790, but the charges against him were dropped (in 1792) and the promise of recompense was never forthcoming. His bitterness encouraged him to enter radical politics and by the late 1790s he was a militant republican with links to both Irish rebels and the French. In 1798 he was arrested and held until 1801 under the suspension of the Habeas Corpus Act. In November 1802 he was arrested again and charged with high treason. The extent and seriousness of the Despard plot remains controversial. In spite of the appearance of Nelson (q.v.) as a character witness, Despard was convicted and executed with six accomplices.

Diez, Juan Martin, see El Empecinado.

Dörnberg, Wilhelm Ferdinand Kaspar, Baron von (1768–1850) German soldier and statesman. Born near Hersfeld in Hesse he served with Hessian troops in the wars against Revolutionary France, later transferring to Prussian service. After Jena he retired to his estates but, in 1807, he accepted an invitation from Jerome Bonaparte to organise the guards of Westphalia. As colonel of

Jerome's guard he plotted an uprising in communication with Stein (q.v.) and Brunswick (q.v.). The rising, in April 1809, was a failure but, helped by sympathetic peasants, he escaped first to Bohemia, then to England. He fought for the Russians in 1812–1813, and with German troops under British command at Waterloo. After the wars he entered Hanoverian service and was ambassador to St. Petersburg 1818–19 and 1825–35. He died in Münster.

El Empecinado (Diez, Juan Martin) (1775–1825) Spanish guerrilla leader. Born into a well-to-do peasant family in Old Castile he ran away to join the army but was brought back by his parents as he was under 16. According to tradition he fought with distinction in the Spanish cavalry against Revolutionary France. Following the peace in 1795 he married and settled down near Aranda. With a small group of about a dozen men he began guerrilla attacks on French lines of communication about the time of the *Dos de Mayo*. He took the *nom de guerre* 'El Empecinado' from the word *pecina* (slime), applied to the mud carried by the stream in the village where he was born. The Central Junta acknowledged his military effectiveness with the rank of captain (April 1809) and then (September 1810) of general. Noted for his generosity and humanity in a particularly savage war, his centre of operations was the province of Guadalajara; by the end of 1810 he is said to have commanded some 5000 men. On the restoration of Ferdinand VII (q.v.) he requested the king to restore the constitution of 1812, and was exiled to Valladolid. During the revolution of 1820 he joined the Liberal regime. Although promised safe conduct by Ferdinand in 1823 he was imprisoned, periodically exhibited publicly in a cage, and finally executed.

Emmet, Robert (1778–1803) Irish rebel. The youngest son of the physician to the Lord Lieutenant of Ireland he entered Trinity College Dublin in 1793 where he showed an aptitude for maths and chemistry, and acquired a reputation as an orator. He left university in 1798 without taking his degree and involved himself with the United Irishmen, a radical and, by this time, revolutionary organisation among whose leaders was his brother Thomas Addis Emmet. He travelled in Europe with his brother, and others, negotiating with the French for assistance in a rising against British rule. He returned to Ireland in October 1802 partly for family reasons, but also because he was one of the few United Irish leaders against whom there was no charge in Ireland and this enabled him to act as a messenger. In July 1803 he was a key figure in an insurrection in

Dublin; he appears to have hoped to restore dignity to Irish republicanism and prove that it was not subservient to the French with
whom he had become disillusioned. The rising received little support; Emmet was captured, tried for high treason, and executed.
During his trial he made a passionate speech from the dock ex-
plaining his beliefs and motives, and which subsequently inspired
generations of Irish nationalists.

Enghien, Louis Antoine Henri de Bourbon Condé, duc d' (1772–
1804) French nobleman. Born in Chantilly the son of the Prince of
Condé and the sister of the Duke of Orleans. During the wars
against the French Revolution he served with the *émigré* army, but
on the dissolution of this army following the Peace of Lunéville he
married and took up residence at Ettenheim in Baden, close to the
Rhine. Early in 1804 Napoleon received information suggesting
that a French prince was about to arrive in France in league with
Cadoudal (q.v.) and Pichegru (q.v.). Acting on orders from Napoleon French gendarmes crossed into Baden and seized d'Enghien
who was then brought to Vincennes, tried by a military court and
shot.

Espoz y Mina, Don Francisco (1781–1836) Spanish guerrilla
leader. Born Francisco Espoz into a well-to-do peasant family near
Pamplona, Navarre, he became head of the family on his father's
death in 1796. During the insurrection against Napoleon in 1808
he joined a battalion of regular Spanish troops in Aragon, but when
this force was defeated he joined a guerrilla band organised by his
nephew Xavier Mina. Xavier was captured in March 1810 and Francisco took command, subsequently (the story goes) adding his
nephew's name to his own becoming known as Espoz y Mina, or
just Mina. The juntas in Aragon and Castile agreed to make him
commander of all the *partidas* in Navarre following which he
brought all the bands in the province under his control. In September 1810 the Central Junta made him a colonel. Mina's men fought
a ferocious war against the French with atrocities and reprisals on
both sides. By 1813 his force amounted to some 13,500 men of all
arms, and was integrated into the Spanish army. Disillusioned with
Ferdinand VII (q.v.), after an abortive rising in Navarre he went
into exile in France, returning during the revolution of 1820 to
command one of the liberal armies. Following the defeat of the revolution he again went into exile, returning to Spain on Ferdinand's
death when he was restored to military command. He died in Barcelona.

Ferdinand IV (1751–1825) King of Naples, King of the Two Sicilies. The third son of Charles, King of Naples, he succeeded in 1759 when his father became King of Spain. A regency ruled for him until 1767. The following year he married Maria Caroline of Habsburg, an intelligent and forceful woman who guided Neapolitan policy towards the Habsburgs and allowed her husband to follow his favoured pursuits of hunting, fishing and agriculture. In December 1798 Ferdinand and Maria Caroline were driven from Naples by the French, escaping to Sicily in Nelson's (q.v.) flagship. Following a rebellion in Naples which toppled the new Parthenopean Republic, Ferdinand returned in 1801. He joined the Third Coalition in 1805, and on its defeat was again forced into exile on Sicily where he remained under British protection from 1806–14. He briefly handed rule over to his eldest son (1809–12), but was encouraged back by Bentinck (q.v.) who also persuaded him to introduce a liberal constitution. Maria Caroline opposed this reform but Bentinck succeeded in having her exiled to Vienna, where she died (Sep 1814). Ferdinand married his mistress and, on the fall of Murat (q.v.), returned to Naples taking the title King of the Two Sicilies. His rule following his restoration was noted for repression. This prompted an abortive revolution in 1820, but one which forced him, once again, into temporary exile.

Ferdinand (Fernando) VII (1784–1833) King of Spain. The eldest son of Charles IV of Spain (q.v.) he developed an intense dislike of his parents and his mother's favourite, Godoy (q.v.). He was involved in conspiracy against his father, discovered in 1807, but the following year he succeeded in forcing his father to abdicate. In turn he was compelled to renounce the throne by Napoleon and from 1808 to 1814 he lived in luxurious exile under military guard at Valençay in France. Returning to Spain in 1814 he rejected the liberal constitution of 1812, persecuted liberals, but also succeeded in alienating loyal army officers who disliked the way in which he surrounded himself with young noblemen who had played no part in the war against Napoleon. A series of military coups reached a successful climax in 1820 and Ferdinand was forced to accept the constitution of 1812. Restored to full power by the intervention of a French army in 1823 he proceeded to alienate the French by a cruel and vengeful persecution of his opponents.

Fesch, Joseph (1763–1839) Born in Ajaccio, Corsica, the son of a Swiss army officer and the widowed mother of Letizia Bonaparte. Archdeacon of Ajaccio, on the outbreak of the French Revolution he retired from the Church and became a military contractor. His fortunes rose with those of the Bonapartes and he re-entered the Church. He played an active role in the negotiations on the Concordat, becoming Archbishop of Lyon (1802), Cardinal (1803) and French ambassador to Rome (1804) where he was caught in the middle in the arguments between Napoleon and the Pope. He retired to Rome first in 1814 and, after supporting Napoleon during the Hundred Days, again in 1815; here he spent the remainder of his life amassing a large art collection.

Fichte, Johann Gottlieb (1762–1814) German philosopher. The son of a ribbon weaver he spent the early part of his adult life as a tutor and writer. In 1793 he published two critical analyses of the French Revolution and was appointed to a chair of Philosophy at the University of Jena. He lost the position in 1799, accused of atheist sympathies in his work, and moved to Berlin. Temporarily driven from the city following the French victory at Jena (1806) he returned in 1807 and the remaining years of his life were most notable for his involvement in political affairs. In 1807–8 he delivered a series of Addresses to the German Nation (*Reden an die deutsche Nation*) in which he equated the idea of 'Germanness' with morality. In 1810–12 he was rector of the new University of Berlin.

Fouché, Joseph (1759–1820) French statesman and noted minister of police. Born near Nantes the son of a merchant sea captain he was educated by the Oratorians and subsequently served as a lay teacher in their schools. He became active in Jacobin politics, was elected to the National Convention in 1792 and, during the following two years, he was prominent in the dechristianising campaign and in ruthlessly suppressing counter-revolution in the provinces. He was involved in the coup which overthrew Robespierre but then sank into obscurity and poverty. He became a protégé of the Director Paul Barras in 1798 making diplomatic missions to Italy and Holland; the following year he became Minister of Police. He retained the position after the coup of Brumaire acting effectively against both Jacobin and Royalist threats to the Consulate. Napoleon became worried by his intrigues and abolished the Ministry of Police in 1802; however, two years later it was re-established with Fouché, again, in charge. Fouché was created Duke of Otranto in 1809, but the following year he was dismissed and banished to Aix for opening secret communications with the British. In 1813 he was appointed governor of the Illyrian provinces. During the first restoration he returned to Paris and though he served as Minister of

Police during the Hundred Days, he also maintained links with Metternich (q.v.) and helped re-establish the monarchy in 1815. Banished as a regicide in 1816, he eventually became naturalised as an Austrian and retired to Trieste where he died.

Fox, Charles James (1749–1806) British statesman. Third son of the 1st Earl Holland he was educated at Eton and Oxford and entered parliament in 1769. He was noted in his early years for a passion for gambling and for his attractive personality which brought great loyalty and devotion from his friends. He was a brilliant parliamentary orator, yet he spent most of his political career in opposition serving in government only briefly under Lord North (1770–72), as a coalition partner with Lord North (1782–83), and as Foreign Secretary in the 'Talents' (1806). He became the principal spokesman for the opposition to Pitt (q.v.). On the outbreak of the French Revolution he warmly embraced its reforming ideals and this support led to a rupture in his own Whig party. He was disliked by George III (q.v.), but the King could not ignore his claims to office on the death of Pitt. As Foreign Secretary he attempted to negotiate peace with France, but his health failed; he was forced to leave the negotiations to colleagues, and he died in September 1806.

Fra Diavolo (Michele Pezza) (1771–1806) Italian guerrilla leader. He began life as a stocking maker, but first came to prominence leading Calabrian partisans (*Sanfedists*) against the Parthenopian Republic in 1799. For this the Bourbons gave him the rank of colonel of militia. In 1806 he resumed his guerrilla activities, though his loyalty was always to the Neapolitan Bourbons rather than to any notion of 'Italy'. Unlike most of the other Calabrian guerrilla leaders he did not confine his activities to his native district; he was shipped by the British Navy from his original area of operations to disrupt French communications north of Naples. He acquired his nickname 'Brother Devil' as he allegedly wore the habit of a friar and enjoyed the reputation among the peasants of being supernatural. He was captured by the French in November 1806 and executed.

Francis (Franz) I (1768–1835) Last Holy Roman Emperor (as Francis II), first Emperor of Austria. Born in Florence the son of Leopold, Grand Duke of Tuscany, and nephew of Joseph II, Holy Roman Emperor. In 1784 he was sent to Vienna to finish his education under his uncle's supervision. When Joseph II died (1790) he acted briefly as regent until his father arrived from Italy to succeed as Leopold II. He succeeded his father in turn in 1792. As Holy Roman Emperor he participated in all of the coalitions against Revolutionary France, but in 1804 he assumed the title of hereditary emperor of Austria and this made it easier for him to yield the title of Holy Roman Emperor when events forced him to do so in 1806. During 1805 he introduced significant changes in the way that Austria was governed, dispensing with a chief minister and taking personal responsibility. He was not a brilliant ruler and administrator, but he had considerable patience and worked hard. From 1809 he relied heavily on the advice of Metternich (q.v.) in foreign affairs and gave him considerable leeway in their conduct. The following year he became Napoleon's father-in-law when he agreed to the marriage betwen the French emperor and his daughter Marie Louise. During the twenty years after Napoleon's final defeat he was closely associated with reactionary policies both at home and abroad. He was married four times, his first three wives all dying comparatively young.

Frederick (Friedrich) I (1754–1816) King of Württemberg. He entered the Prussian army in 1774 but transferred to the Russian army in 1782 when his sister married the future Tsar Paul (q.v.). He served as governor of Finland, then Kherson, and commanded a regiment during the Turkish war. He succeeded his father as Frederick II, Duke of Württemberg, in 1797 and ruled as an enlightened despot, which brought him into confrontation with his parliament. Following French annexations in the Rhineland he was compensated in 1803 with new territories and the title of Elector. He entered into alliance with Napoleon in October 1805. At the beginning of 1806 Napoleon enlarged his territories still further, agreed to Frederick becoming king, and married the new king's daughter to his brother Jerome (q.v.). As king, Frederick suppressed his parliament and began to develop a French-style administration. Following Napoleon's defeat at Leipzig he joined the alliance against him. He rejected attempts at the Congress of Vienna to persuade him to restore his parliament and, in 1815, introduced a conservative constitution.

Frederick VI (1768–1839) King of Denmark. The son of the weak Christian VII he conducted a coup against the autocratic regime of Ove Gulberg in April 1784 and from then, until his father's death in March 1808, he ruled as regent. Initially his rule was enlightened; he was more interested in ceremony and the military, but he chose able men as his ministers. However, increasingly he took a more active role in affairs and began to act in a more authoritarian manner. On his father's death he abolished the cabinet system and began issuing instructions directly. In 1807 he found himself in a difficult position threatened by a British fleet and by a French army. The British struck first, bombarding Copenhagen and seizing his fleet. This led Frederick into a formal alliance with Napoleon (October 1807) which he maintained until 1814. The war ruined the Danish economy and contributed to the loss of the twin kingdom of Norway. He revived cabinet government in 1814, and in spite of the disasters and his autocratic behaviour, he continued to be popular with his people.

Frederick Augustus (Friedrich August) I (1750–1827) King of Saxony. The son of the Elector Frederick Christian, he succeeded his father under a guardianship in 1763 and was declared of age in 1768. Hard-working and conscientious he earned the title 'the Just' (*der Gerechte*). His early alliance with Frederick the Great brought considerable profit to his electorate. In 1791 he was offered the Polish crown, which he refused. He was opposed to the war with Revolutionary France, but participated out of loyalty to the Empire. He sided with Prussia in 1806 and, after the Prussian defeat, he signed the treaty of Posen with Napoleon by which Saxony became a kingdom and entered the Confederation of the Rhine. At Tilsit (1807) he was given nominal sovereignty over Poland as Grand Duke of Warsaw. He sided with Napoleon in the wars of 1809 and 1812 and, even though he made overtures to Austria in April 1813, he remained a loyal ally until Leipzig. In the aftermath of Leipzig he was captured and, at the Congress of Vienna he was compelled to give the northern part of his kingdom to Prussia. Welcomed back by his people in 1814, he spent the remainder of his life and reign seeking to repair the destruction and economic damage wrought by the wars.

Frederick William (Friedrich Wilhelm) III (1770–1840) King of Prussia. The son of Frederick William II, like other Prussian princes he was educated as a soldier joining the army in 1784. He participated in the campaigns of 1792, 1793 and 1794 against Revolutionary France. In 1793 he married Louise, daughter of the Prince of Mecklenburg-Strelitz, and four years later he succeeded his father as king. Queen Louise was a much stronger personality than her husband; she helped him through the disaster of 1806 and encouraged him to appoint capable reforming ministers like Stein (q.v.)

and Scharnhorst (q.v.). She died in 1810. Frederick William was forced to ally with Napoleon against Russia, but broke with him after the retreat from Moscow not because of his own determination but rather more because of the actions of Yorck (q.v.) at Tauroggen. During the War of Liberation he promised his people a constitution, but the promise was never fulfilled and in the aftermath of the wars he went along with the reactionary policies of Austria and Russia.

Gaudin, Charles (1756–1841) French financial administrator. The son of an attorney of the Parlement of Paris he served as a tax official before the Revolution. He was minister of finance throughout the Consulate and Empire, and again during the Hundred Days. He improved French finances, sorting out many of the problems left by the Directory; he founded the Bank of France and established the *grand cadastre*. In 1809 he was created Duke of Gata.

Gentz, Friedrich von (1764–1832) German publicist and statesman. The son of an official in the Prussian government he was brought up in Berlin and studied at the University of Königsberg under Immanuel Kant. He entered Prussian service himself in 1785. Favourable to the early liberal aspects of the French Revolution, in 1794 he translated into German Edmund Burke's *Reflections on the Revolution in France* and thereafter he became increasingly critical of the Revolution while praising the virtues of the British constitution. His political writings over the next few years brought him reward from the Austrian and British governments, which enabled him to finance his libertine lifestyle, but made his position in Prussia difficult since, from 1795, she was neutral. In 1802 he moved to Vienna and entered Austrian service. Together with a stream of anti-French polemic he drafted proclamations and correspondence on behalf of Frederick William of Prussia (q.v.) before the Jena campaign, and the Austrian declaration of war in 1809. His political outlook meanwhile became more and more conservative. From 1812 he became a close confidant and advisor to Metternich (q.v.) accompanying him on diplomatic missions. He acted as secretary to the Congress of Vienna and to subsequent congresses in restoration Europe. He was closely involved in preparing the Carlsbad Decrees (1819). While he took money and gifts from whoever offered, he never made any secret of this, and it is generally acknowledged that Gentz only ever wrote according to his personal convictions, which sometimes led him to be critical of his employers.

George III (1738–1820) King of England. The son of Frederick, Prince of Wales, he became heir to the throne on his father's death (1751) and succeeded his grandfather (George II) as king in October 1760. His domestic life, with his wife Charlotte of Mecklenberg, was noted for its dullness and probity. As king, George was hard-working and conscientious, determined to be an active monarch and to focus on Britain rather than Hanover. His fixed ideas sometimes brought him into serious conflict with his ministers, notably over the question of Catholic emancipation in 1800 and 1807. In 1788 hard work brought on his first attack of 'madness' (now diagnosed as porphyria) which led to talk of a regency. Subsequent bouts occurred in 1801, 1804, and 1810. In 1811, on the death of his favourite daughter, Amelia, his illness became permanent and a Regency Bill was passed giving his powers to his son, George, Prince of Wales (q.v.). He spent his last years in seclusion; his eyesight deteriorated to the point of blindness. The early part of his reign was marked by conflict with, and finally the loss of, Britain's American colonies, and also by the political agitation focusing on John Wilkes. The last part of his reign witnessed the problems emanating from the French Revolution and the wars against Revolutionary and Napoleonic France. Not particularly popular with his subjects during the early years of his reign, the years of the French wars, of his illness and seclusion were notable for a growth in his popularity as a national figurehead.

George, Prince of Wales (subsequently **George IV**) (1762–1830) Eldest son of George III (q.v.). In contrast to the dull domesticity of his parents he embarked on a life of extravagance and profligacy which put him on bad terms with his father. When he came of age (1783) he was given an annual income of £50,000 from the Civil List and £60,000 to pay off his debts; but these sums were never sufficient. He established his own household at Carlton House which became a centre for opposition politicians. In 1785 he contracted a secret, morganatic marriage to a Catholic widow, Maria Fitzherbert. Nine years later, partly to ensure that his father would agree to pay off his debts, he contracted a loveless marriage with Caroline of Brunswick; the couple separated shortly after the birth of their only child, Princess Charlotte. In 1811, following his father's incapacity, he became Prince Regent but, owing to continuing arguments notably about Catholic emancipation, his Whig friends remained out of political office. He was unpopular throughout the country, and continued to be so when he succeeded his father in 1820.

Géricault, Jean-Louis-André-Théodore (1791–1824) French painter. The son of a lawyer in Rouen he left school in 1808 to enter the studio of Carle Vernet; two years later he moved to that of Pierre Guérin, one of David's (q.v.) most active pupils. In 1812 his painting *Officier de chasseurs à cheval* attracted much attention and won him a gold medal. Two years later he again attracted attention with another, but bleaker, military painting, *Cuirassier blessé quittant le feu.* He joined the royal army during Napoleon's exile on Elba and followed Louis XVIII to Ghent during the Hundred Days. In 1815 he prepared several drafts for a series on the retreat from Moscow, but this was never completed. *Radeau de la Méduse* (Raft of Medusa) was exhibited in 1819 and he was disappointed that the state did not purchase it. In 1822 he suffered a severe fall from a horse which contributed to his early death.

Gneisnau, August Wilhelm Anton (1760–1831) Prussian soldier. He enlisted in the Austrian army in 1779; served with German mercenaries on the British side in the American War of Independence and, on his return from America, joined the Prussian army. He won considerable credit for his successful defence of Colberg against the French in 1807. He assisted in the reorganisation of the Prussian army under Scharnhorst (q.v.) and became Quartermaster General to Blücher (q.v.) in 1813, taking a prominent role in the invasion of France (1814) and the Waterloo campaign (1815).

Godoy, Manuel de (1767–1851) Spanish statesman and courtier. He was born into the minor nobility and entered the Royal Bodyguard in 1784. He became the lover of Maria Luisa of Parma, wife of the future King Charles IV (q.v.); he was also a favourite of Charles which led to him being created Duke of Alcudia (April 1792) and prime minister (Nov 1792). Following the Treaty of Basel with France (1795) he was named 'the Prince of the Peace.' He made many enemies at court which led to him being driven from office in 1798, but he was returned to power in 1801. He personally led the Spanish army against Portugal in the War of the Oranges. He encouraged the arts, attempted to strengthen the army, and introduced some economic reforms, especially with reference to church lands. But his foreign policy was generally unsuccessful and his scandalous romantic life outraged opinion. Ferdinand, the heir apparent, was a particular enemy and had him arrested and his property confiscated following the uprising of Aranjuez (March 1808). He went into exile with Charles IV, and was unwelcome in the Spain of Ferdinand (q.v.). He spent the last years of his life in relative poverty in France.

Gogel, Isaac Jan Alexander (1765–1821) Dutch statesman and reformer. As an Amsterdam merchant he had welcomed the French armies. He helped in the creation of the Batavian Republic and briefly edited the influential radical journal *De Democraten*. It was during the Republic that his ability as a financial reformer was first noticed. He served as finance minister under Schimmelpenninck (q.v.) and continued in this position under King Louis Bonaparte. His aim was a centralised government with an efficient, national system of taxation. He refused the offer of serving in the government of the restored Prince of Orange in 1813 and he went to Paris in voluntary exile, until ejected on the return of the Bourbons. He returned to the Netherlands to run a starchworks which he had acquired at Overveen. He agreed to prepare a memorandum for the King on public finance and taxation in 1818, but refused to re-enter public life.

Görres, Joseph von (1776–1848) German man of letters. Born in Coblenz and educated by the clergy at a Latin College he became an ardent supporter of the French Revolution. In 1797 he was a leading figure among the 2000–3000 Rhenish Jacobins urging the creation of the Cisrhenan Republic. One of a deputation to Paris shortly after Brumaire he returned, greatly disillusioned, and retired from active politics for a decade. He lectured at Heidelberg (1806–8) and then at Coblenz; at the same time he published German folk tales and developed his romantic concept of the nation as a popular community defined by language and custom. During the German War of Liberation he founded the influential, anti-Napoleonic journal *Der Rheinische Merkur*. The journal stressed his ideas of the nation and criticised the settlement following Napoleon's fall for being the work of princes and ignoring the people. In 1816 his comments led to the journal being suppressed and to him losing his position at Coblenz. He was forced into exile after the assassination of Kotzebue (q.v.), not because he sought to justify it but because he suggested that political repression could generate such actions. Subsequently he settled in Bavaria where he became Professor of History at Munich and a leading member of that university's group of Catholic romantics.

Gourgaud, Gaspar, baron (1783–1852) French soldier and memorialist of Napoleon. The son of a musician in the royal chapel of

Versailles he enlisted in the artillery in 1802 and fought with distinction in all major Napoleonic battles and campaigns from Ulm onwards. He was created baron for his services in the Russian campaign. He rallied to Napoleon during the Hundred Days and was promoted to general. He then followed his emperor into exile on St. Helena. Short-tempered and proud he quarrelled with Montholon (q.v.) and was forced to leave St. Helena in 1818, though later the two collaborated on memoirs of Napoleon's exile. Having published his own recollections Gourgaud returned to active service in the French Army in 1830. He was one of the veterans who brought Napoleon's remains from St Helena to France in 1840. He was elected to the Assembly in 1849.

Goya y Lucientes, Francisco José de (1746–1828) Spanish painter. Born near Zaragoza. By 1780 he was established as a successful painter and was established at the court in Madrid. In 1785 he became director of the Academy of Arts. A severe illness in the early 1790s left him deaf and following this his paintings became much more sombre in subject and colour. The French invasion prompted some of his most striking work: two canvases *Dos de Mayo* and *Tres de Mayo* illustrate the uprising against the French in Madrid in May 1808 and its cruel aftermath; *Los Desastres de la Guerra* (The Disasters of War), a series of etchings made between 1810 and 1814, portray the savagery of the guerrilla war against the French. Goya worked at King Joseph's court in Madrid, though he also painted the Duke of Wellington (q.v.); there remains debate about his political commitment during these years. He spent most of the last four years of his life, still painting, in Bordeaux.

Grenville, William Windham, Baron (1759–1834) British statesman. Educated at Eton and Oxford he entered parliament in 1782 as MP for the borough of Buckingham. The following year he became Paymaster General in the government of his cousin, Pitt (q.v.), and over the next few years held a variety of posts. In January 1789 he became Speaker of the House of Commons, but resigned in June to become Home Secretary. Created a baron in November 1790 he took charge of government business in the Lords; the following year he became Foreign Secretary. He resigned with Pitt in 1801 over Catholic emancipation. He opposed the Peace of Amiens and refused to join Pitt's administration in 1804 because Fox (q.v.) was excluded. On Pitt's death he formed the Ministry of All the Talents. He played a key role in the bill to abolish the Slave Trade. In 1807 he resigned with the rest of the ministry and thereafter served in opposition. Suffering a paralytic attack in 1823, he retired from public life.

Gros, Antoine-Jean, baron (1771–1835) French painter. Born in Paris, the son of a painter of miniatures, he entered David's (q.v.) studio in 1785. In 1793 he travelled in Italy; three years later he was present when Bonaparte's army won the battle of Arcola which he celebrated with a canvas much admired by the victorious general. Thereafter he travelled with the army and was appointed to select Italian works of art to be sent to the Louvre. Two of his most famous paintings were commissioned by Napoleon to counter critical comment: *Les pestiférés de Jaffa* (1804) showing Bonaparte visiting sick troops during the Egyptian campaign; and *La bataille d'Eylau* (1808), showing the Emperor victorious on the field. Though he subsequently painted for the Bourbons – notably a canvas of Louis XVIII leaving the Tuileries at the beginning of the Hundred Days, and ceilings in the Louvre for Charles X – his fortunes declined with the fall of the empire. There was also a reaction against his style of Neo-Classical art. Gros took over the running of David's studio and sought to preserve the Neo-Classical style. His lack of success and declining appeal contributed to his suicide, by drowning in the Seine.

Grouchy, Emmanuel, Marquis de (1766–1847) French soldier. Born into the nobility he entered the army at the age of 14 and in 1789 was serving in the Royal Bodyguard. He fought loyally for the Revolution, being promoted to general in 1792, and then for Napoleon. He rallied to Napoleon during the Hundred Days and was created marshal. It is Grouchy's actions in the Waterloo campaign for which he is best remembered. After the battle of Ligny he was ordered to pursue Blücher's Prussians and prevent them linking with Wellington. He lost Blücher and, though he heard the artillery at Waterloo, he did not march to join Napoleon but fought the minor action of Wavre. Between 1815 and 1821 he lived in the United States; on his return to France his rank and titles were eventually restored, but his last years were clouded by criticism of his behaviour during the Waterloo campaign and his determination to respond to his critics.

Gustavus IV (1778–1837) King of Sweden. The son of Gustavus III who was assassinated in 1792, he succeeded to the throne on reaching his majority in 1796, though he was not formally crowned until 1800. Interested in agriculture he encouraged reforms in this area (notably enclosures), but he was generally narrow-minded and introspective, and extremely hostile to the ideas of the French Revolution. In 1803–5 he paid a long visit to the court of his father-in-law, the Grand Duke of Baden, which turned him more against Napoleon because of the latter's treatment of many minor German sovereigns and because of his arrest (on Baden soil) and execution of d'Enghien (q.v.). Against the urgings of some of his ministers that he should maintain neutrality, he joined the coalition against Napoleon (October 1805). The consequences of his foreign policy were disastrous and prompted a military coup in March 1809. The following December he and his family were sent to Germany where he assumed the title of the Count of Gottorp; he subsequently called himself Colonel Gustaffson. He separated from his family and divorced his wife in 1812. He finally settled in Switzerland where he died in relative poverty.

Hardenberg, Karl August von (1750–1822) German statesman. He entered the Hanoverian civil service in 1770 but was forced to leave it when his wife became involved with George, Prince of Wales (q.v.). He took service with Prussia and rose rapidly to become a member of the cabinet in 1797. Appointed Foreign Minister in 1804 he initially urged neutrality with France in the hope of acquiring Hanover for Prussia, but he subsequently incurred the wrath of Napoleon who forced his dismissal in 1807. Retiring to Riga he planned a liberal reconstruction of the Prussian monarchy. He was brought back to Prussia as Chancellor in 1810 and continued the far-reaching reforms begun by Stein (q.v.) in the army, the civil service, the economy, the education system and local government. He urged Frederick William III (q.v.) to move against Napoleon towards the end of 1812. He was overshadowed by Metternich (q.v.) at the Congress of Vienna and in the subsequent Congress System. Remaining in government after the final victory over Napoleon he drifted with the tide against liberalism.

Haugwitz, Christian August Heinrich Kurt, Count von (1752–1832) Prussian statesman. In 1792 he became Prussian ambassador to Vienna. He was reluctant to see Prussia involved in the war against Revolutionary France, but helped negotiate the British subsidy in the War of the First Coalition. The Treaty of Basle (1795) by which Prussia left the war, was largely his work. Concerned by French success in 1798 he urged Frederick William III (q.v.) to join the new coalition. In 1804 he was replaced as Foreign Minister by Hardenberg (q.v.) but he remained influential opposing his successor's rapprochement with France. The following year he was recalled to serve alongside Hardenberg, but was diplomatically trounced by Napoleon and instead of delivering a Prussian ultimatum he signed the treaty of Schönbrunn with France (15 Dec 1805). His political career ended with the Prussian disaster of 1806. The last ten years of his life were spent in Italy; he died in Venice.

Hofer, Andreas (1767–1810) Tyrolean patriot. The son of an innkeeper he served in the Austrian army during the Revolutionary wars from 1796 to 1805. When, by the Treaty of Pressburg, Tyrol was transferred to Bavaria, he became a leader of the agitation against Bavarian domination. Following discussions with the Austrian government – which was to use him cynically throughout – he led popular risings in 1809, first against the Bavarians then against the French. Driving the French from the country he ruled in the name of the Austrian Empire for a short period. When the French re-entered Tyrol he attempted to renew the popular revolt, but was defeated, captured and shot.

Humboldt, Karl Wilhelm von (1767–1835) Prussian statesman and man of letters. A reforming Minister of Education (1809–10) and instrumental in the creation of the new University of Berlin, he returned to a diplomatic career in 1810, most notably encouraging Austria to join the anti-French coalition in 1813. The reactionary policies of, and the factional division within, the Prussian government led him to give up political life in 1819, after which he devoted himself to literature and academic pursuits, in particular the comparative study of languages.

Isabey, Jean-Baptiste (1767–1855) French painter best known for his miniatures. The son of a grocer in Nancy he was already recognised as a miniaturist, with commissions from the royal family, while a member of David's (q.v.) studio before the Revolution. He experimented by painting increasingly in the new medium of *aquarelle* rather than *gouache*. In addition to his miniatures he became painter of ceremonies to Napoleon and worked for both of his empresses. Following the restoration he again worked for the Bourbons, and then the July Monarchy; during the Second Empire Napoleon III elevated him to be a commander of the Legion of Honour.

Jahn, Friedrich Ludwig (1778–1852) Founder of German patriotic sports movement (*Turnverein*). He joined the Prussian army after the defeat at Jena then, in 1809, he took up a teaching post in Berlin where he developed his ideas for using gymnastics to restore the morale and boost the patriotism of his fellow countrymen. In 1811 he established the first sports ground in Berlin. During the War of Liberation he served in the Lützow-Korps and assisted in the foundation of the *Burschenschaften*. His classic book on physical education, *Deutsche Turnkunst*, was published in 1816, but his liberal ideas brought him under suspicion. The *Turnen* were abolished in 1819 and Jahn was imprisoned until 1825. He was rehabilitated in 1840, being given the Iron Cross for his bravery in the wars against Napoleon. The *Turnen* were formally re-established and gymnastics was incorporated into the Prussian school curriculum in 1842. In 1848 he was elected as a delegate to the Frankfurt parliament.

Jomini, Antoine Henri, (1779–1869) Soldier and military theorist. Born in the canton of Vaud, Switzerland, he began his adult life as a clerk in a Paris banking house. He became a soldier in the Swiss wars of 1798–9. Returning to his banking career, he published *Traité des grandes opérations militaires* (1804–5). He served as an aide-de-camp in the Austerlitz campaign subsequently reaching the rank of general in the French army, and also accepting a commission in the Russian army. The latter led him to refuse taking part in the invasion of Russia. He served with the Russian army after Bautzen, but refused to participate in the invasion of France. After the wars he helped organise the Russian Staff College. He is best known for his *Précis de l'art de la guerre* (1836) which became influential with European general staffs but which, with its emphasis on a strategy adapted to professional, long-service armies, ran counter to much of the experience of the Revolutionary and Napoleonic wars.

Josephine (1763–1814) French Empress. Born Marie-Rose Josephine Tascher de la Pagerie into the lesser Creole nobility of Martinique. In 1779 she moved to France to marry the vicomte de Beauharnais by whom she had two children, Eugène (q.v.) and Hortense (q.v.). The vicomte sided with the Revolution and held command in the revolutionary armies, but he was arrested and guillotined towards the end of the Terror. Josephine was also arrested, but was released on the fall of Robespierre. She became the mistress of the prominent politician Paul Barras, and it was through him that she met General Bonaparte whom she married in March 1796. She was never brought into her husband's political councils when he was consul or emperor. While she was often subjected to petty jealousy by other Bonapartes, she was noted for her generosity and lack of malice. Dynastic and political considerations led Napoleon to divorce her in 1809, but she retained the rank and title of empress with an annual income of 80,000 francs. She retired to Malmaison where she died in May 1814.

Jourdan, Jean-Baptiste (1762–1833) French soldier. Born in Limoges, the son of a surgeon, he was apprenticed to a silk merchant but, in 1778 he enlisted in the French army. Invalided home from the West Indies (1784) he became a draper in Limoges. In 1791 he was elected lieutenant-colonel of volunteers, two years later he was promoted to general and, in 1795, commanded the Army of the Sambre-et-Meuse. Defeated by Archduke Charles in 1796 he turned to a political career and was elected to the Council of 500 (1797). In 1798 he framed the law on conscription. Opposed to Brumaire, he was soon reconciled to Bonaparte again resuming his military career. Appointed marshal (1804), he became a close advisor of Joseph Bonaparte (q.v.) acting as governor of Naples (1806) and his chief of staff in Spain. He retired after Joseph's defeat at Vitoria (1813). A member of Napoleon's Chamber of Peers during the Hundred Days, he submitted to the Bourbons on the second restoration but refused to serve on the court-martial trying Ney (q.v.). Created a count and a member of the Chamber of Peers in 1819 he was a prominent opponent of the extreme royalists and welcomed the Revolution of 1830.

Junot, Andoche (1771–1813) French soldier. Born in Bussey-le-Grand (Côte d'Or). In 1790, while a student of law he enlisted in the army. He first met Bonaparte while serving as a sergeant at Toulon. He became a favourite of Bonaparte serving first as his secretary, then as an aide-de-camp in Italy. He was promoted to general during the Egyptian campaign. In Egypt he was severely wounded fighting a duel on Bonaparte's behalf. Appointed commandant of Paris under the Consulate he, and his headstrong wife Laure (q.v.), cut figures in society and were noted for their extravagance. Ambassador to Portugal in 1805, two years later he led the army which captured Lisbon; for this he was created Duke of Abrantès and governor of Portugal, but he was not an able administrator. In August 1808 he was defeated by Wellesley at Vimeiro and, following the Convention of Cintra, returned to France with his army; it was probably this failure which prevented him being created a marshal. He served in Spain under Masséna (q.v.) and suffered a serious head wound (1810); he served in the Russian campaign, and was much criticised for not engaging with the Russians and cutting their retreat at Smolensk. In 1813 he was appointed governor of

Illyria but domestic problems, his war wounds and an increasing mental illness led to his suicide in July of that year.

Junot, Laure Permon (1784–1838) Wife of Andoche Junot (q.v.). She was educated in her mother's salon, popular during the Directory. She married Junot on his return from the Egyptian campaign. When he went to Portugal as ambassador in 1805 she sought to establish her own court in Lisbon similar to that in Paris. She was noted for her extravagance and wit, and also for a scandalous liaison with Metternich (q.v.) while he was serving in Paris and her husband was in Portugal (1807). Napoleon called her *la petite peste*. Following Junot's death she became a virtual recluse, but in the early 1830s she began publishing a variety of volumes including her celebrated, gossipy *Mémoires* of Napoleon's court.

Katte, Friedrich Wilhelm von (1770–1836) German soldier. A lieutenant in the Prussian infantry remembered for his attempt to surprise the fortress of Magdeburg and to persuade the Prussian provinces incorporated into the Kingdom of Westphalia to return to their old allegiance (April 1809).

Körner, Karl Theodor (1791–1813) German poet and patriot. Born in Dresden he studied first mining and then law, but his main interest was always writing verse. Between 1811 and 1813 he lived in Vienna writing comedies and librettos for operas. In 1813 he joined the Lützow-Korps; he was seriously wounded at Kitzen in June, and killed in fighting at Gadesbuch in August. He is best known for the patriotic verse and war songs, *Leier und Schwert* (Lyre and Sword), published posthumously in 1814.

Kotzebue, August (1761–1819) German man of letters and Russian civil servant. Born in Weimar he studied law at Jena and Duisburg following which he had a chequered career as a dramatist and essayist (in Weimar, Vienna and St Petersburg) and as an official in the Russian administration. His conservative ideals brought him into conflict with Goethe and the German romantics; he was also a severe critic of the spread of Napoleonic influence in Germany. This led to his appointment as a Russian privy councillor and he accompanied Tsar Alexander (q.v.) during the campaign of 1813–14. Following Napoleon's fall he continued to work for the Tsar, in particular sending him reports of events in Germany. From 1817 he was resident in Weimar and Mannheim where his plays and essays ridiculed the liberal and national aspirations of the *Burschenschaften* and others. In 1819 he was stabbed to death by a revolutionary student of theology, Karl Ludwig Sand.

Kutusov, Mikhail Larionovich (1745–1813) Russian soldier. Joined the army c. 1759 or 1760 and served with distinction in Polish and Turkish campaigns, losing an eye in battle in 1774. During the Revo-lutionary wars he held a series of administrative and diplomatic posts. Recalled to active service he fought, and was wounded, at Austerlitz. His criticism of Tsar Alexander led to him being given a distant posting, but he was recalled again to take command of the army opposing Napoleon's invasion in 1812. He masterminded the Russian campaign of that year and, following his defeat of the French at Smolensk in November, he was created Prince of Smolensk. He took command of the combined Russian and Prussian armies at the beginning of 1813, but died before the opening of the campaign season.

Lannes, Jean (1769–1809) French soldier. The son of a stable keeper in Lectoure (Gers) he was apprenticed to a dyer. A volunteer in the Revolutionary wars he served with distinction on the Spanish front. He left the army in 1795, but re-enlisted the following year where, in the Army of Italy, he came to the notice of Bonaparte and was rapidly promoted to general. In 1800 he led the advance guard of the French army across the Alps, winning the battle of Montebello. Inspector General of the Consular Guard (1800); Ambassador to Portugal (1801); Marshal (1804); Duke of Montebello (1808). He served in all of the major campaigns of the Empire until mortally wounded at Aspern-Essling; Napoleon openly wept over his loss. He was noted for his extreme courage, but also a tendency to violence; with Davout (q.v.) and Masséna (q.v.) he is regarded as one of Napoleon's three most able generals.

Las Cases, Emmanuel Auguste Dieudonné, comte de, (1766–1842) Memorialist of Napoleon. Born into the minor French nobility he was educated at a military school, joined the navy in 1782, and served in the West Indies. An *émigré* during the Revolution he served briefly in the royalist forces and supported himself in London by teaching and writing. In 1799 he published his *Atlas Historique et Généalogique* which met with considerable success. He returned to France during the Consular period and sought employment. In 1809 Napoleon appointed him as his chamberlain, and he made him a count the following year. Rallying to the Emperor during the Hundred Days, Las Cases acted as Napoleon's spokesman during negotiations with the British on board HMS Bellerophon, and travelled with him into exile on St. Helena. While in exile he compiled the *Mémorial de Sainte-Hélène*, a record of his conversations with Napoleon on the latter's life. In November 1816 he was arrested and removed from the island for his criticism of its governor. He was confined on the Cape of Good Hope, but then returned to Europe. On Napoleon's death he was permitted to return to France. In 1831 he was elected to the Chamber of Deputies.

Lebrun, Charles François (1739–1824) French statesman and financier. Educated in law he became secretary and assistant to Chancellor Maupeou during his attempts to reform the old regime monarchy. On Maupeou's fall (1774) he retired from public life, but came back into prominence in the early years of the Revolution urging moderate reform. Imprisoned during the Terror, he was later elected to the Council of Ancients (1795). Though he was apparently not involved in the Brumaire coup he was named Third Consul. Greatly interested in financial reform, he was made Arch-Treasurer of the Empire in 1804; he also contributed to the administrative and legal reforms of the Consulate and Empire. He was governor general of Liguria from 1805–6 and effected its annexation to France. He disapproved of Napoleon's recreation of the nobility, but was persuaded to accept the title Duke of Piacenza in 1808. After the annexation of the Netherlands he administered them as governor general. He accepted the first restoration, but rallied to Napoleon during the Hundred Days and was appointed Grand Master of the University. On the return of the Bourbons in 1815 he was suspended from the House of Peers, but was reinstated in 1819.

Louis XVIII (1755–1824) King of France. The brother of Louis XVI his official title was the comte de Provence; technically he became king on the death of his nephew, Louis XVII, in 1795, but effectively he did not succeed until the fall of Napoleon. Critical of the way in which the Revolution was developing he emigrated in 1791 and spent the next 24 years in exile. When restored as king he accepted many of the changes of the Revolutionary period and reigned as a constitutional monarch steering a mid course between the reactionary faction, which centred on his brother Artois (q.v.), and more liberal elements.

Lowe, Sir Hudson (1769–1844) British soldier, best known for being governor of St. Helena during Napoelon's exile. An Irishman, and son of a military surgeon, he joined the army in 1787.

During the Revolutionary and Napoleonic wars he led a brigade of Corsican exiles – the 'Corsican Rangers' – seeing service in Minorca, Egypt and Italy. In October 1808 he commanded the garrison on the Isle of Capri when it was attacked and forced to surrender by the forces of Murat (q.v.); by the terms of his surrender he and his men agreed not to take arms against the French for a year. A man of limited vision, he had little time for Napoleon and his entourage on St. Helena; he was, and has been, much criticised for this. From 1825 to 1830 he commanded the imperial forces in Ceylon (Sri Lanka), and in 1842 he was appointed colonel of his old regiment, the 50th Foot.

Lubienski, Feliks Franciszek, Count (1758–1848) Polish statesman chiefly remembered for his role as Minister of Justice in the Duchy of Warsaw. He studied law in Italy and shortly before the battle of Jena was active in a project for the restoration of Poland under the Prussian Hohenzollerns. After the Prussian defeat he co-operated with the French and was appointed Minister of Justice in the new duchy. As such he pushed through legal reforms based on the French model and was responsible for the decree of December 1807 which nominally abolished serfdom. His Francophile sentiments brought him some unpopularity and he was passed over for the presidency of the Council of State. He refused to co-operate with the Russians in 1814 and never again held a government post, retiring to his estates where he busied himself with agricultural improvements.

Lützow, Adolf (1782–1834) Prussian soldier. Born in Berlin he joined the Prussian army in 1795. In 1813 he was authorised by Scharnhorst (q.v.) to organise a *Freikorps*, the Lützow-Korps, to operate in the French rear and to rally the smaller German states to the anti-French coalition. He fought his way out of the massacre at Kitzen and reorganised the corps; he was wounded at Gohrde in 1814. He led a regiment of Uhlans during the Waterloo campaign, notable for riding down and injuring Blücher (q.v.) in the Prussian defeat at Ligny.

Mack von Leiberich, Charles (Karl), Baron (1752–1828) Austrian soldier. Joined the army in 1770 and created a baron for his services in the Turkish War of 1788–9. He held different commands during the Revolutionary wars; in 1798 he was put in charge of the Neapolitan army where he met with little success and was captured by the French. In 1805 he was called from retirement to be chief of staff; his entire command was surrounded by Napoleon at Ulm and he was forced to surrender. On repatriation to Austria Mack was court-martialled, sentenced to two years in prison and stripped of his honours; the latter were finally restored by the Emperor in 1819.

Malachowski, Stanislaw (1736–1809) Polish statesman. Born in Warsaw he became a member of the *Sejm* (Polish Diet) in 1764 and was elected as its President in 1788. He was a key figure behind the Polish Constitution of 1791 which established a constitutional monarchy. In 1792 he was forced into exile in Vienna and he remained there until 1807. Napoleon made him President of the provisional Committee of Government and then President of the Council of Ministers. He resigned following arguments with the Francophile Lubienski (q.v.), but was then appointed President of the Senate.

Malet, Claude-François de (1754–1812) French soldier. Born into the minor nobility at Dôle he joined the Royal Household troops in 1771, retiring to his estates in 1775. In 1789 he was elected captain of the Dôle National Guard. He served in the campaigns of the Revolution rising to the rank of brigadier-general. A staunch republican he opposed Napoleon but continued in the army until cashiered in 1807. He became involved in conspiracy and was arrested the following year. In 1810 he was transferred from prison to a mental institution. Two years later he escaped and, with a small group of conspirators attempted a coup in Paris which came close to success convincing many senior officers that Napoleon had been killed in Russia and that the Republic was to be restored. Malet and 16 others were tried and shot (October 1812).

Maret, Hughes-Bernard (1763–1839) French statesman. The son of a Dijon physician he studied law, becoming an advocate. His interest in literature and revolutionary politics led him to begin taking down the speeches in the National Assembly and printing them as the *Bulletin de l'Assemblée* which later merged into the larger *Moniteur*. In 1792 he entered the Ministry of Foreign Affairs and undertook missions to London and Naples; on his way to the latter he was captured by the Austrians (1793) and not released until 1795. He became associated with Bonaparte, supported the Brumaire plot and was made secretary general to the Consulate, a task which involved co-ordinating the work of the ministers. He subsequently became the head of Napoleon's personal office to which all ministers, except Talleyrand (q.v.), sent their official papers. Maret was trusted to select documents and stories from these papers for publication in the *Moniteur* (from 1800 the official organ of government). Created Duke of Bassano (1809) and Minister of Foreign Affairs (1811–13). He sided with Napoleon during the Hundred Days and was consequently forced into exile (1816–20). In 1831 King Louis Philippe made him a peer.

Marie Louise (1791–1847) Austrian princess and French Empress. The daughter of Emperor Francis I (q.v.) who, for reasons of state, reluctantly agreed to her marriage with Napoleon in 1810. She was married by proxy in Vienna (1810) and in a religious ceremony when she reached Paris (April 1810). In March 1811, following a labour which nearly cost her life, she bore Napoleon a son. She played no part in politics, but was appointed regent by Napoleon in his absence in May 1813. Following the first abdication she travelled to Vienna with her son, and made no reply to Napoleon's requests to join him on Elba. She remained in Vienna during the Hundred Days. In 1816 she was granted the Italian duchies of Parma, Piacenza, and Guastalla which she ruled in an enlightened fashion. Count Adam Neipperg, the Austrian general who had escorted her to Vienna in 1814, became her constant companion, advisor and a minister in her duchies; she bore him a son and, following a morganatic marriage on Napoleon's death, three more children. Neipperg died in 1829 and five years later she married, again morganatically, Count Charles René de Bombelles. She died in Vienna.

Marmont, Auguste-Frédéric-Louis-Viesse de (1774–1852) French soldier. Born at Châtillon-sur-Seine the son of an army officer. He was intended for a career in the artillery and met Bonaparte as a fellow student. He served with Bonaparte at Toulon, then as an ADC in Italy and Egypt. He became Inspector General of Artillery (1801), a grand officer of the Legion of Honour (1804), governor of Dalmatia (1805). As the latter he seized Ragusa from the Russians (1807) and was created Duke of Ragusa (1808). During the Wagram campaign he was made a marshal on the battlefield (1809) and was subsequently appointed Governor-General of Dalmatia. In 1810 he replaced Masséna (q.v.) in Spain, where two years later he was severely wounded at Salamanca. It took a year for him to recover from his wound, and early in 1814 he was given command of an army corps in northern France. Rather than defending Paris he signed a convention with the allies and yielded the city to them. Napoleon and his supporters never forgave him for this and during the early nineteenth century the verb *raguser* (taken from his title) was used with the meaning 'to betray'. In July 1830 he was commander of the royal troops in Paris; he failed to suppress the revolution and went into exile with Charles X. He moved to Vienna where he became tutor to the Duke of Reichstadt (q.v.) and finally settled in Venice, where he died. His memoirs devote considerable time to justifying his actions in 1814.

Masséna, André (1756–1817) French soldier. Born in Nice the son of a small wine merchant, he began life as a cabin boy. He served in the French army between 1775 and 1789 rising to non-commissioned rank. He re-enlisted in 1791 winning rapid promotion and becoming one of Napoleon's most trusted generals during the Italian campaign. He was created a marshal in 1804, Duke of Rivoli in 1808 and Prince of Essling in 1809. Between 1810 and 1811 he commanded the French Army of Portugal against Wellington and came close to beating him at Fuentes de Oñoro. Wellington considered him the best of his opponents in the Peninsular War, but Masséna never commanded an army in the field after 1811. He served Louis XVIII during the first restoration, refused to participate during the Hundred Days, but also refused to serve on the court martial which tried Marshal Ney.

Maximilian I Joseph (1756-1825) King of Bavaria. The second son of a marshal in the army of the Holy Roman Empire he also began life as a soldier, joining the French army and reaching the rank of colonel in the Royal Alsace Regiment. He was also greatly influenced by the ideas of the Enlightenment. In 1795, on the death of his brother, he became Duke of Zweibrücken and also heir to the childless Elector of Bavaria; the following year he took Maximilian von Montgelas (q.v.) as his principal advisor and they began planning reforms for the electorate. In 1799 he became Maximilian IV Joseph, Elector of Bavaria. He saw his territories enlarged under the *Reichsdeputationshauptschluss* and by his own treaties with Napoleon. In 1805 he allied with the French; the next year Bavaria became a kingdom and he took the title Maximilian I Joseph. He remained an ally of Napoleon until 1813; this alliance, and his subsequent shift to Napoleon's enemies, both helped enlarge his kingdom. Considerable reforms were introduced into the kingdom on the French model, and in 1818 he renounced some of his prerogatives granting a liberal constitution and creating a two chamber legislature.

Melzi d'Eril, Francesco (1753–1816) Italian statesman. The son of a Lombard noble and a Spanish mother, by whom he was related to the Spanish patriot Palafox (q.v.). In his youth he travelled widely in Europe before entering public service in the Italian lands of the Habsburgs and becoming involved in the implementation of the liberal reforms of Joseph II and Leopold II. A liberal himself, and inspired by both enlightenment ideas and anti-clericalism, he was also sympathetic to some French revolutionary ideas. He was involved in the negotiations with General Bonaparte in the mid 1790s and in the creation of the Cisalpine Republic. In 1798 he retired to his Spanish estates near Zaragoza, but was summoned to Paris by Bonaparte in 1801 and participated in the creation of the Italian Republic. When Bonaparte became President of the latter, he became vice-president and was charged with much of the day-to-day government. He introduced a large number of reforms sweeping away the privileges of provinces, cities and guilds, and reducing the influence of the church. He was lukewarm towards the transformation of the Republic into the Kingdom of Italy and hoped to develop independent Italian links with other states, notably Austria. He continued to serve in the kingdom, often deputising for Eugène de Beauharnais (q.v.), the viceroy. Napoleon showered him with honours; he became Duke of Lodi in December 1807, but his political influence waned. He stood by Eugène in April 1814 hoping to keep the kingdom intact. He died in Milan in 1816.

Metternich, Clemens Lothar Wenzel, Prince (1773–1859) Austrian statesman. Brought up in the Rhineland where his father was the Austrian representative to several small principalities, he attended the universities of Strasbourg and Mainz. His studies at the latter were interrupted by the French Revolution. He served under his father in The Netherlands, briefly travelled to England, before moving to Vienna where he made a good marriage (1795) and entered court society. He was appointed to several minor diplomatic missions until November 1803 when he was made ambassador to Berlin. Napoleon was impressed with him and, following his request, Metternich was sent as ambassador to Paris (Aug 1806). Interned briefly in France at the outset of the Wagram campaign he returned to Vienna and was appointed Minister of State (Aug 1809) and Foreign Minister (Oct 1809). He held the latter office for the next forty years. Initially he pursued a shrewd policy maintaining links with France but also keeping Austria's freedom of manoeuvre. Following the disaster of the Moscow campaign he offered his services to Napoleon as a mediator, but then joined with the allies always cautious to preserve a balance of power and wary of Russia or

Prussia becoming too strong. Among many honours he was created an hereditary prince of the Austrian Empire (Oct 1813). His charm, prestige, and ability enabled him to wield considerable influence at the Congress of Vienna. The dominant statesman in Germany after the wars, his policy was guided by a desire to maintain a balance of power and stability. While he was aware of the need for some change and reform in the Austrian system of government he was associated with conservatism and the policy of the crowned heads of east and central Europe to suppress all liberal and revolutionary manifestations. He was forced to resign by the Viennese Revolution of 1848 and went briefly into exile in London and Brussels. He returned to Austria in 1851 but never again held office.

Miot, André-François (1762–1841) French administrator. Born in Versailles the son of a state bureaucrat, he followed his father's footsteps entering the War Ministry. He continued to serve during the Revolution transferring to the Foreign Ministry in 1793. Surviving a charge of moderation during the Terror he undertook a series of diplomatic service missions under the Directory and the Consulate. He was appointed to the Tribunate and the Council of State in 1800 and was governor of Corsica 1801–2. In 1806 he accompanied Joseph Bonaparte (q.v.) to Naples as Minister of the Interior; Joseph made him Count of Melito, and thereafter he was known as Miot de Melito. He followed Joseph to Spain and served as his Chief of Household. He retired from public life in 1815. His *Mémoires sur le Consulat, l'Empire, et le roi Joseph* (published 1858) are regarded as fairly reliable.

Molé, Louis-Mathieu (1781–1855) French financial administrator and statesman. Born into a noble family, his abilities brought him to the attention of Napoleon whose favouritism helped his rapid rise through the administration: Prefect of the Côte d'Or (1806); Director of Bridges and Highways (1809); Minister of Justice (1813). The speed of his promotion meant that he was not always aware of the needs of, nor in possession of the necessary expertise for his offices, and his arrogance annoyed his subordinates. However, the experience he had gained during the Empire led subsequent regimes to call on his services, notably as Minister of the Navy (1817–19), Foreign Minister (1830), Prime Minister (1836–9). He was a deputy during the Second Republic, and subsequently rallied to the Second Empire.

Mollien, Nicholas-François (1758–1850) French financial administrator. The son of a Rouen merchant he became a clerk in the office of the Tax Farms in 1775; from 1781 he was chief clerk in the office of the *Contrôle Générale* which supervised the Tax Farms and was noted here for his involvement in improving the taxation system. He established himself as a cotton manufacturer in 1791. Imprisoned during the Terror, he returned to state employment at the end of the revolutionary decade as Director of the Sinking Fund (*caisse d'amortissement*) (1800). As Treasury Minister (1806–14) he introduced a variety of reforms to prevent peculation and to reduce the opportunities for error, but his financial policy remained cautious. While he refused an invitation to serve as Minister of Finance under the restoration, he continued to give financial advice to both this regime and the July Monarchy. He was appointed to the Chamber of Peers in 1819.

Montalivet, Jean-Pierre Bachasson, comte de (1766–1823) French administrator. The son of an army officer he enlisted in the cavalry when only 13, but left to study law becoming an attorney at Valence and a councillor of the Parlement of Grenoble. Sympathetic to the liberal reforms of the early revolution he disliked its radical shifts. He had met Bonaparte in 1789, and when the latter became Consul, Montalivet's administrative career began: Prefect of the Manche (1801), Seine-et-Oise (1804), Director of Bridges and Highways (1806), Minister of the Interior (1809). He played an important role in the training of the imperial prefects and ensuring the selection of capable men; he was responsible for organising a large number of public works across the Empire.

Montgelas, Maximilian von, Count (1759–1838) German statesman. Born in Munich the son of a soldier and diplomat in Bavarian service. Educated at Nancy and Strasbourg he entered the Bavarian civil service, but resigned in 1785 believing that his advancement was blocked because of his membership of the Illuminati. He entered the service of the Duke of Zweibrücken, but was dismissed in 1793 as his liberal ideas led to him being suspected as a Jacobin. In 1796 he became advisor to the new duke, Maximilian Joseph (q.v.) who was also heir to the Electorate of Bavaria and receptive to his reforming ideas. When Maximilian Joseph succeeded as Elector in 1799 Montgelas became Foreign Minister and also served as Minister of the Interior (1806) and Finance Minister (1803–6 and 1809). He dominated Bavarian politics for almost two decades introducing reforms on the French model, maintaining the French alliance, but also maintaining Bavaria's independent sovereignty. His reluctance to concede a liberal constitution, however, led to his fall from favour in 1817.

Montholon, Charles-Tristan, comte de (1783–1853) French soldier and memorialist of Napoleon. Educated at the Brienne Military Academy he joined the cavalry, but saw little action in Napoleon's campaigns serving as chamberlain to Josephine (after 1809) and on several diplomatic missions. Created a general and a count in 1811 he rallied to Napoleon during the Hundred Days and acted as an aide-de-camp. He volunteered to go to St. Helena and, with his wife, shared Napoleon's exile. He was an executor of Napoleon's will and received a legacy of 2m. francs. In 1823 he published *Mémoires de Napoléon à Sainte Hélène* with Gourgaud (q.v.) and subsequently his own *Récits de la captivité de Napoléon à Sainte Hélène*. Reinstated into the army he joined the future Napoleon III in his attempted coup at Boulogne (1840) for which he served seven years in prison. In 1849 he was elected as a deputy to the Assembly.

Moore, Sir John (1761–1809) British soldier. Born in Glasgow, the son of a well-to-do doctor and man of letters. He joined the army in 1776 and served in the American War. During the Revolutionary wars he fought in Corsica (1794), the West Indies (1796–7), Ireland (1798), Holland (1799), and Egypt (1800–1801) where he was seriously wounded. In 1803 he was nominated to command a brigade encamped at Shorncliffe which he proceeded to train as light infantry introducing new drill, new manoeuvres and less severe discipline. In 1808 he was sent to Sweden to assist Gustavus IV (q.v.), but he had a serious difference of opinion with the King; he escaped from Swedish custody and brought his army home to Britain. He was then ordered to Portugal and replaced the officers responsible for the Convention of Cintra. He marched his army into Spain, but, finding no assistance from Spanish armies, was forced to embark on a retreat of 250 miles culminating in the victorious battle of Corunna, where he was mortally wounded.

Moreau, Jean Victor (1763–1813) French soldier. Born in Britanny, Moreau was studying law at Rennes during the unrest which brought about the Revolution. He was a leader of the students and became an ardent democrat. In 1791 he joined the army, and three years later was a general distinguishing himself in Germany and in Italy. His friendship with Pichegru (q.v.) led to accusations of royalism, which were unfounded though Moreau's military ability and popularity made him a threat to Napoleon. In 1804 he was arrested and sentenced to two year's imprisonment for conspiring against the First Consul, but the sentence was commuted to exile. Moreau spent much of the next eight years in Pennsylvania. Following the defeat of Napoleon in Russia he was persuaded to become a military advisor to Tsar Alexander. He was mortally wounded at the battle of Dresden.

Murat, Joachim (1767–1815) French soldier, subsequently King of Naples. The son of a Gascon innkeeper he gave up the study of canon law to join the army. He served alongside Napoleon on 13 Vendémiare, in Italy and Egypt. In January 1800 he married Napoleon's youngest sister, Caroline. He was created a marshal in 1804 and, following his distinguished service commanding cavalry during the Austerlitz campaign, Grand Duke of Berg and Cleves (1806). He commanded the French cavalry in the great battles of 1806 and 1807, and the French army which occupied Madrid in 1808. In August 1808 Napoleon made him King of Naples where he carried out major reforms, but also established an ostentatious court. Relations grew frosty between him and Napoleon, but he served in the Russian campaign. Following the battle of Leipzig he entered into negotiations with the allies, but only Austria was prepared to accept his claim to Naples. Complex diplomatic moves continued until the Hundred Days when Murat tried to secure his throne by mobilising the Neapolitan army and calling for a united Italy. He was defeated by the Austrians, escaped to France, but Napoleon rejected his services. In turn Murat rejected Metternich's offer of a position and a pension. He returned to southern Italy with a small force in October 1815; he was captured, court-martialled and shot.

Napoleon I (1769–1821) Born Ajaccio 15 Aug 1769, the son of a member of the minor Corsican nobility. He was sent to school in France – to Autun (Jan 1779), military school in Brienne (May 1779), the Ecole Militaire in Paris (Sep 1784) and gazetted as an artillery officer (Sep 1785). He was elected Lieutenant Colonel in the Corsican National Guard (1791), but serious differences with the Corsican patriot leader Pasquale Paoli, forced him to flee Corsica with his family in 1793. In France he rejoined the army as a captain of artillery and first came to prominence commanding the artillery at Toulon (Dec 1793) – a position engineered for him by his fellow Corsican Saliceti (q.v.) and which brought promotion to General of Brigade. Linked with the Jacobins he was briefly imprisoned on the fall of Robespierre (Aug 1794). The following year he helped suppress the Vendémiaire rising and was made commander of the Army of the Interior (Oct). In March 1796 he married Josephine de

Beauharnais (q.v.) and almost immediately left Paris to take command of the Army of Italy. During 1796–7 he won a series of spectacular victories over the Austrians in Italy which brought about the Peace of Campo Formio (Oct 1797). Appointed commander of the Army of England he persuaded the Directory that an attack in the Middle East would be of more benefit than an invasion across the Channel. In July 1798 his army landed in Egypt but, in spite of victories over Turkish–Egyptian armies and a march into Syria, the campaign was not a success. In August 1799 he left his army and returned to France. By the coup of Brumaire (Nov 1799) he established the Consulate with himself as First Consul. In August 1802 he became Consul for life, in May 1804 Emperor of the French, and in March 1805 King of Italy. As Consul and then Emperor he presided over widespread administrative, economic and legal reforms which can be regarded as the climax of those begun by the French Revolution. The spectacular military successes of his armies and the spread of his Empire brought these reforms to other parts of Europe. Concerned about his lack of an heir (but convinced by the pregnancy of Marie Walewska (q.v.) that he could father children) he divorced Josephine (Dec 1809) and married Marie Louise (q.v.), the daughter of the Austrian Emperor (Mar 1810); a son, named the King of Rome, was born the following year (Mar 1811). His disastrous Russian campaign of 1812 encouraged all of his old enemies, and many of his allies, into a new coalition against him and, in spite of a brilliant campaign in northern France during the winter of 1813–14, he was compelled to abdicate (Apr 1814). The allies allowed him to keep the title of Emperor and granted him the island of Elba. Early in 1815 he returned to France; troops sent to arrest him instead went over to him, and the restored Bourbons fled. The government which he promised France on his return was to be more liberal than the old empire, but military defeat at Waterloo forced his second abdication (June 1815). He was exiled to St. Helena, a British possession in the South Atlantic, where he justified his actions and dictated memoirs to a variety of individuals, notably Las Cases (q.v.); these recollections played a significant part in the creation of the Napoleonic legend. He died on the island. In 1840 his remains were removed from St. Helena and reinterred in the Hôtel des Invalides in Paris.

Napoleon II, see Reichstadt, Duke of.

Nelson, Horatio Nelson, Viscount (1758–1805) British sailor. Born the son of a clergyman in Norfolk he first went to sea on a warship in 1770 but also served on a variety of merchant vessels before being gazetted lieutenant in 1777; post captain in 1779. He first saw active service during the American War of Independence commanding a frigate in the North Sea, in American waters and in the West Indies. He was kept on the active list following the peace and when war broke out with Revolutionary France (1793) he was appointed to command a 64-gun battleship, HMS Agamemnon. He served principally in the Mediterranean, distinguishing himself at the battle of St. Vincent (14 Feb 1797) shortly after which he became a rear-admiral by seniority. He lost an arm leading an attack on Santa Cruz de Tenerife (24 July 1797) but returned to the fleet of Cadiz in April 1798. At the end of that month he was ordered in pursuit of the French expedition to Egypt, and on 1 August he destroyed the French fleet at Aboukir Bay (battle of the Nile) where he received a head wound. As a reward for his success he was created a baron. From September 1798 to January 1800 he served in Italian waters and became embroiled in Neapolitan politics, partly because of his intimacy with Emma Hamilton, the wife of the British ambassador to Naples. He returned to England in November 1800 in company with the Hamiltons. The following January he was made vice-admiral and appointed a second in command of the fleet ordered to break up the Armed Neutrality. He destroyed the Danish fleet at the battle of Copenhagen (2 April 1801). He spent the period of the Peace of Amiens in the company of Emma Hamilton and her husband, largely ignoring his own wife. In 1803 he was ordered to command the Mediterranean fleet and blockaded Toulon. Early in 1805 the French avoided the blockade, sailed to the West Indies, and united with the Spanish fleet. The climax to the ensuing campaign was the battle of Trafalgar (21 October 1805) in which Nelson's masterly tactics destroyed the enemy fleets, but during which he was mortally wounded.

Ney, Michel (1769–1815) French soldier. Born in Saarlouis the son of a cooper, he began life as a clerk (1782), joining the army in 1788. He distinguished himself during the Revolutionary wars rising to the rank of general. Napoleon made him a marshal in 1804 and Duke of Elchingen in 1808. He served under Masséna in the Peninsular War, but quarrelled with him and was removed from his command. Noted for his impetuosity and bravery he was created Prince of Moskowa on the evening of the battle of Borodino. He led the rearguard of the *Grande Armée* heroically during the retreat from Moscow. Prominant among those who urged Napoleon to abdicate in 1814 he served Louis XVIII during the first restoration. He was ordered to arrest Napoleon on his return from Elba but, instead, rallied to him. He led a succession of fruitless cavalry charges at Waterloo. With the second restoration royalists insisted that he be tried for his actions; he was court-martialled, and shot.

Oberkampf, Christophe-Philippe (1738–1815) French businessman and manufacturer. The son of a dyer in Weissenbach, Bavaria, he became an engraver at Mulhouse, was next employed as a manufacturer by the court of Lorraine, and then moved as a dyer and colourer to the Arsenal factory in Paris. In 1759 he founded, at Jouy-en-Josas, the first factory for making printed calicoes using engraved copper plates, and rapidly cornered the market. In 1770 he was naturalised French, and was granted a patent of nobility in 1787. Napoleon gave him the Legion of Honour in 1806. Between 1806 and 1810 he invested more than 1.5m. francs in a cotton mill at Essonnes; but peace in 1815 brought the return of British competition and ruined the enterprise.

Ouvrard, Gabriel-Julien (1770–1846) French financier and speculator. Born near Clisson he began life working for a merchant in Nantes, but his gift for speculation was revealed early when, anticipating the expansion of the newpaper press in the Revolution, he invested heavily and successfully in paper. He moved to Paris after the Terror and developed his fortune, notably winning contracts for the French and Spanish navies, but he overextended himself and, unable to meet his obligations, he was placed under supervised residence in 1800. Released by Napoleon in 1802, he became a partner in a successful company organised for bringing grain to Paris. In 1804 he organised a commercial group, the *Négociants - réunis,* which speculated in bringing Spanish-American silver through the British blockade. The scheme failed and precipitated a financial crisis in France. He acted as Fouché's (q.v.) go-between in secret negotiations with the British and this led to a period of imprisonment (1810–13). In 1814 he contracted to supply the allied armies in France; during the Hundred Days he did the same for Napoleon. He continued his activities during the restoration, notably providing financial advice to the French government in 1817 and contracting to supply the French army in Spain in 1823. Convicted of fraud he spent a brief period in prison in 1825. He died in London.

Palafox y Melzi, José Rebolledo de (1776–1847) Spanish soldier. Born into a noble Aragonese family he enlisted in the Royal Bodyguard and rose to officer rank. During the French invasion of Spain in 1808 he took an independent stance becoming a populist military dictator in Zaragoza and defending the city against the French in two sieges, June – August 1808 and December 1808 – February 1809. Partly as a result of Palafox's military incompetence, Spanish losses during the appalling second siege were enormous and the city was captured; nevertheless he became a popular Spanish hero and was imprisoned in France. He and his family were the centre of a faction which constantly intrigued against the Central Junta; and during his imprisonment this faction was instrumental in the Junta's fall. In December 1813 Napoleon sent him back to Spain on a secret mission to attempt to bring the Peninsular War to an end. On his return to Spain he was created Duke of Zaragoza, subsequently becoming a senator for the city and also director of the Spanish veterans hospital.

Palm, Johann Philip (1768–1806) German patriot. Born in Schorndorf he became a bookseller in Nuremburg. In June 1806 he was arrested by the French for publishing an anonymous pamphlet *Deutschland in seiner tiefen Erniedrigung* (Germany in her deepest humiliation). Tried by court-martial, he was sentenced to death and shot, becoming the first martyr to German liberation.

Paul I (1754–1801) Tsar of Russia. The son of Peter III and Catherine the Great, Paul was convinced that his mother was responsible for his father's death in a palace coup; this belief contributed to his mental instability. On becoming Tsar in 1796 he sought to reverse his mother's policies and reforms and to strengthen his own autocratic powers. Hostile to the French Revolution he joined the coalition against France in 1798, then reversed his policy having developed an intense dislike of Britain. In December 1800 he organised the Armed Neutrality. But his policies and actions had made him many enemies. A palace coup was engineered by a group of Guards officers in March 1801 during which Paul was strangled.

Perceval, Spencer (1762–1812) British statesman. The second son of the 2nd Earl of Egmont, he was educated at Harrow and Cambridge. Called to the bar in 1786, he became a King's Counsel in 1796 and entered parliament in the same year. A staunch supporter of Pitt (q.v.) he nevertheless served in Addington's (q.v.) administration as Solicitor General (1801) and then Attorney General (1802). He was Chancellor of the Exchequer in the Duke of Portland's (q.v.) ministry (1807) and succeeded the duke as Prime Minister in 1809. He received much of the blame for the economic difficulties of the next few years and on 11 May 1812 he was shot dead in the lobby of the House of Commons by a bankrupt, John Bellingham, who blamed him for his personal misfortunes.

Pezza, Michele, see Fra Diavolo.

Pichegru, Jean-Charles (1761–1804) French soldier. The son of poor peasants from the Jura, he was educated by friars and joined the army in 1783. The Revolution gave him the opportunity to rise in rank and by October 1793 he was a general. He fought several successful campaigns in Germany, Belgium and Holland, and in 1795 was instrumental in suppressing the Germinal rising in Paris. Increasingly sympathetic to royalism he was elected to the Council of Five Hundred where he became a leader of the royalists. He was deported to Guiana following the coup d'état of Fructidor (1797), but escaped to England and served as a Russian staff officer in the campaign against France in 1799. In league with Cadoudal (q.v.) he was arrested on a mission to France in 1804, and was found strangled in prison while awaiting trial.

Pitt, William 'the Younger' (1759–1806) British statesman. The second son of William Pitt ('the Elder'), Earl of Chatham. He was educated intensively by a home tutor, which brought on his precocity, and went to Cambridge in 1773 aged 15. Called to the bar in 1780 he entered parliament in 1781 and was appointed Chancellor of the Exchequer in Shelburne's ministry (1782–83). On the fall of the Fox-North coalition in December 1783, George III (q.v.) invited him to form a ministry. During the next few years Pitt's ministry carried out a series of significant reforms which restored the nation's finances, but his attempt at parliamentary reform (1785) was rejected. From 1792 his policies were increasingly dictated by the need to respond to the French Revolution – which led him to oppose proposals for political reform – and by the demands of war. Following the Irish Rebellion of 1798 he proposed the union of Ireland with Britain and the abolition of the political bars against Catholics (and Protestant dissenters). George III refused to contemplate the latter and Pitt resigned. He supported his successor, Addington (q.v.), until the rupture of the Peace of Amiens when he became increasingly critical of the government's war policy. He was reappointed Prime Minister in May 1804, but the strains of conducting the war broke his health. He died 23 January 1806.

Pius VII (Luigi Barnabà Chiaramonti) (1740–1823) Chiaramonti entered the Benedictine Order in 1758. He became Bishop of Tivoli in 1782, and Bishop of Imola and a cardinal three years later. In 1800 he was elected Pope. A man of liberal leanings he sought to restore links with France by the Concordat, but was displeased by the Organic Articles which Napoleon added to the agreement without consultation. He hoped to get the Articles modified when he agreed formally to consecrate Napoleon's coronation, but failed and thereafter relations deteriorated between the Empire and the papacy. In 1808 the French occupied Rome, annexing it in the following year; Pius excommunicated the invaders and was imprisoned for so doing. The Papal States were restored to his control on Napoleon's fall, and while some liberal reforms were introduced from then until his death Pius followed a policy critical of the Revolution and its works.

Poniatowski, Josef Anton (1763–1813) Polish soldier. The son of an officer in the Austrian army and a nephew of the last King of Poland, he also served intermittently as an Austrian officer against the Turks between 1778 and 1788. From 1792 to 1794 he fought for Poland against the Russians, but with the Polish defeat he was allowed to retire to his family estates near Warsaw. In 1806 the King of Prussia made him governor of Warsaw, but he welcomed Napoleon's defeat of Prussia and, in consequence, was invited to command the Polish division of the Imperial Army and to serve as Minister of War in the Grand Duchy of Warsaw. He liberated Cracow from the Austrians in July 1809, and commanded a corps composed of Poles and Saxons in the Moscow campaign. Appointed a Marshal of the Empire on the morning of the battle of Leipzig, he was drowned in the Elster at the end of the battle covering Napoleon's retreat.

Portalis, Jean-Etienne-Marie (1746–1809) French jurist. Born at Bausset, Var, the son of a notary he studied law and became a distinguished lawyer in pre-Revolution Provence. Imprisoned in Paris during the Terror he was elected to the Council of Ancients in 1795 where he became a leader of the right-wing *Clichian* faction. He was forced into exile after the coup of Fructidor, but returned after that of Brumaire. Appointed a Councillor of State in 1800, he was given responsibility for drawing up the provisions of the Concordat and the Organic Articles. In 1801 he was put in charge of the department of *cultes*, or public worship, and in 1804 he became Minister of Ecclesiastical Affairs. His legal expertise led to his appointment to the commission charged with preparing the Civil Code; he was, reputedly, the hardest working member of the commission and personally responsible for many of its key provisions. He died in Paris.

Portland, William Henry Cavendish Bentinck, 3rd Duke of (1738–1809) British statesman. Educated at Eton and Oxford. As Marquis of Titchfield he entered parliament in 1761 as member for Weobly, Herefordshire; the following year he succeeded his father as Duke of Portland. He associated with the Whig faction in parliament and from 1783, when he briefly acted as Prime Minister, he was regarded as the leader of the group. During the 1780s he left the organisation of Whig politics to Fox (q.v.) and Edmund Burke, devoting himself to his favourite country seat at Bulstrode and his passionate interest in music. He re-emerged during the French Revolution, breaking with Fox and entering a coalition with Pitt (q.v.) in 1794. Home Secretary 1794–1801, he continued to hold office as Lord President of the Council under Addington (1801–3) and then again under Pitt. He retired to Bulstrode during the administration of the 'Talents' but accepted the position of Prime Minister, unwillingly, in 1807; it was considered that he was the best man to hold together a cabinet made up of Pitt's former colleagues. The duel between Canning (q.v.) and Castlereagh (q.v.) greatly upset him and this, together with ill-health, hastened his resignation in September 1809. He died the following month.

Potocki, Stanislaw Kostka Count (1752–1821) Polish statesman, one of a celebrated landed family. A member of the *Sjem* (Diet) 1788–92 he was a strong supporter of the liberal constitution of 1791. He commanded the artillery in the war with Russia in 1792, but remained in Poland following the final partition. In 1807 Napoleon appointed him to the provisional Committee of Government in Warsaw; he subsequently became a senator and President of the Council of State (1809). He played a key role in educational reform and continued this as Director of the Commission for Religious Denominations and Public Enlightenment in Congress Poland (1815–21). He was instrumental in the foundation of the University of Warsaw (1816) and the thousand primary schools in operation by 1821. However, he clashed with the Catholic Church over the secularisation of education and was forced to resign shortly before his death.

Récamier, Jeanne-Françoise-Julie-Adelaide (Juliette) (1777–1849) Noted French beauty and salon hostess. The daughter of a Lyon banker. She moved to Paris in 1792 and, the following year, married Jacques Récamier, a wealthy banker aged 42. For most of the period from the Consulate to the Revolution of 1848 she ran a salon in Paris welcoming a variety of literary personages (Mme de Staël (q.v.), Constant (q.v.), Chateaubriand (q.v.)) and critics of Napoleon such as Bernadotte (q.v.) and Moreau (q.v.). Never overtly political herself she displeased Napoleon particularly in 1803 when she declined the request that she be a lady attendant on Josephine (q.v.). Towards the end of the Empire she was exiled from Paris. Her husband became bankrupt in 1805, and she lost most of her own fortune in the early years of the restoration. From 1817 she became the close companion of Chateaubriand.

Regnier, Claude (1736–1814) French administrator and statesman. A distinguished lawyer in Nancy during the old regime he became a deputy to the Estates General in 1789 and busied himself with the legal changes of the early stages of the Revolution. He had no public role during the Legislative Assembly or the Convention, but became President of the Council of Ancients under the Directory. He participated in the Brumaire coup and Bonaparte appointed him to the Council of State where he was involved in drafting the Civil Code. As Minister of Justice (1802–13) he worked under the supervision of Cambacérès (q.v.); as President of the Commission of Claims (*des affaires contentieuses*) of the Council of State (1806–13), which prepared draft laws and decrees and heard accusations brought by private citizens against state functionaries for arbitrary behaviour, he earned a reputation for impartiality and fairness. Created Duke of Massa (1809), he retired in November 1813 with the title of Minister of State and the office of president of the *Corps législative*.

Reichstadt, Napoleon Francis Joseph Charles, Duke of (1811–1832) 'Napoleon II'. The son of Napoleon and Marie Louise, proclaimed the King of Rome on his birth. In April 1814 Napoleon sought to abdicate in his favour, but the proposal was unacceptable and overtaken by events. When Napoleon was exiled to Elba, Marie Louise and their son were moved to Vienna; they remained there throughout the Hundred Days. In 1816 the Austrian court refused to let the boy succeed to his mother's possessions in Italy; two years later he was given the title the Duke of Reichstadt. Educated as an Austrian prince, his tutors kept from him as much as possible of his father's achievements and the history of France. He remained the hope of the Bonapartists, especially during the Revolution of 1830. Never particularly strong, and noted for a weak chest, he died in 1832.

Reitzen, Sigismund von (1766–1847) German statesman. Born into the minor nobility he became a career civil servant and from 1796 to 1803 he acted as foreign envoy in Paris for the small Duchy of Baden. During the reorganisation of southern Germany he successfully pressed Baden's case and, as a result, Baden made the largest territorial gains of the German states. Appointed minister by Charles Frederick (q.v.) in May 1809 he initiated a vigorous policy of internal reorganisation on Napoleonic lines. Briefly removed from power in 1810 he served again as minister 1813–18 and 1832–42.

Riego Nunez, Rafael del (1785–1823) Spanish soldier and liberal martyr. Educated at the University of Oviedo he subsequently joined the Royal Bodyguard. He fought the French during the invasion of 1808 and was promoted to the rank of captain by the Asturias Junta. Captured at the battle of Espinosa he was taken to France. He travelled briefly in England and Germany before returning to Spain (1814) and resuming his military career. Inspired by liberal ideas, while only a major, he was a key figure in military pronunciamentos against Ferdinand VII (q.v.). During the Revolution of 1820 he was promoted to general and commanded a liberal army. In 1823 he was captured by supporters of the King and executed.

Roederer, Pierre-Louis (1754–1835) French politician and administrator. Born in Metz, the son of a prominent lawyer, he also studied law becoming a councillor in the Parlement of Metz, an industrialist and a spokesman for industrial interests in north-east France. He became a member of the Constituent Assembly in October 1789 where he gained a reputation for his work on tax reform. He defended Louis XVI during the *journée* of 10 Aug 1792, and was forced to go into hiding during the Terror. He re-emerged after Thermidor developing liberal socioeconomic theories to bring stability and rational government. He was involved in the Brumaire coup and during the Consulate he was president of the Section of the Interior in the Council of State, and frequently dined with Bonaparte. Quarrels with Chaptal (q.v.) and Fouché (q.v.) led to his dismissal in 1802, but he was appointed a senator. He served as Minister of Finance under Joseph Bonaparte (q.v.) in Naples (1806–8) successfully reforming the tax system; these reforms were kept by the Bourbons on their return. He was administrator of the Grand Duchy of Berg (1810–13), imperial commissioner of Strasbourg (1813–14), and of south-east France (during the Hundred Days). In 1815 Napoleon created him a peer, but the returning

Bourbons stripped him of his titles and he retired from public life to write histories, plays and his memoirs (generally regarded as useful and reliable particularly for the Consular period). He recovered the title of peer of France in 1832.

Romana, Pedro Caro y Sureda, Marqués de la (1761–1811) Spanish soldier. Appointed to command Spanish troops sent to Denmark in 1807 he rebelled against the French and, in 1808, escaped with the bulk of his troops via Britain, back to Spain. At the end of the year the Central Junta gave him command in Galicia, where he conducted a successful guerrilla campaign which helped secure the French withdrawal in June 1809. He spent most of 1809 defying the Junta, seeking its overthrow and the creation of a dictatorship. His intriguing continued even when the Junta sought to bring him under control by making him a fellow member. In 1810 he went to Lisbon to support Wellington's defence. Returning to Spain the following January he died suddenly, probably of syphilis. A favourite of Wellington, his favourable reputation among British military historians is probably undeserved.

Saliceti, Antoine-Christophe (1759–1809) French–Corsican politician and administrator. Born in Corsica the son of Italian parents he studied law at the University of Pisa becoming a magistrate deputy to the Corsican Estates and an *avocat* before the French Royal Council in Bastia. In 1789 he was chosen as a Corsican deputy to the Third Estate of the French Estates General and secured the island's annexation. He identified increasingly with the Jacobins, was elected to the National Convention and voted for Louis XVI's death. As a political representative with the army at Toulon he arranged for Captain Bonaparte to take command of the artillery. He survived the fall of Robespierre, acted as a supply agent for the Army of Italy and helped organise the Cisalpine Republic. After Brumaire he rallied many Jacobins to Bonaparte and thus helped secure his own political survival. He served the Consulate on a variety of missions to Corsica, Elba and Italy. In general Napoleon seems to have preferred him to be out of France. In 1806 he accompanied Joseph Bonaparte (q.v.) to Naples where he served as Minister of Police, a post which he combined with that of Minister for War (from April 1807). In these posts he organised the brutal war against the Calabrian brigands/partisans. When Murat (q.v.) replaced Joseph he was concerned about Saliceti's power; he removed him from the Ministry of War and sought to limit police activities. On Napoleon's behalf Saliceti assisted in the seizure of the Papal States and the arrest of Pius VII. On his death in Naples there were rumours of poison, but the autopsy ordered by Napoleon revealed nothing.

Savary, Anne Jean Marie René (1774–1833) French soldier and policeman. The son of a cavalry officer he volunteered for the cavalry in 1790 and served throughout the Revolutionary wars becoming aide-de-camp to Bonaparte after Marengo. Promoted to general (1803) and created Duke of Rovigo (1808) he was used by Napoleon to carry out a variety of unpleasant tasks: the execution of d'Enghien (q.v.) and duping the Spanish royals into the trap at Bayonne. In 1810 he replaced Fouché (q.v.) as Minister of Police, but he lacked his predecessor's abilities and subtlety and acted in ways that were often brutal and clumsy. During the conspiracy of General Malet (q.v.) he was captured in bed by the plotters, but Napoleon continued to rely on him and Savary responded with blind loyalty. He attempted to go to St. Helena with Napoleon, but was arrested on board HMS Bellerophon and briefly imprisoned on Malta. Eventually returning to France he was restored to his citizenship. He returned to favour during the July Monarchy and served briefly as commander-in-chief in Algeria (1831). His memoirs, in which he attempts to justify his activities under Napoleon, are regarded as unreliable.

Scharnhorst, Gerhard Johann David von (1755–1813) German soldier. He began his military career in the army of Hanover (1778) and fought alongside the British army in the early campaigns against Revolutionary France. He published two military textbooks which were highly regarded and entered Prussian service in 1801 as director of the War Academy in Berlin, becoming Chief of the General Staff in 1806. Following the Prussian disasters at Jena and Auerstädt he began to rethink the organisation of the Prussian army and was instrumental in creating a new national army based on universal service. He served as Minister of War 1808–10, and died as a result of wounds received at the battle of Lützen.

Schill, Ferdinand Baptista von (1776–1809) German soldier. Born in Saxony he entered the Prussian army at the age of 12. As a subaltern he was wounded at Auerstädt, but subsequently organised a band of 1000 partisans who harried the French armies across northern Germany. After the Treaty of Tilsit his corps was incorporated into the Prussian army. In May 1809 he attempted to spark a German rising against Napoleon, marching his men out of Berlin and into Westphalia where he declared a national uprising. He had some initial military success but his small force was forced to withdraw into Swedish Pomerania and was overwhelmed at Stralsund. Schill was killed in the fighting.

Schimmelpenninck, Rutger Jan (1761–1825) Dutch statesman. Born into a Mennonite family he was educated as a lawyer making his name defending radical patriots, and making a fortune through investments in America. A pragmatic reformer he was involved with the politics of the Batavian Republic from its beginning. He served as its ambassador in Paris (1798 and 1802) and in London (1801), and represented it in the conferences negotiating the Peace of Amiens. In 1805 he was installed as Grand Pensionary of the Republic by Napoleon, but he resigned the following year refusing to go along with the Emperor's plans to make Louis Bonaparte King of Holland. His period as Grand Pensionary witnessed a variety of reforms geared towards making the Netherlands a centralised state; it also coincided with a serious deterioration in his eyesight, leading eventually to blindness. When Holland was annexed to France in 1810 he was made a member of the French Senate. After Napoleon's fall he served as a deputy in the legislative assembly of the Kingdom of the Netherlands.

Schwarzenberg, Karl Philipp zu, Prince (1771–1820) Austrian soldier. He entered the Austrian army aged only 16 fighting first against the Turks then in the campaigns against Revolutionary France. In 1796 he was promoted to general. Vice-president of the Imperial War Council in 1805. In 1809 he was sent to St. Petersburg to dissuade Tsar Alexander (q.v.) from an alliance with Napoleon. He commanded the Austrian cavalry at Wagram, subsequently serving as ambassador in Paris (1809–12). At Napoleon's request he was put in command of the Austrian contingent (13,000 men) serving with the *Grande Armée* in the Russian campaign; he endeavoured to keep these out of the action and avoided the worst of the disaster. In 1813 he sought to mediate between the French and Russian armies, but subsequently became commander-in-chief of the allied armies against Napoleon and fought, as such, at Leipzig. He planned the allied campaign in northern France (1813–14) and was appointed President of the Imperial War Council in 1814. During the Hundred Days he commanded an Austrian army organised on the Upper Rhine but not engaged in the fighting. He was struck down by paralysis in 1817. He died in Leipzig.

Sidmouth, Viscount, see Addington, Henry.

Soult, Nicholas-Jean de Dieu (1769–1851) French soldier. The son of a notary in the Tarn he was intended for the bar himself but, on his father's death in 1785, he enlisted as a private in the French infantry. Commissioned in 1792 he came to prominence as one of Masséna's subordinates towards the end of the Revolutionary wars. Created a marshal in 1804 he was appointed to command the army at Boulogne destined for the invasion of England. He played a key role in the battle of Austerlitz, and further distinguished himself at Jena and Eylau. Created Duke of Dalmatia in 1808, the following year he was entrusted with the pursuit of Moore (q.v.) to Corunna. During the next four years he fought in the Peninsula; most notable was his conduct of the campaign in southern France early in 1814. He sided with Louis XVIII during the first restoration, rallied to Napoleon during the Hundred Days, and after Waterloo was banished from France until 1819. He was made a peer in 1827 and served Louis Philippe as Minister of War from 1830–34 and from 1840–45. In 1838 he represented France at the coronation of Queen Victoria, and there met his old enemy Wellington. He died in 1851; his son edited a volume of his memoirs which were published three years later.

Speranski, Mikhail Mikhailovich (1772–1839) Russian statesman. The son of a village priest he was educated at an ecclesiastical seminary in St. Petersburg where he subsequently became professor of maths and physics. His considerable ability brought him to the notice of the court. Between 1809 and 1812 Tsar Alexander entrusted him with full powers as virtually his sole minister. He introduced plans for constitutional and governmental reform, but court intrigues and Alexander's desire for a scapegoat led to his dismissal. Later restored to favour he became Governor General of Siberia (1816) and a member of the Council of State (1821).

Stadion, Johann Philipp von (1763–1824) Austrian statesman. Born into the imperial nobility in Mainz he entered the service of the Emperor and was appointed ambassador to Stockholm when only 24. He became the ambassador to London in 1790, but resigned five years later in protest over imperial foreign policy. By the turn of the century he was back in diplomatic service first as ambassador to Berlin (1801), then to St. Petersburg (1803). After the Austro-Russian defeat at Austerlitz he was appointed Foreign Minister and he urged reforming policies on the Emperor Francis (q.v.), in particular he sought to promote popular education and a spirit of German patriotism. He resigned following the Austrian defeat in the Wagram campaign. In 1813 he negotiated Austria's entry into the alliance against Napoleon. Following Napoleon's defeat he was given charge of Austrian finances and introduced a series of reforms seeking to resolve the financial problems created by two decades of war. He died in Vienna.

de Staël (or de Staël-Holstein), Germaine (1766–1814) Woman of letters and critic of Napoleon. The daughter of Jacques Necker, the Geneva banker and popular finance minister of Louis XVI, she was born in Paris and spent her early years there and on her father's estate at Coppet in Switzerland. She began writing at an early age publishing her first novel, *Sophie*, anonymously in 1786. The same year she married a Swedish diplomat, later made Swedish ambassador to France, Eric Magnus, Baron of Staël-Holstein. An early supporter of the Revolution she left France during the Terror, returning with the fall of Robespierre. During the Directory she ran an influential salon sympathetic to the regime; at the same time she became intimate with Benjamin Constant [q.v.] and separated amicably from her husband. Initially sympathetic to Napoleon she rapidly became one of his sharpest critics which prompted him to ban her from Paris. She spent the years 1804–14 either travelling in Europe or at Coppet. In 1811 she married a young Swiss officer named Rocca, 23 years her junior. She returned to Paris with the first restoration, and reopened her salon there in 1816–7.

Staps, Friedrich (1791–1809) German patriot. Born in Saxony, the son of a Lutheran pastor. While a student he became inspired by the idea of a German Fatherland of which Napoleon was the main enemy. He attempted to assassinate Napoleon with a knife at a military review at Schönbrunn. Napoleon sought to demonstrate his magnanimity by offering Staps his life for an apology, but Staps steadfastly refused and was executed.

Stein, Heinrich Friedrich Karl, Baron vom und zum (1757–1831) Prussian statesman. After studying law he entered Prussian service in 1780. He distinguished himself administering part of the Westphalian lands of Prussia. Dismissed early in 1807 for criticising policies of Frederick William III (q.v.), but was recalled as Minister of Home Affairs with wide powers after the Treaty of Tilsit. He began a major reform programme which involved freeing the serfs, abolishing caste distinctions of all kinds, and reorganising land tenure and municipal government. At the same time he encouraged Scharnhorst's (q.v.) military reforms. Napoleon put pressure on Frederick William to dismiss him in 1808 and in January 1809 he was forced to flee Berlin taking refuge first in Austria, then in Russia. After Napoleon's retreat from Moscow he urged Tsar Alexander (q.v.) to liberate Europe. He became the administrator of the provinces of East and West Prussia following the French withdrawal. He retired after the Congress of Vienna to devote himself largely to the study of history.

Suchet, Louis-Gabriel (1770–1826) French soldier. The son of a silk manufacturer in Lyon, his first military experience appears to have been as a volunteer in the national guard cavalry of Lyon in 1791. He met Bonaparte while serving as a battalion commander at Toulon; thereafter he served in the Revolutionary wars in Italy and Holland, and in the Austerlitz and Jena campaigns. Much of his work during these campaigns was as a staff officer and this kept him out of the limelight. In 1808 he was made a count, he married a niece of Joseph Bonaparte's wife, and marched into Spain with the imperial army. It was for his role in Spain that he is most remembered. As military commander and governor of the province he successfully brought Aragon under French control. However, in doing this he secured the collaboration of the local gentry only by maintaining feudal dues, now exacted with the support of well-disciplined French troops. While running an efficient and honest administration and supplying money for Joseph's generally bankrupt treasury, he refused to accept the officials sent by Joseph to administer the territories under his control. In spite of this, and as a reward for his successes, Napoleon created him a marshal in 1811, and following his military conquest of Valencia he was created Duke of Albufera de Valencia (1813). French defeats forced him to withdraw his army from Spain early in 1814. Louis XVIII created him a peer of France. He rallied to Napoleon during the Hundred Days commanding the army on the Alpine frontier; he was consequently stripped of his titles, though only briefly. He died near Marseilles leaving his memoirs of the Peninsular War unfinished; these were edited and subsequently published by his former chief of staff.

Talleyrand (or Talleyrand-Périgord), Charles Maurice (1754–1838) French statesman. Born into the nobility in Paris, a club foot prevented him from joining the army so, without any profound religious calling, he entered the Church. In 1788 he was made Bishop of Autun and as such he was predominant among the liberal clergy in the early years of the Revolution. He welcomed the Civil Constitution of the Clergy (1791) but shortly after renounced his bishopric for a diplomatic career first in England (1792) then in the United States. He returned to France during the Directory and served as Foreign Minister 1797–9, resigning shortly before the Brumaire coup during which he backed Bonaparte. He was reappointed Foreign Minister at the end of 1799 and during the Consular period and the early years of the Empire he played an influential role in getting the laws relaxed against *émigrés*, non-juring priests, and royalists. While his private life, corruption and cynicism were notorious, he nevertheless sought to moderate some of Napoleon's foreign adventures and his treatment of defeated enemies. In 1807 he resigned as a minister though he remained on the fringes of public life. In 1814 he worked to bring back Louis XVIII as king and subsequently represented France at the Congress of Vienna. He served very briefly as Foreign Minister at the beginning of the second restoration and was subsequently appointed High Chamberlain. After the Revolution of 1830 King Louis Philippe invited him to be Foreign Minister, but he opted instead for the embassy in London.

Villeneuve, Pierre-Charles-Jean-Baptiste-Silvestre de (1763–1806) French sailor. Born into the nobility in Valensoles, Basses-Alpes, he joined the French navy in 1778. Sympathetic to the Revolution he became a captain in 1793 and an admiral in 1796. He was censured for his conduct at the battle of the Nile when he succeeded in escaping (with four ships) Nelson's (q.v.) destruction of the French fleet. In 1804 Napoleon appointed him to command the Toulon squadron with orders to divert Nelson from the surveillance of European coasts so as to enable the invasion of England to take place. The subsequent naval campaign reached its climax with the battle of Trafalgar. He showed personal bravery during the battle, but was completely outmanoeuvred by Nelson. Briefly a prisoner in England, he returned to France in April 1806, where, at Rennes, he committed suicide.

Walewska, Marie (1789–1817) Polish countess and Napoleon's mistress. Born Marie Laczinski, the daughter of a Polish nobleman killed in the fighting leading to the third partition of Poland, she was married in 1804 to a rich regional governor, Count Anastase Walewski, 49 years her senior. Napoleon met her during his Polish campaign and made her his mistress. He had already fathered two illegitimate children (a son by Elénore Denuelle, and a daughter by the actress Pellapra), but he had doubts about the fidelity of these earlier mistresses. The news of Walewska's pregnancy convinced him of his ability to father children and finally determined him to divorce Josephine (q.v.). His son, Alexandre Walewski (who was to become a leading French diplomat and politician), was born in May 1810. Marie and Alexandre visited Napoleon secretly on Elba; they were denied by Murat (q.v.) the possessions promised them in Naples. They visited Napoleon at Malmaison following his second abdication, and Marie, ever romantic and loyal, offered to follow him into exile. Widowed in February 1815, in October 1816 she married General Philippe d'Ornano, a distant relative of the Bonapartes, and died in childbirth.

Wellington, Arthur Wellesley, 1st Duke of (1769–1852) British soldier and statesman. The fourth son of Garrett Wellesley (or Wesley), 2nd baron and 1st Earl of Mornington, he was born in Ireland and educated at Eton and at a French academy for young noblemen in Angers. He joined the army in 1787 as an ensign; he purchased his lieutenant colonelcy in 1793. He first saw active service in the Holland campaign 1794–5. The following year he accompanied his regiment to India where he fought with distinction in several campaigns, most notably winning a succession of victories against the Mahrattas. Returning to England as a major-general in 1805 he entered parliament and was appointed Chief Secretary for Ireland in Portland's (q.v.) ministry. He commanded the British troops in the Copenhagen expedition (August 1807), and the following year was a divisional commander in the first expedition to Portugal. Unlike his superiors he was exonerated in the court-martial following the Convention of Cintra and returned to Portugal to command the Anglo–Portuguese armies in the Peninsular War. It was here from 1809–14 that he confirmed his military reputation with a succession of victories over Napoleon's marshals and brother Joseph (q.v.). He commanded the British troops in Belgium during the Hundred Days, most notably at Waterloo; he subsequently commanded the army of occupation in France. The victories brought him honours from the British and from foreign governments: viscount (1809), earl (1812), duke (1814), prince (of the Netherlands, 1815). In 1818 he entered the cabinet as Master General of the Ordnance and thereafter played a leading role in the Tory party. Prime Minister in 1828, for pragmatic reasons he accepted Catholic emancipation, but he remained opposed to parliamentary reform. He served in Peel's cabinets (1834 and 1841–6), and planned for the military defence of London during the Chartist disorders of 1848.

William I (1772–1844) King of the Netherlands. The son of William V, Prince of Orange and hereditary *stadtholder* of the Netherlands, and a Prussian princess. In 1791 his Prussian links were extended by his marriage to the daughter of Frederick William II of Prussia. He fought with distinction in the French Revolutionary wars but, following the French victories in 1795 he was forced into exile with the rest of his family; he moved first to London, then to Berlin. During the peace following the Treaty of Amiens he met Napoleon and was given territory adjoining his family's hereditary German lands. In 1806, on the death of his father, he became William VI, Prince of Orange. In the same year he fought with the Prussian army and was present at Jena; in response Napoleon seized his territories. In 1809 he held command in the Austrian army and was wounded at Wagram. He returned to the Netherlands at the end of 1813 following the revolts against Napoleon. He was recognised as sovereign and took the title of William I, King of the Netherlands. His new kingdom included Belgium, but William failed to acknowledge the differences between the Dutch and the Belgians which led to the latters' rising for independence 1830–31. Even when Belgian independence had been won and guaranteed by other powers, William refused to accept it until 1839. Liberal changes in the Netherlands towards the end of the 1830s were not to his liking; this, and popular hostility to his proposed second marriage to a Belgian, Catholic countess led him to abdicate in 1840. He retired to an estate in Silesia where he died.

Windham, William (1750–1810) British statesman. Educated at Eton, where he was a contemporary of Fox (q.v.), and Oxford. He entered parliament as MP for Norwich in 1784 and joined the Whig opposition faction. Alarmed by the French Revolution he shifted his allegiance to Pitt (q.v.) and with the Pitt-Portland coalition (1794) he entered the cabinet as Secretary at War. He resigned with Pitt over Catholic emancipation (1801), but his opposition to the Peace of Amiens cost him his seat in 1802. He re-entered parliament as MP for St. Mawes, a Cornish borough controlled by the Grenvilles (1802), and subsequently served as MP for New Romney (1806), and Higham Ferrers (1807–9). He sided with Grenville (q.v.), refusing to join Pitt's administration in 1804 without Fox. He was Minister for War and the Colonies in the Talents Ministry, introducing measures to improve the army. He went into opposition when the Talents resigned and became the foremost critic of Castle-reagh's policies as Minister of War, but he was also a warm supporter of the British involvement in the Peninsular War.

Yorck von Wartenburg, Hans David Ludwig (1759–1830) German soldier of English extraction. He joined the Prussian army in 1772 but was dismissed for insubordination seven years later. After a brief period serving in the Dutch army in the East Indies he was allowed to rejoin the Prussian army (1785) where he became noted as a commander of light infantry. He fought in the campaign of 1806 and was wounded at Lübeck. In 1812 he was in command of the Prussian corps demanded by Napoleon to assist in the Russian campaign; he neutralised this corps by signing the Convention of Tauroggen with the Russians at the end of the year. He led a corps throughout the War of Liberation and was given the addition to his name for distinguished service leading his men over the Elbe near Wartenburg in October 1813. He was made a count in 1814, and a field marshal in 1821.

Battles

See map 12 on page 312.

Alba de Tormes 28 November 1809 (Peninsular War) About 22,000 Spanish troops were separated from the bulk of Del Parque's army by a river. They were surprised by Gen. Kellerman who, initially, had only a few thousand cavalry. A French victory: 3000 Spanish casualties, about 300 French.

Albuera 16 May 1811 (Peninsular War) 35,000 British, Portuguese and Spanish, under Marshal Beresford, defeated 24,000 French under Soult. The battle is notable for the casualties sustained by the units most heavily engaged, in particular two-thirds of the 6000 British infantry engaged were killed or wounded. The total casualties were 6000 among the allies and 7000 French.

Arcis-sur-Aube 20–21 March 1814 (Campaign of 1814, Northern France) 23,000 French under Napoleon were forced to withdraw by an allied force of 20,000, mainly Austrians, commanded by Schwarzenberg. 3000 French and 4000 allied casualties.

Aspern-Essling 21–22 May 1809 (Wagram Campaign) 70,000 French led by Napoleon had entered Vienna but the Austrians had destroyed the bridges over the Danube. French troops led by Lannes and Masséna crossed by means of pontoon bridges and occupied Aspern–Essling where they were attacked by 90,000 Austrians under Archduke Charles. The French were forced to withdraw; Lannes was mortally wounded. 21,000 French and 23,000 Austrian casualties.

Auerstädt, see Jena-Auerstädt

Austerlitz 2 December 1805 'The Battle of the three Emperors' (Napoleon, Alexander and Francis) This was the climax to the 1805 campaign when Napoleon, with 73,200 men defeated the combined Austrian and Russian armies (85,400) inflicting 27,000 casualties for the loss of 9000. The result brought the third coalition to the point of collapse.

Bailén (or Baylén) 19 July 1808 (Peninsular War) Gen. Dupont with a French army of 20,000 was caught between two Spanish armies of 30,000 and compelled to surrender his entire force.

Barrosa 5 March 1811 (Peninsular War) 5000 British, Portuguese, and Spanish under Sir Thomas Graham sallied out of Cadiz and attacked the rear of the besieging French army under Victor. Some 7000 of the French army were engaged and defeated. 1200 allied casualties and 2000 French.

Basque Roads 11–12 April 1809 (Naval battle) French Admiral Williamez avoided British Admiral Gambier's blockade and broke out of Brest with eight battleships and four smaller craft. He sailed into Basque Roads, at the mouth of the Charente, and was joined by three battleships from Rochefort. The French were then attacked by Admiral Cochrane with fireships and frigates. Two French battleships and a frigate were burnt and two surrendered. The French commanders were court-martialled; one was shot, one cashiered, three imprisoned.

Bautzen 20–21 May 1813 (Leipzig Campaign) Napoleon with 200,000 men forced the withdrawal of 90,000 Prussians and Russians well entrenched behind the River Spree. Roughly 20,000 casualties on each side.

Berezina 27–28 November 1812 (Russian Campaign) Rearguard action to enable the remnant of the *Grande Armée* (perhaps 49,000 strong) to cross the River Berezina, opposed by 64,000 Russians. 25,000 French casualties (plus some 30,000 non-combatants) and 20,000 Russian casualties.

Bidassoa 7–9 October 1813 (Peninsular War) Wellington fought his way across the River Bidassoa into France with 32,000 British, Portuguese and Spanish troops, opposed by 14,000 French under Soult. 16,000 allied and 11,000 French casualties.

Borodino 7 September 1812 'The Battle of Moscow' (Russian Campaign) Drawn battle fought between the *Grande Armée* of 133,000 commanded by Napoleon and 120,000 Russians under Kutuzov. The Russians withdrew leaving the road to Moscow open. 30,000 French and 44,000 Russian casualties.

Brienne 29 January 1814 (Campaign of 1814, Northern France) Napoleon with 34,000 men forced the withdrawal of 25,000 Prussians led by Blücher. Blücher and Gneisnau were nearly captured. 3000 French and 4000 Prussian casualties.

Busaco 27 September 1810 (Peninsular War) 50,000 British and Portuguese under Wellington defeated Soult's 60,000 French inflicting 5000 casualties for the loss of 1300.

Caldiero 29 October 1805 (Northern Italy) Masséna, with 46,000 French, attacked an Austrian army under Archduke Charles holding a rocky position in the Alps. The battle was inconclusive with 5700 Austrian casualties and 6300 French; but, preoccupied with the Austrian disaster at Ulm, Charles proceeded to withdraw from Italy.

Castalla 13 April 1813 (Peninsular War) An inconclusive battle between 17,000 British, German and Italian troops under Sir John Murray, and 15,000 French under Suchet. The French withdrew, with 800 casualties; the allies suffered 600.

Champaubert 10 February 1814 (Campaign of 1814, Northern France) 5000 Russians under Olssufier were routed by 24,000 French under Napoleon. Only about 1000 Russians escaped, for some 200 or so French casualties.

Ciudad Real 18 February 1809 (Peninsular War) 12,000 Spanish under Cartoajal marching on Toledo were intercepted and forced to retreat by 10,000 French under Sebastiani.

Copenhagen 2 April 1801 (Naval battle) Nelson, with 12 battleships, five frigates and some smaller craft, attacked the Dutch fleet at anchor inflicting heavy casualties: about 3500, including 2000 prisoners, for 1000 British. The action forced the Danes out of the Armed Neutrality.

Corunna 14 January 1809 (Peninsular War) 20,000 French under Soult attempted to prevent Sir John Moore's force of 15,000 British troops from embarking after the initial British campaign in the Iberian peninsula. The British lost 1000 men, including Moore, but inflicted 2000 casualties on the French and succeeded in escaping.

Craonne, see Laon.

Dresden 26–27 August 1813 (Leipzig Campaign) The last of Napoleon's great victories. 120,000 French defeated 170,000 Austrians, Prussians and Russians inflicting 38,000 casualties for the loss of about 10,000.

Eckmühl 22 April 1809 (Wagram Campaign) 60,000 French under Napoleon defeated Archduke Charles's 35,000 men. There were about 6000 French casualties, and perhaps twice as many Austrian.

Espinosa 10 November 1808 (Peninsular War) In Napoleon's drive over the Ebro 23,000 Spanish troops under Blake were routed by a French column under Victor. Blake was only able to rally 7000 men when the flight was halted at Reynosa on 12 November. Probably about 11,000 Spanish casualties, and about 1000 French.

Eylau 8 February 1807 (Polish Campaign) 75,000 French, under Napoleon, fought a savage but inconclusive battle in a snowstorm with 76,000 Russians. 25,000 French and 15,000 Russian casualties.

Friedland 14 June 1807 (Polish Campaign) Napoleon, with 80,000 men, heavily defeated Benningsen's 60,000 Russians. The French inflicted 20,000 casualties for the loss of 8000 men. The defeat led Alexander to seek an armistice.

Fuentes de Oñoro 5 May 1811 (Peninsular War) Masséna, with 45,000 men, attacked an Anglo–Portuguese army of 33,000 under Wellington in an attempt to relieve Almeida. The battle was inconclusive with 1500 Anglo–Portuguese casualties and some 2000 French. It was the nearest thing to a defeat experienced by Wellington in the Peninsular, but the French failed to relieve Almeida.

Gamonal 10 November 1808 (Peninsular War) In Napoleon's drive from the Ebro 12,000 Spanish regulars under Belvedere, backed by about 8000 armed peasants were completely routed by the French under Soult. Spanish losses were put at 2500 dead and 900 prisoners; French losses were extremely small.

Hanau 30 October 1813 (War of Liberation) Withdrawing to the Rhine after Leipzig, Napoleon, with 60,000 men, swept aside 50,000 Austrians, Bavarians and Cossacks who sought to bar his retreat. 6000 French and 5000 allied casualties.

Heilsberg 10 June 1807 (Polish Campaign) Napoleon with 49,000 men sought to isolate Benningsen's 53,000 attacking them in a fortified position. The Russians inflicted heavy casualties on the French (over 10,000) for the loss of about 8000, but Benningsen decided to withdraw.

Hohenlinden 3 December 1800 (Revolutionary Wars) Crucial battle towards the end of the Revolutionary wars in which General Moreau, with 60,000 French, defeated 70,000 Austrians under Archduke John inflicting 20,000 casualties (including 12,000 prisoners).

Isle d'Aix, see Basque Roads.

Jena-Auerstädt 14 October 1806 (Prussian Campaign) Two devastating defeats inflicted by the French on the Prussians. Napoleon, with 96,000 men, crushed 53,000 Prussians at Jena inflicting 25,000 casualties for 5000 French, while 27,000 men under Davout withstood the attacks of 63,500 Prussians at Auerstädt inflicting 13,000 casualties for the loss of 7000. Davout was eventually supported by fresh troops under Bernadotte; in many respects his success was the more striking, but it was underplayed by Napoleon.

Kitzen 17 June 1813 (War of Liberation) Incident during the armistice of Poischwitz when the French destroyed the Lützow Korps claiming that they had violated the terms of the armistice. Napoleon dismissed the French commander, Nisas, when he protested that Lützow had not broken the terms.

Laon 7–10 March 1814 (Campaign of 1814, Northern France) Indecisive battle between 47,500 French under Napoleon and 85,000 allied troops under Blücher. The French began with a successful assault on allied troops on the plateau of Craonne on 7 March. The subsequent attack on the main allied force at Laon on 9 and 10 March was unsuccessful. The French withdrew suffering 6000 casualties for the allies' 4000.

La Rothière 1–2 February 1814 (Campaign of 1814, Northern France) Napoleon's 40,000 men clashed with 110,000 allied troops and, after an initial success, were forced to retire primarily because of bad weather and the difficulty of moving their artillery over the heavy ground; about 6000 casualties on either side.

Leipzig 16–18 October 1813 'Battle of the Nations'/*Völkerschlacht* (War of Liberation) Napoleon's 195,000 men were confronted by 365,000 Austrians, Prussians, Russians and Swedes in the climax of the War of Liberation. The French were defeated losing about 73,000 men; allied casualties were about 54,000.

Ligny 16 June 1815 (Waterloo Campaign) 80,000 men under Napoleon inflicted an indecisive defeat on 84,000 Prussians under Blücher; 11,000 French casualties and 25,000 Prussian. Following the battle Napoleon sent Grouchy in pursuit of Blücher but Grouchy lost the Prussians thus enabling them to link with Wellington at Waterloo.

Lundy's Lane 5 July 1814 (Anglo–American War) Confused and indecisive battle between about 3000 British, under Sir George Drummond, and about 5000 Americans under Gen. Winfield Scott, who were withdrawing from Canada. About 1000 casualties on each side; the Americans continued their withdrawal.

Lützen 2 May 1813 (War of Liberation) Indecisive victory by Napoleon, with 110,000 men, over 73,000 allies. Approximately 20,000 French casualties and 18,000 allied.

Maida 4 July 1806 A small British force under Sir John Stuart made a pinprick raid from Sicily on the Calabrian coast. Stuart's 5200 men met 6400 French under Gen. Reynier inflicting 2200 casualties for the loss of only 330. Stuart did not follow up the victory, but tactically the battle is generally regarded as an important precursor of those fought in the Peninsular.

Maloyaroslavets 24 October 1812 (Russian Campaign) Napoleon, with 24,000 French was checked by a similar number of Russians under Kutusov. Napoleon had hoped to march south and winter in Lithuania, but the battle forced him to retreat along the route his invasion had come. 6000 French and 8000 Russian casualties.

Marengo 14 June 1800 (Revolutionary Wars) Napoleon, with 28,000 men, believed that he had the Austrians on the run and divided his army to impede the enemy's retreat. The Austrian Gen. Melas, however, had 31,000 men and the French position was desperate until Desaix rejoined the army with his division and saved the day. 7000 French casualties (including Desaix who was killed) and 14,000 Austrian.

Medellin 28 March 1809 (Peninsular War) 23,000 Spanish troops under Cuesta were routed by about 18,000 French under Victor. The Spanish were believed to have suffered about 10,000 casualties (8000 dead and 2000 prisoners); French losses were about 1000.

Medina de Rio Seco 14 July 1808 (Peninsular War) About 22,000 Spanish under Cuesta and Blake were decisively defeated by Bessières with 14,000 French. French casualties were about 500, Spanish over 3000.

Montmirail 11 February 1814 (Campaign of 1814, Northern France) 18,000 Prussians under Sacken were attacked by Napoleon with 20,000 French. Sacken withdrew with 4000 casualties for the French 2000.

New Orleans 8 January 1815 (Anglo–American War) 5300 British under Sir Edward Pakenham made a frontal assault on 5000 Americans under Andrew Jackson. The Americans were entrenched behind felled trees and cotton bales with the Mississippi on one flank and a cypress swamp on the other. Pakenham was killed and the British called off the attack with heavy casualties – some 2000 men. The Americans lost eight killed and 13 wounded. The battle was pointless as the war was already over.

Nive 9–13 December 1813 (Peninsular War) Wellington pushed 60,000 British, Portuguese and Spanish across the Nive. He was attacked first on one flank, then on the other by Soult with a similar number of men. The French were repulsed with 7000 casualties to the allies' 5000.

Nivelle 10 November 1813 (Peninsular War) Soult, with 63,000 men in a strong defensive position, attempted to hold up the advance of Wellington's 80,000 British, Portuguese and Spanish. Wellington's attack split Soult's army and forced it to retreat with 4300 casualties; the allied loss was 2700.

Ocaña 18 November 1809 (Peninsular War) Spanish disaster in which 50,000 men under Areizaga were defeated by 34,000 French under Joseph and Soult. The Spanish lost 12,000 killed and wounded and 14,000 prisoners; the French casualties were 2000.

Orthez 27 February 1814 (Peninsular War) Soult, with 36,000 men attempted to halt Wellington's advance with 44,000 British, Portuguese and Spanish. The French were defeated with 4000 casualties for the allies 2,000. Wellington was slightly wounded in the leg.

Pultusk 26 December 1806 (Polish Campaign) Indecisive battle between 25,000 French under Lannes and 36,000 Russians under Benningsen. The Russians withdrew with losses of 5000 to 6000 on each side.

Pyrenees 25 July – 1 August 1813 (Peninsular War) Series of engagements in the mountains as Wellington broke off the sieges of Pamplona and San Sebastien to meet Soult's relieving force. Some 40,000 British, Portuguese and Spanish were engaged against some 53,000 French. 7000 allied casualties and 13,500 French.

Quatre Bras 16 June 1815 (Waterloo Campaign) Indecisive battle which was a prelude to Waterloo. 36,000 British and allied troops under Wellington fought some 25,000 under Ney. 4300 allied and 4700 French casualties.

Raab 14 June 1809 (Wagram Campaign) 33,000 French and Italians under Eugène de Beauharnais attacked an Austrian army of 30,000 under Archduke John so as to prevent its juncture with the army of Archduke Charles facing Napoleon. The Austrians were forced to retreat suffering 6000 casualties, half of them prisoners; French losses were 2500.

Ratisbon 23 April 1809 (Wagram Campaign) Realising that Arch-duke Charles could rebuild the Austrian army and attack the French lines of communication from Ratisbon, Napoleon attacked Charles's 47,000 with 72,000 men. The city was taken largely through the courageous example of Lannes. About 2000 casualties on each side. Napoleon was slightly wounded in the right foot.

Roliça 17 August 1808 (Peninsular War) Unnecessary battle at outset of the Peninsular War, probably the result of the impetuosity of some British officers who made a frontal assault on a strong French position and drove them from it. The battle involved about 9000 British under Wellesley and 5000 French under Laborde. 480 British casualties, 600 French.

Salamanca 22 June 1812 (Peninsular War) Wellington was with-drawing to Portugal with 48,000 men pursued by Marmont with 50,000. Initially reluctant to fight, Wellington seized the oppor-tunity when Marmont was manoeuvring and inflicted a heavy defeat. The blow to Marmont would have been greater but for a Spanish army vacating a key position on the French line of re-treat. 4800 allied casualties; at least 14,000 French, including 7000 prisoners.

Smolensk 17–18 August 1812 (Russian Campaign) 45,000 French under Napoleon engaged 30,000 Russians under de Tolly. Two Rus-sian armies converged on Smolensk, one led by Barclay de Tolly, the other by Bagration. French attacks failed to take the city, but Barclay de Tolly decided to evacuate it fearing that the French would by-pass it and press on to the Smolensk–Moscow highway. De Tolly was much criticised by many on the Russian General Staff. 12,000 French and 6000 Russian casualties.

Somosierra Pass 30 November 1808 (Peninsular War) 9000 Span-ish troops sought to check Napoleon's march on Madrid. The ac-tion is most notable for Napoleon's impatient order to his Polish Light Horse to seize 16 Spanish guns; the first charge was a disaster, but the second, supported by infantry in the surrounding hillsides, was successful. Napoleon omitted all reference to the first charge in his bulletin reporting the action.

Sorauren 26 July 1814 (Peninsular War) First clash of the allied army under Wellington and the French under Soult during the battle of the Pyrenees (q.v.).

Talavera 27–28 June 1809 (Peninsular War) Wellesley moved on Madrid with 55,000 British and Spanish troops. Attacked by 46,000 French led by Victor and Joseph. The main burden of the attack fell on Wellesley's 20,000 British troops who withstood the assaults until the French withdrew fearing a Spanish move on Madrid. 5600 allied casualties, 7300 French.

Tolentino 3 May 1815 (Italy, during the Hundred Days) About 100 miles north-east of Rome Murat's Neapolitan army clashed with an Austrian army under Bianchi. Probably both sides engaged about 11,000 men. Murat's army was routed, suffering some 4000 casualties for the Austrians' 1000.

Toulouse 10 April 1814 (Peninsular War) 50,000 British, Portuguese and Spanish attacked the city's defences forcing Soult to withdraw with his 42,000 men. An unnecessary battle since the allies moving from the north were already in Paris, though Wellington was unaware of this until two days later. 4500 allied casualties, 3200 French.

Trafalgar 21 October 1805 (Naval battle) Nelson with 27 battleships and two frigates attacked the Franco–Spanish fleet of 33 battleships and four frigates. 18 of the allied ships were captured (three of these sank). 1500 British casualties (including Nelson, mortally wounded); 2600 allied casualties, with another 4400 made prisoner. The British victory largely put paid to Napoleon's plans for an invasion of Britain.

Tudela 23 November 1808 (Peninsular War) In Napoleon's drive from the Ebro 45,000 Spanish troops under Castaños were routed by Lannes's 35,000 French. Only about half of the Spanish troops were engaged as Gen. La Peña ignored orders to bring his men into the battle and Gen. Grimarest was too slow. About 4000 Spanish casualties.

Uclés 12 January 1809 (Peninsular War) 12,000 Spanish under Venegas attacked and defeated by Victor with 16,000 French. The Spanish lost about 1000 killed and 6000 prisoners; French casualties were about 200.

Vimeiro 21 August 1808 (Peninsular War) 13,000 French under Junot made a series of assaults on Wellesley as he disembarked the last of 17,000 men. The French were severely beaten suffering 2000 casualties to the British 720. Wellesley's superiors failed to follow up the victory.

Vitoria 21 June 1813 (Peninsular War) 79,000 British, Portuguese and Spanish under Wellington decisively defeated 66,000 French under Joseph. The latter lost all his guns, supplies and treasure, and all hope of maintaining his kingdom. 4900 allied casualties, 5200 French.

Wagram 5–6 June 1809 Hard fought battle forming the climax to the campaign of 1809. 170,000 French under Napoleon beat 146,000 Austrians under Archduke Charles. Enormous casualties on both sides: 32,000 French and 40,000 Austrians. The victory was not as decisive as Austerlitz or Jena; exhaustion limited the French attempts at immediate pursuit.

Waterloo 18 June 1815 Last great battle of the Napoleonic Wars. Wellington, with 67,000 British and allied troops, withstood a succession of attacks from 72,000 French under Napoleon. After several hours of fighting, 53,000 Prussians under Blücher joined the battle which resulted in a French rout. 22,000 allied casualties, 32,000 French.

Wavre 18 June 1815 (Waterloo Campaign) Grouchy with the right wing of Napoleon's army (33,000) men, in pursuit of Blücher after Ligny, fought a fruitless battle with 17,000 Prussians under Thielemann. About 2500 casualties on each side. Blücher, meanwhile, was effecting his junction with Wellington at Waterloo.

Alliances, coalitions and leagues

Armed Neutrality (The League of) December 1800 to March 1801. Encouraged by Napoleon, the Armed Neutrality involved Denmark, Prussia, Russia and Sweden. The prime mover was Tsar Paul who took as his model the similar confederacy entered into by the same powers against Britain during the American War of Independence in 1780. Angered by the Royal Navy's claim to be able to search neutral ships the Armed Neutrality laid down, as principles of natural equity, five articles of international law which Britain had not recognised:

1) All neutral vessels had the right of free navigation from port to port and along the coasts of combatants during a war.

2) All goods belonging to the subjects of belligerent powers, with the exception of contraband, were to be inviolate if on neutral shipping.

3) A port was only to be considered as 'blockaded' if the blockading ships were so close that they made entrance by neutrals dangerous; and no neutral ship was to be deemed to have broken a blockade unless she had been specifically warned off by the commander of the investing fleet.

4) Neutrals could only be stopped for clear reasons; there was to be no delay on adjudication and a uniformity of procedure; compensation was to be paid to any who suffered loss through no fault of their own; and satisfaction was to be given for insult to a neutral flag.

5) The declaration by the commander of neutral warships convoying merchant vessels, that the vessels under his charge contained no contraband, was to be sufficient to prevent a search of those ships.

The Armed Neutrality crumbled following the assassination of Tsar Paul in March, and the British destruction of the Danish fleet at Copenhagen, 2 April 1802.

Coalition A series of coalitions were organised against first, Revolutionary France, and then Napoleon. Most of the military manpower was drawn from the continental states, and the finance came from Britain.

The First Coalition, 1792–7, began with Austria, Prussia and Sardinia in 1792, and was joined in the following year by Britain, the Netherlands, Spain, Portugal, Naples and various Italian and German states. By the end of 1795 French victories, and various other interests (such as the Partition of Poland) had reduced it to Britain and Austria.

The Second Coalition, 1799–1801, involved Austria, Britain, Naples, Portugal and the Ottoman Empire, with only the two former continuing the conflict through into 1801 and the respective treaties of Lunéville and Amiens.

The Third Coalition, 1805. An alliance of Austria, Britain, Russia, Naples and Sweden, with only the three former active. The coalition collapsed after the battle of Austerlitz.

The Fourth Coalition, 1806–7. An alliance between Britain, Prussia, Saxony and Russia. The German powers were virtually eliminated following the French victories of Jena-Auerstädt; the Russians fought on until Friedland.

The Fifth Coalition, 1809, hardly merits the name involving only Austria and Britain with the former being rapidly beaten in the Wagram campaign.

The Sixth Coalition, 1812–14, beginning with the alliance between Britain and Russia at the time of Napoleon's Russian campaign, then attracting Prussia, Austria and other German powers in 1813. The coalition came to an end with Napoleon's first abdication.

The Seventh Coalition, 1815, the alliance between Austria, Britain, Prussia, Russia and various lesser powers to defeat Napoleon during the Hundred Days.

The Confederation of the Rhine (*Rheinbund*) Formed 12 July 1806, dissolved 4 November 1813. The Confederation was organised by Napoleon in the hope that it would lead Germany to develop into a unity with a central government and an administration based on the French model. His ideas were shared by Karl Theodor von Dalberg, the Archbishop of Mainz, whom Napoleon created Prince-Primate (*Fürstenprimas*) of the Confederation. But the Confederation never became anything more than a military alliance primarily because of each state's, and each prince's, determination to preserve independence. From the beginning of the Spanish campaign Napoleon appears to have accepted the military side of the Confederation and to have left the other aspects alone. German states, kings, princes and dukes joined the Confederation as follows:

12–16 July 1806: the Prince-Primate; the Kings of Bavaria and Württemberg; the Grand Dukes of Baden, Berg, and Hesse-Darmstadt; the Dukes of Nassau-Usingen, and Arenberg (his territory was annexed to the French Empire, 13 December 1810); the Count von der Leyen; the Princes of Nassau-Weilburg (united with Nassau-

Usingen later in 1806), Hohenzollern- Sigmaringen, Hohenzollern-Hechingen, Salm-Salm, Salm-Kyrburg (his territory was annexed to the French Empire, 13 December 1810), Isemburg-Birstein; Liechtenstein.

23 September 1806: the Grand Duke of Würzburg.

11 December 1806: the King of Saxony.

15 December 1806: the Dukes of Saxe-Weimar, Saxe-Gotha, Saxe-Meiningen, Saxe-Hildburghausen, and Saxe-Coburg.

11 April 1807: the Dukes of Anhalt-Dessau, Anhalt-Bernburg, Anhalt-Coethen; the Princes of Lippe-Detmold, Schaumburg-Lippe, Waldeck, Schwarzburg-Rudolstadt, Schwarzburg-Sonderhausen, and the four Princes of Reuss.

15 November 1807: the King of Westphalia.

12 February 1808: the Duke of Mecklenburg-Strelitz.

22 March 1808: the Duke of Mecklenburg-Schwerin.

14 October 1808: the Duke of Oldenburg (his territory was annexed to the French Empire, 13 December 1810).

16 February 1810: the Grand Duke of Frankfurt (this title and territory were given to Prince-Primate Dalberg, though Eugène de Beauharnais was to be his heir).

The Holy Alliance An agreement signed between the monarchs of Austria, Prussia and Russia in September 1815 (published the following January) to preserve the peace in Europe and to support each other in achieving this end. The document was originally drafted by Tsar Alexander and was profoundly religious in its language insisting that Christian principles should guide princes and that the governments and peoples of Europe should all regard themselves as members of the same Christian nation. The document was dismissed by Castlereagh as 'a piece of sublime mysticism and nonsense'; Metternich had little time for many of the ideas in it, but used it nevertheless to maintain the status quo in Restoration Europe. The alliance was subsequently signed by most of the European monarchs, though not by the British King.

'The Holy Alliance' was also the term used pejoratively by some contemporary liberals, and by later historians, to describe the reactionary attitudes and actions of the conservative monarchies in Restoration Europe.

The Quadruple Alliance Signed between Austria, Britain, Prussia and Russia on 20 November 1815. The four powers agreed to maintain the Second Peace of Paris (signed the same day) and to prevent the return of Napoleon. They also agreed to hold periodic conferences of sovereigns or chief ministers to maintain the stability of Europe and discuss matters of common interest. At the Congress of Aix-la-Chapelle in 1818 France was reacknowledged as one of the great powers of Europe and, to all intents and purposes, the Quadruple Alliance became the Quintuple Alliance.

Codes, decrees and declarations

Additional Act, *l'Acte additionel,* promulgated by Napoleon during the Hundred Days (22 April 1815) this 'Act Supplementing the Constitutions of the Empire' sought to replace the authoritarian image of the imperial regime with more liberal institutions. It established a Chamber of Peers, nominated by Napoleon with hereditary rights, and an elected Chamber of Deputies; ministers were to have some responsibility to the chambers, and debates were to be public; all judges were to be nominated by the Emperor, but trial by jury was maintained; censorship was suppressed; tax quotas were lowered. The act was submitted to a plebiscite, but the results were disappointing: of 5 million electors only 1.5 million voted in favour, 4,800 voted against, and the remainder abstained. The largest number of abstentions were in the west and the south; the countryside was more favourable to the act than the towns.

Berlin Decree, issued by Napoleon, 21 November 1806. The formal beginning of the economic warfare between Napoleon's Empire and Britain. The decree claimed that the British Order in Council of 16 May, declaring a blockade on the entire coast of Europe, was a paper blockade and illegal as it could not be enforced. Napoleon therefore declared the British Isles to be in a state of blockade and forbade all those parts of Europe under French control from buying British goods or goods carried in British ships.

Borgö, Act of Guarantee of, issued on 27 March 1809 by Tsar Alexander. Russia had seized Finland from Sweden during the war of 1808; by this guarantee Alexander promised to respect the religion, rights and privileges of the Finns. Finland became a semi-independent Grand Duchy of the Russian Empire with the Tsar as Grand Duke.

Carlsbad Decrees, prepared in August 1819 at a meeting of the principal ministers of the nine largest German states called by Metternich in the Bohemian spa town of Carlsbad, these decrees were subsequently passed by the deputies of the Frankfurt Diet on 20 September and applied to the territories of the German Confederation. They outlawed the *Burschenschaften* and Jahn's gymnastic clubs, imposed strict censorship on the press (particularly periodicals), put the universities under the surveillance of 'curators' charged with supervising the behaviour of both professors and students, and established a commission of enquiry in Mainz to investigate a suspected revolutionary conspiracy across the whole of Germany.

Code Napoleon, the *Code Civile des Français*, promulgated 21 March 1804, and officially called the Code Napoleon from September 1807. The Civil Code was the culmination of attempts begun during the Revolution to remake the civil law in the image of a new and better society, and to reform and simplify it in the terms of natural law. The code maintained many of the key principles of the Revolution – equality before the law, freedom of conscience, the secular state, and economic freedom in the sense of free enterprise and competition. The family was held up as the basis of civilised society, with authority vested in the male head; women were relegated to a subordinate position throughout the code. In accordance with the achievements of the Revolution the feudal nobility was irrevocably abolished. There was considerable concentration on landed property throughout the code; limits on primogeniture maintained the wide degree of small land-ownership. The code continued the prohibition of labour organisations introduced by the Le Chapelier Law (1791), and put the employee in an inferior position to the employer in industrial disputes. The code was implemented throughout the Empire and continued to influence European civil law after Napoleon's fall. It continued in force in France after the Restoration, but reverted to its original title in 1818.

Five other codes were also prepared during Napoleon's reign: the Code of Civil Procedure (April 1806); the Commercial Code (August 1807); the Criminal Code (October 1808); the Penal Code (February 1810); the Rural Code (drawn up but never adopted). Each combined, to different degrees, progressive ideas from the early period of the Revolution, with rather more authoritarian ideas.

Constitutional Charter (*la Charte Constitutionelle*), bestowed on the French people by Louis XVIII on 4 June 1814 recognising the fundamental principles of liberty, equality and property, and establishing the political system of the restoration regime. There were to be two chambers: the House of Peers and the Chamber of Deputies. The former were to be appointed by the King, and subsequently recognised as hereditary peers; the latter were to be elected by men, and from men, paying a set sum in direct taxes – a *cens*, hence the expression applied to the form of government in France from 1814–48, *la monarchie censitaire*. Trial by jury and an independent judiciary were established. Freedom of religion was maintained, but Catholicism was declared the state religion. The 79 articles of the charter reflect an English influence and also the influence of the experiment in constitutional monarchy of the early years of the Revolution.

Continental System / Continental Blockade, the policy of economic warfare waged by Napoleon with the intention of closing the continent of Europe to Britain, thus bankrupting her and forcing her to sue for peace. Attempts at closing European ports to Britain were made from the very beginning of the Napoleonic wars, but the term *blocus continental* was first used in the 15th Bulletin of the *Grande Armée* (10 October 1806). The policy was formally begun with the Berlin Decree and reached its most effective period following the treaties of Tilsit and the Milan Decree. The system was also closely linked with Napoleon's overall economic policy by which, given that France was cut off from overseas markets and had lost her colonies to Britain, he intended to establish French economic dominion over Europe.

Fontainebleau Decrees,
   a) 18 October 1810, ordered the seizure and burning of all British manufactured goods found in France or parts of the French Empire.
   b) 25 October 1810, established 41 tribunals to decide on questions arising out of the earlier decree, to reward those helping to enforce it and to punish anyone found importing British goods into Europe.

Milan Decrees
   a) 23 November 1807, any ship which put into a British port was to be considered as denationalised and subject to seizure.
   b) 17 December 1807, any ship which complied with the British Orders in Council was to be considered denationalised and subject to seizure.

Orders in Council, the directives by which the British government responded to the Continental System, the most significant being:
   a) 7 January 1807, forbidding all neutrals from trading between the ports of France and her allies, or between ports observing the Berlin Decree, under pain of seizure and confiscation of ship and cargo.
   b) 11 November 1807, all countries from which British ships were excluded were to be subject to the same restrictions as if they were blockaded. Neutrals were only to trade with France providing they did so via a British port and paid a duty.

Reichsdeputationshauptschluss, Literally the main resolution of the *Reichsdeputation,* a committee of eight appointed on the suggestion of Francis II to negotiate compensation for the German princes dispossessed by the French occupation of the left bank of the Rhine. The resolution was accepted by the Imperial Diet of the Holy Roman Empire (*Reichstag*) on 25 February 1803. Essentially it reorganised west and south Germany. All of the ecclesiastical principalities (except Mainz) and the imperial cities were secularised and lost their status of being subject to the Empire alone. Of the 51 imperial cities 45 were absorbed by their more powerful neighbours, as were 112 small principalities and counties. Prussia and the middle states of the south and west of Germany (Baden, Bavaria and Württemberg) were the principal beneficiaries and were all considerably increased in size.

Saint-Ouen, Declaration of, issued by Louis XVIII on 2 May 1814 just before he returned to Paris. By this declaration Louis promised to establish a representative system of government in France.

Conferences, congresses and treaties

Aix-la-Chapelle, Congress of, October-November 1818. The first session, held on 1 October, was attended by Tsar Alexander, Frederick William III, Francis I, Metternich, Wellington and Castlereagh. Richelieu attended for France. The initial discussion focussed on the evacuation of allied troops from France; terms were quickly agreed and a treaty signed on 9 October. The former allies went on to consider what action to take in the case of future French aggression and signed a secret protocol renewing the Quadruple Alliance. Britain opposed Alexander's proposal for a 'universal union of guarantee' based on the Holy Alliance, but a public declaration was made to maintain a union for the preservation of peace.

Amiens, Peace of, brought about the end of the French Revolutionary wars. Following the preliminary Treaty of London the peace was signed 27 March 1802 between France and Britain. The former agreed to respect the integrity and independence of the Batavian Republic, Naples and Portugal. Britain agreed to return all the colonial conquests she had won from France and her allies except for Ceylon (taken from the Dutch) and Trinidad (taken from the Spanish). She also agreed to evacuate Elba and Malta, returning the latter to the Knights of St.John. The Ionian Islands were to become an independent republic; Egypt was to be handed back to Turkey.

Aranjuez, Treaty of, signed between Spain and France 21 March 1801, confirming the Convention of San Ildefonso (q.v.).

Badajoz, Treaty of, signed between Spain and Portugal 6 June 1801 concluding the War of the Oranges. Portugal agreed to close her ports to British shipping, ceded the province of Olivenza to Spain, and promised to pay France an indemnity of 2m. francs. Much to the annoyance of Spain Napoleon was unhappy with the treaty and initially refused to ratify it.

Bartenstein, Convention of, signed 26 April 1807 between Prussia and Russia. The two powers agreed to fight for the common cause of ousting the French from Germany. Austria, Britain, Denmark and Sweden were to be asked to join in a general war of liberation. The Italian problem was to be resolved at a later date, but old rights were to be restored.

Brno, Treaty of, signed 12 December 1805 between France, Baden and Württemberg. The treaty followed the Austro–Russian defeat at Austerlitz and was a step in Napoleon's reorganisation of Germany in favour of princes who had acted as his allies. It further dismant-led the last vestiges of the Holy Roman Empire in favour of Baden and Württemberg.

Bucharest, Peace of, signed 28 May 1812 between Russia and Tur-key. The Tsar had the treaty prepared hastily and by it agreed to withdraw from Moldavia and Wallachia. He thus had his hands free for the approaching war with Napoleon.

Charlottenburg, Convention of, signed 16 November between Napoleon and a group of Prussian envoys. Following the Prussian defeats of Jena and Auerstädt Napoleon agreed to an armistice on condition that French troops occupy the territory between the Oder and the Vistula, that fortresses on the Vistula be surrendered to him, and that Russian troops, with the surviving Prussian armies, be dismissed. Frederick William III of Prussia refused to ratify the terms at a council held at Osterode on 21 November.

Chatillon, Conference of, February 1814. At a meeting between the allies and the French the former set out peace terms requiring France to give up all conquered territories in Europe and to return to her pre-Revolution boundaries. Britain was to restore some col-onies by way of recompense. Napoleon refused to accept the propo-sals and the conference closed.

Chaumont, Treaty of, signed 9 March 1814 by Austria, Britain, Prussia and Russia. Following Napoleon's rejection of the proposals made at the Conference of Chatillon (q.v.) each of the allies agreed not to sign a separate peace and to prosecute the war until France was reduced to its former size. The treaty outlined the military com-mitment required of each signatory, with Britain guaranteeing fin-ancial aid.

Cintra, Convention of, signed 30 August 1808 between the British general, Sir Hew Dalrymple, and the French general, Andoche Junot. The latter had been defeated by Dalrymple's subordinate, Wellesley, at Vimeiro, yet was virtually permitted to dictate his own terms. The Convention arranged the evacuation of Junot's army, together with much of its booty, from Portugal. It was much criticised in both Britain and Portugal.

Concordat, signed 15 July 1801; published 18 April 1801. The agreement signed between Napoleon and Pope Pius VII, intended by the former to disassociate the Catholic Church from royalist op-position to his regime. It acknowledged the Pope as head of the

Catholic Church, but it ensured the ultimate authority of the French state over the Church in France. Catholicism was recognised as the religion of the majority of Frenchmen, but it was not to be a state religion and the Code Napoleon subsequently granted freedom of religion. Bishops were to be nominated by the First Consul and were to choose their own lower clergy. All clergy, however, were to be paid by the government; Church lands sold during the Revolution were to remain in the hands of the purchasers.

The subordinate position of the Church within the state was emphasised by the Organic Articles (q.v.) which Napoleon published with the Concordat, but without consulting the Pope.

Erfurt, Convention of, signed by Napoleon and Alexander, 12 October 1808. France agreed to the Russian possession of Finland and to her acquisition of Moldavia and Wallachia. France was to remain neutral in the event of war between Russia and Turkey; Russia was to assist France if she was attacked by Austria. Both France and Russia guaranteed remaining Turkish possessions.

Florence, Treaty of, forced on Ferdinand IV of Naples by a French army under Murat, and signed on 28 March 1801. Ferdinand agreed to yield Taranto to the French and to maintain a French garrison of 15,000 there. He also agreed to cede Elba to France and to close his ports to British trade.

Fontainebleau, Conventions of,

a) Austro–French Convention signed 11 October 1807. French agreed to evacuate Brannau in Bavaria; the frontier of Napoleon's Italian possessions was extended to the River Isonza at Austrian expense.

b) Secret Convention between France and Spain signed 27 October 1807 agreeing to dismember Portugal and to divide most of it between Godoy and Charles IV's son-in-law, the erstwhile King of Etruria.

c) Military Convention between France and Spain signed 27 October 1807 specifying the military commitment required of the two powers to carry out b); 28,000 French, aided by 27,000 Spanish were to march on Portugal; another 40,000 French were to be stationed at Bayonne in case of a British attack.

Fontainebleau, Treaty of, signed between Napoleon and the allied powers, 11 April 1814. In return for sovereignty over the Isle of Elba Napoleon agreed to renounce all claims of his own and his family to sovereignty over France and Italy. The Empress Marie

Louise was to keep her title and was given territory in Italy which was to pass to Napoleon's son.

Frankfurt, Proposals of, agreed by the allies on 9 November 1813, following the battle of Leipzig, and forwarded to the French. The allies proposed that France withdraw to her 'natural' boundaries – the Alps, the Rhine, the Pyrenees and the ocean (this would have enabled France to keep Belgium, Savoy and Nice). Austria was to acquire a part of Italy, but the remainder of the peninsula was to be independent. The French were to withdraw from Holland and Spain and these were to be independent. Britain was to hand back conquered French colonies. Napoleon made no initial response; when eventually he decided to accept the proposals the allies had already withdrawn them.

Fredrickshamm, Treaty of, signed between Russia and Sweden 17 September 1809 concluding the Russo–Swedish war. Sweden ceded Finland and Aaland to Russia.

Ghent, Treaty of, signed 24 December 1814, by Britain and the United States. The treaty brought an end to the War of 1812. Both sides agreed to revert to the status quo *ante bellum,* but Britain retained islands in Passamaquoddy Bay (off Maine), and outstanding problems on fishing rights and navigation remained unresolved. Britain acknowledged the territorial integrity of the United States; the United States acknowledged the territorial integrity of Canada.

Hartford, Convention of, met Hartford, Connecticut, 15 December 1814 to 5 January 1815. Members of the New England elite were opposed to the War of 1812 because of its detrimental effect on their trade. The war also brought other New England concerns to a head, particularly the rise of slaveholder power enhanced by the Louisiana Purchase. Some radicals contemplated secession. The Convention was a meeting of delegates from New England to discuss the situation. Connecticut, Massachusetts and Rhode Island were officially represented by delegates sent from the state legislatures; the delegates from New Hampshire and Vermont were chosen at county level. While the radicals were in a minority, the Convention agreed to send a delegation to Washington to press for constitutional amendments. The delegation arrived in the capital at the same time as the news of the peace with Britain and the victory at New Orleans; nothing came of its proposals.

Jönköping, Peace of, signed 10 December 1810, between Denmark and Sweden. It ended the Dano–Swedish war (1808–10) with neither side gaining any new territory or advantage.

Kalisch, Treaty of, signed 26 February 1813, but not made public until 13 March. The treaty was signed between Prussia and Russia; they agreed to provide 80,000 and 150,000 troops respectively in a war against France. Prussia was also to acquire territory in North Germany, and by a secret article Tsar Alexander agreed to restore Prussia to the status which she had enjoyed before the defeats of 1806.

Kiel, Treaty of, signed 14 January 1814 between Britain, Denmark and Sweden. It brought to an end Denmark's disastrous participation in the wars on Napoleon's side; by it she yielded Heligoland to Britain and Norway to Sweden, receiving a small indemnity in Germany.

Königsberg, Treaty of, Supplementary to the Treaty of Tilsit (q.v.) providing for the withdrawal of French troops from Prussia when the full payment of a war contribution was made by Prussia to France. The amount of this contribution was eventually set at 35m. thalers (120m. francs). Prussia was also to pay the costs of the French troops occupying the fortresses on the Oder.

Laibach, Congress of, met in January 1821 to consider Austrian intervention in the revolutionary disorders in Italy. Britain and France were opposed to intervention, but Austria received the support of Prussia and Russia.

La Palud, Convention of, signed 8 April 1815. The duc d'Angoulême had led a royalist army against Napoleon in the south of France at the beginning of the Hundred Days. This army was checked at Valance and, by the Convention, d'Angoulême and his officers were allowed to go free while his men were pardoned on condition of laying down their arms.

London, Treaty of, signed 1 October 1801 between Britain and France ceasing hostilities prior to the Peace of Amiens (q.v.).

Lunéville, Peace of, signed between Austria and France, 9 February 1801; a key treaty in bringing an end to the Revolutionary wars. The terms were hard on Austria reflecting her defeats. France was to obtain all German territories west of the Rhine, was confirmed in possession of Belgium and Luxembourg, and was to be guarantor of her sister republics (Cisalpine, Ligurian, Batavian and Helvetic). The frontier of the Cisalpine Republic was extended to the Adige. Tuscany was established as the Kingdom of Etruria under Louis, Duke of Parma; and the Pope was confirmed as ruler of the Papal States.

Moss, Convention of, signed between Sweden and the Norwegian representatives 14 August 1814. The Convention brought an end to the Norwegians' move for independence under King Christian Frederick. They were compelled to surrender the fortress of Halden which had been holding out against the invading Swedish army, and demobilise; the Swedes were to keep sufficient troops in Norway to prevent further conflict. It was agreed to convene a meeting to establish the terms of union between Norway and Sweden. Christian Frederick was to yield executive authority to his ministers; the King of Sweden accepted the new, liberal Norwegian constitution as the basis for the union.

Organic Articles, attached by Napoleon to the Concordat (q.v.) without either the knowledge or approval of the Pope. The Organic Articles enabled the French state to exercise a close supervision of the current situation and the future development of the Catholic Church there. Seminaries in France were to be regulated by the government; all of the teachers in them were to be French and were to profess the principles of Gallican liberties. All communications from the Pope, including bulls, had to be approved by the government before they could be published in France; and any legate sent by the Pope also needed government approval. The articles specified that there was to be one catechism for the whole of France; this was not completed until after Napoleon had become emperor and it contained sections sanctifying his regime as God-given.

Paris, Treaties of,

a) signed 30 May 1814, between France (represented by Talleyrand) and the four major allies. France was to be reduced to her boundaries of 1792 with Belgium being annexed to Holland and Lombardy and Venetia ceded to Austria. France was to return the colonial territory of San Domingo acquired from Spain in 1795; Britain was to keep the former French colonies of Tobago, St. Lucia and Ile de France (Mauritius). France was not required to pay any reparations, she was not to be subjected to military occupation, and she was to participate in the setting of European boundaries at the Congress of Vienna.

b) signed 20 November 1815 between France and the allies, and much harsher than its predecessor. France lost more territory on her Belgian and eastern frontiers, including most of Savoy; she was to pay an indemnity of 700 million francs, and to support an allied army of occupation of 150,000 men for five years.

Poischwitz (Pleschwitz), Armistice of, signed 4 June 1813 between France and Russia and Prussia. It was designed to give a breathing space to the armies during the War of Liberation, but worked much more to the advantage of the Russians and Prussians than the French.

Posen, Treaty of, signed 11 December 1806 between France, Prussia and Saxony. The Elector of Saxony was given the title of king, his kingdom joined the Confederation of the Rhine and was to provide Napoleon with 20,000 men to assist in his current campaign.

Potsdam, Treaty of, signed 3 November 1805 between Russia, Austria and Prussia. The latter agreed to offer armed mediation between Russia, Austria and France; if Napoleon refused the offer then Prussia would enter the war. The Prussian terms to Napoleon demanded the restoration of the King of Sardinia, the independence of Naples, Holland and Germany and an extension of Austria's Italian frontier. By the time that the Prussian envoy, Haugwitz, set out to meet Napoleon, however, the French had occupied Vienna. Rather than armed mediation Prussia signed the Treaty of Schönbrunn (q.v.).

Pressburg, Treaty of, signed 26 December 1805 between Austria and France at the conclusion of the Austerlitz campaign. Austria ceded her possessions in northern Italy to France and recognised the recent changes made by France on the Italian peninsula. The Electors of Bavaria and Württemberg were recognised as kings and Austria ceded her Swabian territories to them and the new Grand Duchy of Baden. She also ceded Tyrol and Vorarlberg to Bavaria. France guaranteed the sovereignty of the new rulers of Baden, Bavaria and Württemberg. Austria received some small compensation, notably Salzburg.

Reichenbach, Treaties of, signed June 1813 establishing a new coalition against Napoleon. On 14 and 15 June Britain signed treaties with Russia and Prussia with each party promising not to make a separate peace with France. Britain promised an annual subsidy of £1m. to Russia and £500,000 to Prussia. Russia promised to maintain an army of 160,000 in the field, and Prussia 80,000. On 27 June Austria signed a similar treaty with Russia and Prussia agreeing to enter the war if the French refused her mediation; by a secret article Britain promised her £500,000 when she joined the allies.

Ried, Treaty of, signed between Austria and Bavaria 8 October 1813. Austria agreed that, on the liberation of Germany, Bavaria would be recognised as a separate kingdom. Bavaria agreed to restore Austrian territory recently ceded to her.

San Ildefonso, Convention of, signed 7 October 1800. A secret agreement by which Spain gave Louisiana and six warships to France in exchange for Tuscany which was to be ceded to the heir of the Duke of Parma, son-in-law to the King of Spain. The convention was confirmed by the Treaty of Aranjuez (q.v.).

Schiarino-Rizzino, Convention of, signed by Eugène, Viceroy of Italy and the Austrian Field Marshal Bellegarde on 16 April 1814. This was an armistice agreed following the news of Napoleon's abdication. The French troops under Eugène's command were to withdraw from Italy, but the territory which the Viceroy still held was left in the hands of his Italian troops. Eugène was permitted to send a delegation to the victorious allies in Paris and, until turbulent events in Milan overtook matters, it seemed possible that the Kingdom of Italy would survive with Eugène as its monarch.

Schönbrunn, Peace of, signed between France and Austria on 15 October 1809 at the conclusion of the Wagram campaign. Austria agreed to recognise Joseph as King of Spain; to cede territory to the French Empire (Friuli, Carinthia, Cariola, Trieste, parts of Croatia and Dalmatia) to Bavaria (Salzburg and the Inn-viertel), to Russia and the Duchy of Warsaw (parts of Gallicia); to pay an indemnity; to exclude all British products; to limit her army to 150,000 men.

Schönbrunn, Treaty of, signed by Prussian envoy Haugwitz and Napoleon 15 December 1805. Haugwitz had met Napoleon with a Prussian ultimatum following the Treaty of Potsdam (q.v.). Napoleon countered the ultimatum by offering Hanover to Prussia in return for Ansbach (to go to Bavaria) and Cleves and Neufchâtel (to go to France). By the same treaty France and Prussia entered into a defensive and offensive alliance mutually guaranteeing each other's territory, and Prussia agreed to uphold the independence of Turkey.

Stockholm, Treaty of, signed 3 March 1813 between Britain and Sweden. Britain agreed to a compact made between Russia and Sweden the previous April whereby Russia was to help the Swedes acquire Norway and, in return, Sweden would field an army to assist the Russians against Napoleon. Britain was to pay £1m. towards supporting the Swedish army against Napoleon, and ceded Guadeloupe on the stipulation that the Swedes would not import slaves into the island but actively suppress the slave trade. (When, at the Congress of Vienna, Guadeloupe was returned to France, Britain paid the Swedes an indemnity.)

Tauroggen, Convention of, signed 30 December 1812. General Yorck, commanding a Prussian contingent in Napoleon's army, signed the Convention with the Russians whereby he and his men became neutrals.

Teplitz, Treaties of,
   a) Formal treaty of alliance giving substance to the earlier treaties of Reichenbach (q.v.) and signed between Austria, Prussia and Russia 9 September 1813. It also agreed that the future of Poland should be settled amicably between the three signatories.
   b) Formal treaty of alliance between Austria and Britain, signed 30 October 1813 and giving substance to the agreement made at Reichenbach.

Tilsit, Treaties of, signed July 1807 establishing an alliance between Russia and France and ending the Franco- Prussian War.
   a) Signed between France and Russia, 7 July. France agreed to restore to Prussia the province of Silesia and land between the Elbe and the Niemen, but Polish lands seized by Prussia in the Second and Third Partitions (1793 and 1795) were to form the new Duchy of Warsaw. Danzig became a free city while Oldenburg, Mecklenburg-Schwerin and Saxe-Coburg were returned to their dukes; French garrisons were to remain in the first three. Russia recognised the changes made by Napoleon in Naples, Holland and Germany – in particular the creation of the Kingdom of Westphalia to be ruled by Jerome Bonaparte.
   b) Signed between France and Prussia, 9 July. Prussia was to pay an indemnity and to suffer military occupation until this was complete; to limit her army to 42,000 men; to close her ports to British shipping and join the Continental System.

Trachenberg, Compact of, agreed 12 July 1813. Friction had developed between the allies against Napoleon. Bernadotte was criticised for not engaging his Swedish forces against the French; he complained that the Russians had not been forthcoming with the 35,000 troops they had promised him for a campaign to acquire Norway from Denmark. At Trachenberg, a castle north of Breslau, Bernadotte met the Tsar and Frederick William of Prussia. They made up their differences and agreed first, to turn their main forces against Napoleon's main army; second, that any allied unit that threatened Napoleon's flanks or lines of communication should take immediate action against them; and third, that the salient of Bohemia offered the best chance of attacking Napoleon's main army. The first and third of these resolutions were specifically designed to encourage Austria to join the war; the second prevented Bernadotte from waging war merely against Denmark.

Troppau, Congress of, met October 1820 to discuss great power response to the revolutionary disorders in Italy and Spain. Britain was hostile to the idea of intervention and refused to sign the Protocol of Troppau agreed between Austria, Prussia and Russia (19 November) which asserted the right of intervention when the order of Europe was threatened and when a European government was unable to defend itself. France also refused to sign.

Verona, Congress of, met October–December 1822, the last congress of the five great powers in the post-war 'Concert of Europe'. Britain hoped that the discussions would concentrate on Turkey and Spanish America, but events were overshadowed by disorders in Spain and the French determination to intervene there. In an attempt to appease Britain, who opposed this intervention, and Russia, who supported it, Metternich proposed that the powers send simultaneous notes of protest to Madrid. Britain refused insisting that the alliance had no right to interfere in Spain's internal affairs; this action led to her final separation from the other powers. Although France agreed to Metternich's proposal she subsequently refused to present her protest note with those of the others and, in April 1823, embarked on military intervention.

Vienna, Congress of, met October 1814–June 1815. Its aim was the reconstruction of the internal boundaries of Europe following 22 years of war and revolutionary upheaval, and to establish the conditions which would best enable these boundaries and the whole reconstructed European order to survive. There were 41 sittings of the congress before the Final Act was signed on 9 June 1815. Much of the work was done in a series of specialist committees, staffed by diplomats from a variety of European states big and small, which considered issues as varied as diplomatic precedence, the slave trade and population statistics. The principal representatives of the four great powers allied against Napoleon (Austria, Britain, Prussia and Russia), subsequently joined by France, reserved for themselves the major task of redistributing territory.

Between November 1814 and January 1815 the proceedings were dominated by the problem of the Polish and Saxon territories. There were sharp divisions between Prussia and Russia on the one hand (who proposed that Poland be taken over by Russia and Saxony by Prussia) and Britain and Austria on the other. The friction led to a secret defensive alliance being signed in the first week of January 1815 between Britain, Austria and France. The content of the alliance was deliberately leaked to Russia with the desired effect of achieving a compromise: the Tsar became king of a reduced, semi-independent Poland ('Congress Poland') with other Polish territories divided between Austria and Prussia; Prussia got only 40 percent of Saxony, but considerable new territory on the left bank of the Rhine. Austria became the dominant power in Germany, and was put at the head of a new German Confederation; she was also re-established in Lombardy and Venetia thus becoming the dominant great power on the Italian peninsula.

In different ways the leading diplomats in Europe (Tsar Alexander, Castlereagh, Metternich and Talleyrand) saw the congress as the first act of a permanent system of diplomacy, a 'Concert of Europe'; and Vienna was indeed the first of a series of congresses (Aix-la-Chapelle, Laibach, Troppau, and Verona) which met in an endeavour to resolve European problems in the decade following Napoleon's overthrow.

Glossary

Afrancesados Pro-French Spaniards, among the most progressive and talented of their countrymen. The term was initially applied to those who admired French culture and ideas and who subscribed to the ideas of the eighteenth-century Enlightenment. After 1808 the name was given to supporters of King Joseph Bonaparte (along with *Joséfinos*) and those who collaborated with the French. The number of collaborators varied with French success in Spain: it was high in the early summer of 1808, but then declined; it rose again when the French came close to subduing the country in 1810–11, and fell with the decline of Joseph's fortunes. At least 12,000 families sought refuge in France when Joseph left Spain in 1813; many of those identified as *Afrancesados* who remained, were cruelly punished.

Auditeurs au Conseil d'état The *Conseil d'état* (Council of State) was the centre of the Napoleonic administrative system. The *auditeurs* were the professional officials established in 1803 and who made the system work. While the majority of these men were French, Napoleon also recruited young nobles from the annexed departments to be *auditeurs*. Experience in this position was regarded as the ideal preparation for administrative service elsewhere in the Empire.

Bulletin of the *Grande Armée* An official report of military operations, often dictated by Napoleon himself, ostensibly to give troops and the home population an account of events but also designed for morale and propaganda purposes. The bulletins were printed as broadsheets, sometimes with an illustration; they were reprinted in the official government newspaper, *Le Moniteur*, and other papers. The first such bulletin was issued at the beginning of the Austerlitz campaign on 7 October 1805; the most cynical was the 29th, issued at Molodetchno on 3 December 1812, which reported that a disaster had overtaken the Russian expedition, but reassured the peoples of the Empire that the Emperor's health had never been better. Among the army there was a popular saying: *Menteur comme un bulletin* (Liar/false like a bulletin).

Burschenschaften German students' associations initially organised at the University of Jena in the aftermath of the War of Liberation, they rapidly spread to other parts of Germany. They were inspired by liberal and patriotic ideas and sought to promote Christian conduct; they took as their colours those of the *Freikorps* (q.v.) of Adolf Lützow. The associations provoked official displeasure by their destruction of symbols of reaction at their Wartburg Festival (Oct 1817). A radical element, known as the Blacks (*Schwarzen*) was organised at the University of Giessen by Karl Follen; it was one of his admirers, Karl Sand, who assassinated Kotzebue in 1819. The *Burschenschaften* were suppressed by the Carlsbad Decrees of 1819 and again in 1833; the laws against them were repealed in the Revolution of 1848 but thereafter they were largely a social, rather than a political organisation.

Carbonari A secret society, most notable in Italy during the Napoleonic period. It appears to have been taken to Italy by French troops who were members of the *Charbonnerie*. The Italian *Carbonari* covered many tendencies: those in Naples were given some degree of official tolerance by Murat's government; those in Sicily were opposed to Murat. By 1814 the *Carbonari* had spread into northern Italy; it had become generally anti-French; and some of its lodges favoured a united Italy.

Charbonnerie A French secret society whose origins are obscure. A confraternity of charcoal-burners meeting for social and philanthropic purposes in the Jura was in existence before 1789. Soldiers stationed in the area during the Revolution appear to have been initiated, and the organisation increasingly lost contact with the business of charcoal burning. The *Charbonnerie* were loyal to the Napoleonic regime, and celebrated the Emperor's birthday with one of their feasts. By the early 1820s a revitalised, political and conspiratorial *Charbonnerie* was seen as one of the biggest threats to the restored Bourbons.

Chouans Royalist insurgents, mainly drawn from the peasantry of western France, especially Brittany. The word itself is Breton, meaning 'screech owl' and was the nickname of Jean Cotterau one of the *Chouans'* early leaders. The *chouannerie* was at its peak in the years 1794–6. It revived briefly during the War of the Second Coalition, but was a spent force by 1801.

Cortes The legislative assembly of Spain. That which met for the first time in Cadiz on 24 September 1810 was particularly liberal because of the peculiar situation under which it was elected and under which it met. Voting for the *Cortes* in 1810 could only be conducted in areas not occupied by the French. Delegates for the occupied areas had to be selected from inhabitants of those areas who were resident in Cadiz. But the city had a reputation for liberalism, and consequently it was men of a liberal persuasion who tended to be chosen. Even though the liberals did not have an overall majority, their coherent policy and their organisation enabled them to push through a series of reforming policies, including the Constitution of 1812.

Détenu A civilian held captive in France while his country was at war with France. By the decree of 2 Prairial Year XI (23 May 1803) Napoleon authorised the detention of all Englishmen in France aged between 18 and 60 holding a military commission in the militia. The decree was given a broad interpretation by the departmental prefects. Perhaps 500 or so were held in all, but following escapes and releases only just over a hundred men appear to have been interned in this way by the end of the war.

Deutsche Gesellschaften Patriotic societies founded in Germany, notably in the Rhineland and Nassau, in 1814. They took their inspiration from E.M. Arndt and the earlier *Tugendbund* (q.v.). After Napoleon's defeat they were regarded with suspicion by the authorities in Germany and began to be suppressed.

Domaine extraordinaire Established early in 1810, this was a special fund for the management of confiscations, indemnities, and other exactions levied in conquered territories.

Emigré An individual who left France for political reasons during the Revolution. By no means all of the original *émigrés* were nobles, but those prominent during and immediately after the Napoleonic period generally were. The decree of 28 Vendémiaire Year IX (20 October 1800) struck off the proscribed list male *émigrés* from the lower classes, women and children; only those who had fought against France or who had accepted office under the *émigré* princes remained. A *Senatus Consultum* of 6 Floréal Year X reduced the numbers proscribed still further, limiting them largely to leading supporters of the Bourbons. These amnesties encouraged considerable numbers to return to France, notably Chateaubriand; but some chose to go into exile again, particularly after the execution of the duc d'Engien.

Freikorps Armed volunteer units prominent in the War of Liberation who, following Napoleon's Russian disaster, sought to rouse the German lands to resistance and subsequently fought alongside regular armies. The corps raised by Adolf Lützow, with its distinctive uniform of red, black and gold, is the best known and most distinguished, and these colours became those of the German national flag.

Gewerbefreiheit The freedom to practise a trade introduced among the liberal reforms in Prussia following the defeat of 1806. Some historians have tended to see financial motives as central to these reforms and have seen the *Gewerbefreiheit* as a way of introducing a new tax (*Gewerbesteuer*) designed to help remedy the fiscal problems caused by war, defeat and the indemnity demanded by the French; such arguments probably overstate their case.

Grand Cadastre An assembly established in 1807 whose task it was to prepare a land survey (*cadastre*) used for tax registration. The idea was taken from an earlier survey in Lombardy and Piedmont; it was not completed in France until the Third Republic, in 1880.

Grande Armée The term was first used in an order of 29 April 1805. Technically it refers only to a mass army of some 500,000 to 600,000 men commanded by Napoleon in person, but the term is often used as a description for the whole imperial army.

Guerrilla Literally 'little war' but applied to the Spanish irregulars who organised against Napoleon. By the end of 1812 they may have numbered as many as 38,500 men organised into 22 different *partidas* (q.v.). Some of the guerrilla leaders were intent on establishing themselves as local warlords; they refused to co-operate with their neighbours and suppressed any bands that threatened their authority within a district. They were particularly successful in northern Spain notably in Navarre where Espoz y Mina built up a force of about 13,500 men and established an effective provincial administration. (For the Italian equivalent see *Masse.*)

While the Napoleonic period is generally seen as significant in the development of German nationalism it is worth stressing that there was little guerrilla activity against Napoleon's armies in Germany.

Jäger Literally 'huntsman', but also used for German light infantry. In February 1813 the Prussian government invited young men who could afford to provide their own uniforms and equipment to volunteer as *Jäger* and thus avoid the possibility of having to serve alongside men of a lower social class. Some 12,000 men enlisted in these units; they performed well on the battlefield, but they were increasingly diluted as their officers were transferred to regular infantry regiments.

Joséfinos Spanish supporters of King Joseph Bonaparte (see *Afrancesados*).

Junta Literally an assembly, council or meeting. A series of *juntas* was established all over Spain in opposition to the French invasion of 1808. A Central Junta (*Junta Suprema Central de Gobierno*) was organised in September 1808, but it was riven with internal divisions and the internal situation of the country militated against its plans for reform and reorganisation.

Krümpersystem Short-service training established by Scharnhorst in 1808 to circumvent the restrictions on the size of the Prussian army. It provided for a steady turnover of recruits and the creation of a reserve. The traditional myth has it that the system produced an additional 36,000 men in 1813; in fact the number was probably closer to 10,000.

Landsturm Home guards established in Prussia in April 1813 to draw on men not already serving in other forms of military unit. The force was rarely mobilised and for as short a time as possible. The Prussian authorities were more interested in the rhetoric of national war than in unleashing something similar to the Spanish experience.

Landwehr Militia established in Austria in 1809 and Prussia in 1813. The Prussian example was the most significant and was proposed by the military reformers after the disasters of 1806. Established in February 1813 it was intended to be 120,000 men strong recruited from volunteers with the numbers made up by ballot. *Landwehr* units were significant at Leipzig, though large numbers of them deployed in the battle, deserted.

Levée en masse Originally the law of 23 August 1793 which mobilised the French nation for the Revolutionary war effort, and subsequently applied to similar mass mobilisations. In July 1803 the British parliament passed the Levy en Masse Act requiring county authorities to draw up lists of the men resident in them, and making provision for their arming and training. The enormous number of volunteer corps rendered the act superfluous.

Livret ouvrier By the law of 22 Germinal, Year XI (11 April, 1803) all French workers were required to carry a workbook (*livret*) so that a future employer might know about their previous employment. The *livret* did not contain comments on the worker's ability or loyalty, but a man without a *livret* was considered a vagabond and was liable to six months' imprisonment. The system continued until 1890.

275

Luddite An English machine-breaker, taking his name from a mythical Ned Ludd. Luddites were particularly active 1811–12 among industrial groups in three areas: the framework-knitters of the Midlands; the croppers in the West Riding woollen industry; and cotton operatives in Lancashire. There was a notable fusion of radical politics with Luddism in the Lancashire case.

Majorats Imperial land gifts which were given the status of entailed estates. They were first established for members of the imperial nobility on 14 August 1806.

Masse The term used by Calabrian partisans to describe themselves. These partisans, generally dismissed as brigands by the French, fought a guerrilla war against the French, which while on a smaller scale and less successful than the war of the Spanish guerrillas, was equally savage and cruel. The conflict was at its height during 1806, but sporadic outbreaks continued at least until 1812. Most of the leaders were local men who confined their activities to their native district; the principal exception was Michele Pezza, better known as Fra Diavolo, who conducted his operations in conjunction with the British admiral Sir Sidney Smith, but who was captured and executed by the French in November 1806.

Négociants réunis (United Brokers) A group of speculative financiers assembled by G.-J. Ouvrard in 1804 to assist in public finances. The intention was to ship Spanish–American silver from Cuba and Mexico to Europe, avoiding the British blockade. The failure of the project precipitated a financial crisis in France at the end of 1805 and beginning of 1806 since the Bank of France had been underwriting much of the speculation. The Treasury Minister Barbé–Marbois was made the scapegoat and dismissed; the Bank of France was brought under much stricter control.

Partidas A Spanish guerrilla band (see *guerrilla).*

Pays alliés States, nominally sovereign, allied to France.

Pays conquis Conquered territories organised as subject states of France.

Pays réunis Non-French territories annexed to France (e.g. Belgium).

Préfet The prefect was the administrative head of a *département*. The post was created by the law of 28 Pluviôse Year VIII (17 Feb 1800). Centrally appointed the prefect was assisted by a small prefectoral council which advised him on administration, fiscal and legal disputes, and by a larger general council, which sat for two weeks a year to allocate taxes. Initially drawn from men with experience in the revolutionary assemblies, the prefects were increasingly appointed from a growing professional bureaucracy within the Empire.

Not to be confused with the departmental prefects was the Prefect of Police in Paris who had responsibility for the smooth running of the city – the traffic, the markets, the safety of buildings, etc. – as well as the supervision of public order and the prevention and detection of crime. Louis Dubois served as Prefect of Police from March 1800 to October 1810, and Etienne Pasquier from October 1810 until May 1814.

Prud'hommes, conseils de Literally Councils of Wise Men, established in France by law on 18 March 1808 and authorised to resolve employer-worker disputes involving not more than 60 francs. The first council was established in Lyon and had jurisdiction only over the extensive silk industry of the city; by 1810 such councils existed in 26 towns and cities. Each had between five and 15 members; appointment was by election, but the eligibility requirements were such that only a minority of workers was able to stand. The structure of the councils was such that the employers always had a majority.

Regjeringskommission The Government Commission appointed to supervise the government of Norway between 1807 and 1810 when the Anglo–Danish war severed links between that territory and Denmark. The Commission was presided over by Prince Christian Augustus. Its major problem was always food supply as a result of a succession of bad harvests, the Swedish invasion of 1808 and, above all, the British blockade. The Commission was required to act through Copenhagen rather than on its own initiative but, increasingly, sought authority to act alone, notably in February 1809 when it sought authority to make its own foreign policy, clearly hoping to negotiate peace with Sweden. Frederick VI of Denmark disliked its growing independence; he limited its powers at the beginning of 1810, and by the end of the year it had ceased to function. The Commission's significance lay in the fact that it gave the Norwegians a greater degree of self-rule than they had known for centuries.

Republican Calendar On 5 October 1793, the National Convention resolved to replace the Gregorian Calendar with a republican one commemorating the new era in human history which the deputies considered had begun with the overthrow of the monarchy (10

August 1792) and the Convention's declaration of the republic (22 September 1792). Retrospectively the latter date became the 1st day of the month of Vendémiare of Year I of the Republic.

In the new calendar each month had 30 days; five extra days were added to the end of each year (six to each leap year) originally known as *sans-culottides* (after the revolutionary activists, the *sans-culottes*) and later, from August 1795, as *jours complémentaires*. The months were given names to link them with the phenomena of nature as follows:

Vendémiaire	the month of vintage	(Sep–Oct)
Brumaire	the month of fog	(Oct–Nov)
Frimaire	the month of frost	(Nov–Dec)
Nivôse	the month of snow	(Dec–Jan)
Pluviôse	the month of rain	(Jan–Feb)
Ventôse	the month of wind	(Feb–Mar)
Germinal	the month of germination	(Mar–Apr)
Floréal	the month of flowering	(Apr–May)
Prairial	the month of meadows	(May–June)
Messidor	the month of harvest	(June–July)
Thermidor	the month of heat	(July–Aug)
Fructidor	the month of fruit	(Aug–Sep)

The calendar remained in use until the end of 1806.

Romanticism A cultural movement of the period roughly 1790 to 1830 which put a new emphasis on imagination and Nature in contrast to rule-bound Neo-Classicism and the rationalism of the Enlightenment. Romanticism took rather different forms in different countries, largely because of the individual cultural and social environments against which it was a reaction. In England there was little theoretical element and the most popular manifestations are to be found in poetry ranging from that of Wordsworth and Coleridge, to that of Shelley. In Germany, in contrast, the movement was profoundly philosophical and linked with emerging nationalist sentiment. Romanticism in France ranged itself against the conservative neo-classicism of the influential French Academy and consequently was centred particularly in drama and literary criticism. Its prime mover in France was Chateaubriand, and while he could be ambivalent towards Napoleon, the Napoleonic adventure inspired many French Romantic artists, notably, Théodore Géricault and Jean- Antoine Gros among painters and, among writers, Alfred de Musset, Alfred de Vigny, and Stendhal.

Senatus consultum A procedure first used in January 1801 which empowered the Senate, through its right to preserve and amend the Constitution, to sanction constitutional change and new laws. Napoleon appointed men to the Senate and used this procedure in a variety of ways, and notably as a means of bypassing other legislative bodies.

Standesherren Imperial knights and princelings whose territories were swallowed in the reorganisation of south- west Germany 1803–6, but who were granted special protection for their privileges by Napoleon. At least one reason for the peasant emancipation in Württemberg was the fact that it undercut the authority of these men within the kingdom.

Storting Literally 'grand assize'; an archaic term deliberately used in the Eidsvoll Constitution (1814) for the elected legislature of Norway. The drafters of the constitution wanted a bi-cameral legislature to discourage rash decisions, but did not want an 'upper' and 'lower' house, disliking the aristocratic privilege which tended to go with the former. The *Storting* was therefore to be chosen as one body, but to function as two: the *Odelsting* with three-quarters of the members, where legislation was introduced; and the *Lagting* which received and debated the proposals. A proposal became law only when accepted by both chambers; if a proposal failed in one chamber it could be debated by the whole *Storting* in plenary session and passed on a two-thirds majority. Financial matters were similarly discussed by the whole assembly.

Tugendbund The League of Virtue, a patriotic association founded originally in April 1808 in Prussia involving pro-reform army officers, young nobles and men of letters belonging to the Königsberg Freemason's lodge. The association was not a formal body but a network of sympathisers seeking to revive religion, morality and public spirit as well as patriotism. At its peak it had some 700 sympathisers, and was supported by Scharnhorst and Stein. Concerned at the response the *Tugendbund* might provoke from the French, the King of Prussia dissolved it by decree (12 Dec 1809), but the association continued to function and provided the basis for other patriotic bodies formed in 1814 such as the *Deutsche Gesellschaft* (q.v.).

Wehrpflicht Conscription, introduced into Prussia by Scharnhorst in 1813 and regularised by Boyen's law of 3 September 1814. All men, from all ranks of society, were obliged to serve.

Bibliographical notes

The following bibliographical notes are divided, roughly, by themes. Given the monoglot propensities of the English in general, and students in particular, the notes concentrate on works in the English language. Books marked with an asterisk thus * may be consulted for detailed bibliographies and particularly for books in other languages. The best bibliographical guide to the Napoleonic period is Jack Allen Meyer, *An annotated bibliography of the Napoleonic Era*, (New York, 1987). Unless otherwise stated the place of publication of the books mentioned below is London.

Napoleonic Europe: general texts

Most student texts tend to lump Napoleonic Europe with Revolutionary Europe and survey the whole period from 1789 to 1815. Among the best, and by one who is specifically a Napoleonic scholar, is Owen Connelly, *French Revolution/Napoleonic Europe* (New York, 1979). Connelly was the principal editor of the *Historical Dictionary of Napoleonic France 1799–1815* (Westport, Conn. 1985) which surveys much more than simply France, and has also published a key monograph on the way in which the satellite Kingdoms of Naples, Italy, Holland, Spain and Westphalia were created and administered: *Napoleon's Satellite Kingdoms* (New York, 1965). Stuart Woolf, * *Napoleon's Integration of Europe* (1991) is even more ambitious. Drawing on a wealth of sources in five languages Woolf offers, for the first time, a comparative study of the impact of Napoleonic hegemony on Europe from the point of view of both the imperial bureaucrats and soldiers who carved out and administered the Empire, and the subject peoples. Much briefer is the broad overview, largely from the French perspective, provided by Geoffrey Ellis, *The Napoleonic Empire* (1991); this is an excellent introduction to recent research and current debates.

Of the general texts covering a broader period but which might usefully be explored are Franklin L. Ford, *Europe 1780–1830* (1970) and C.W. Crawley, ed. *War and Peace in an Age of Upheaval, 1793–1830*, (vol IX of the *New Cambridge Modern History*, Cambridge, 1965). The latter is particularly useful for its essays on individual countries and regions, as well as for the thematic surveys of diplomacy, the arts, religion etc.

Napoleon and France: general texts

Biographies of Napoleon are legion. The most authoritative modern biography is Jean Tulard, *Napoleon: The Myth of the Saviour* (1984), a translation (which occasionally leaves something to be desired) of a prize-winning French text first published in 1977. Tulard is a key figure in Napoleonic studies in France and edited the massive *Dictionnaire Napoléon* (Paris, 1987) which can usefully be consulted on most aspects of France and Europe during Napoleon's career. Of the older biographies Georges Lefebvre, *Napoleon* (English translation in 2 vols, 1969 and 1974) and Felix Markham, *Napoleon* (1963) still repay the reader, as does Pieter Geyl, *Napoleon: For and Against* (English translation, 1949) which is both a biography and a masterful analysis of the way Frenchmen wrote about Napoleon and his career between 1814 and 1935. Two short, but useful texts designed specifically for students are Irene Collins, *Napoleon: First Consul and Emperor of the French* (1987) and D.G. Wright, *Napoleon and Europe* (1984). There is an interesting collection of primary material in J. Christopher Herold, ed. *The Mind of Napoleon: A Selection from his Written and Spoken Words* (New York, 1955).

Napoleonic France

While the biographies of Tulard and Lefebvre give considerable, useful detail on France itself the best introduction to the domestic history of Napoleonic France is Louis Bergeron, *France under Napoleon* (English translation, Princeton, 1981). A social historian who has researched and published widely on the elites of Napoleonic France, Bergeron's text outlines the social, economic and administrative structures and the shifting attitudes of different social groups. For a general survey of Napoleon's reforms in France the best book in English remains Robert B. Holtman, *The Napoleonic Revolution* (Philadelphia, 1967). Holtman's earlier study *Napoleonic Propaganda* (Baton Rouge, 1950) is the best English-language study of the topic, and covers both France and the Empire.

On the French economy Geoffrey Ellis, *Napoleon's Continental Blockade: The Case of Alsace* (Oxford, 1981) is vital. While the text concentrates on economic development in eastern France it also describes Napoleon's attempt to create a European market dominated by France. Also important, particularly for its comparative dimension, is François Crouzet, 'Wars, Blockade, and Economic Change in Europe, 1792–1815', *Journal of Economic History*, XXIV (1964).

Politics and administration are best surveyed by, respectively, Irene Collins, *Napoleon and his Parliaments, 1800–1815* (1979), and chapter 8 of Clive H. Church, *Revolution and Red Tape: The French Ministerial Bureaucracy 1770–1850* (Oxford, 1981). E.A. Whitcomb, 'Napoleon's Prefects', *American Historical Review*, LXXIX (1974) is a valuable analysis of the origins and careers of these administrators, as is the same author's *Napoleon's Diplomatic Service* (Durham, North Carolina, 1979) for the men who conducted his foreign affairs. For the administrative organisation of the Napoleonic 'police state' see Eric A. Arnold, Jr. *Fouché, Napoleon and the General Police* (Washington D.C., 1979); and Hubert Cole, *Fouché: The Unprincipled Patriot* (1971) is also interesting. But for a corrective to the notion that all policing in Napoleonic France was concentrated on politics or bringing in refractory conscripts and deserters see Clive Emsley, 'Policing the Streets of Early Nineteenth-Century Paris', *French History*, I (1987).

The problems which recruitment created for administrators as well as the reactions of the population to the military demands are assessed in Alan Forrest, *Conscripts and Deserters: The Army and French Society during the Revolution and Empire*, (Oxford, 1989); and see also Isser Woloch, 'Napoleonic Conscription: State Power and Civil Society', *Past and Present*, 111 (1986).

For relations between the Napoleonic state and the Church see E.E.Y. Hales, *Napoleon and the Pope: The Story of Napoleon and Pius VII* (1962), though, as the subtitle suggests, its principal concern is with the personal relations between the two men. The older text, H.H. Walsh, *The Concordat of 1801: A Study of the Problem of Nationalism in the Relations of Church and State* (1933), remains important, especially for the broader considerations.

The Empire and the satellite states

Connelly's *Napoleon's Satellite Kingdoms* and Woolf's *Napoleon's Integration of Europe* are the key texts in the area. A good starting point is also the collection generated by a colloquium held in Brussels, *Occupants-Occupés 1792–1815* (Brussels, 1968); this contains essays on many of the territories occupied by the French (Belgium, the

Netherlands, the Rhineland, Switzerland, the Duchy of Warsaw) and résumés of the debates at the colloquium.

Unfortunately there is a lack of good, recent English-language books for many of the imperial territories and allies. For Germany James Sheehan, *German History 1770–1866* (Oxford, 1990) provides an excellent overview incorporating much of the recent research; but while Sheehan emphasises the significance of the Napoleonic impact on Germany it constitutes only a small part of his story. A useful brief survey of current German research, and again stressing the sheer extent of change in the Napoleonic period, is to be found in John Breuilly, 'State-building, modernisation, and liberalism from the late eighteenth- century to unification: German Peculiarities', *European History Quarterly*, 22 (1992). In particular Breuilly draws attention to the way in which Prussia pursued progressive social and economic policies while resisting constitutional demands, in contrast to the expanded states of south Germany which tended to do the opposite. T.C.W. Blanning, *Germany and the French Revolution: Occupation and Resistance in the Rhineland 1792–1802* (Cambridge, 1983), while an exciting and stimulating account, ends as the territories under examination are annexed to France. The opening chapter of William Carr, *The Origins of the German Wars of Unification* (1991) illuminates the end of the period. Much older, though still valuable given its detail and coverage, is H.A.L. Fisher, *Studies in Napoleonic Statesmanship: Germany* (Oxford, 1903). Jeffrey M. Diefendorff, *Businessmen and Politics in the Rhineland 1789–1834* (Princeton, 1980) presents a valuable assessment of the political education of bankers, manufacturers and merchants and their relationships with successive regimes in Aachen, Cologne and Crefeld. Among the most recent and useful texts for readers of German are Helmut Berding, *Napoleonische Herrschafts- und Gesellschaftspolitik im Königreich Westfalen 1807–1813* (Göttingen, 1973) and W. Demel, *Der bayerische Staatsabsolutismus 1806/08–1817* (Munich, 1983).

Italy is similarly badly served. R.M. Johnston, *The Napoleonic Empire in Southern Italy* (2 vols 1904) is a very old book, yet it remains a mine of useful information. The first two chapters of R. John Rath, *The Fall of the Napoleonic Kingdom of Italy (1814)* (New York, 1941) provide a useful background to the book's central theme with a broad survey of the origins and development of Napoleonic domination and Italian national sentiment. More recent are Dorinda Outram, 'Education and Politics in Piedmont, 1796–1814', *Historical Journal*, XIX (1976) and Michael Broers, 'Revolution as Vendetta: Napoleonic Piedmont 1800–1814', *Historical Journal*, XXXIII

(1990), both significant essays. Franco Della Peruta, 'War and society in Napoleonic Italy: the armies of the Kingdom of Italy at home and abroad', in John A. Davis and Paul Ginsborg, eds. *Society and Politics in Italy in the Age of the Risorgimento* (Cambridge, 1991) describes the impact of Napoleon's military demands and the role of the Italian troops notably in Spain and Russia. Of the general texts on Italy which, while covering a much wider time-span, have useful comment on the Napoleonic period see in particular Harry Hearder, *Italy in the Age of the Risorgimento, 1790–1870* (1983) and Stuart Woolf, *A History of Italy 1700–1860: The Social Constraints of Political Change* (1979). For a modern Italian text-book surveying the whole peninsula under Napoleon see P. Villani, *Italia napoleonica* (Naples, 1978).

The best general survey of the Netherlands in the period is Simon Schama, *Patriots and Liberators. Revolution in the Netherlands 1780–1813* (1977); but the relevant pages of E.H. Kossmann, *The Low Countries 1780–1940* (Oxford, 1978) provide a pithy account.

Given the running sore of the guerrilla war in Spain it is a moot point whether that country is best included here as a satellite or in the next section as an opponent. The fullest account is to be found in Gabriel H. Lovett, *Napoleon and the Birth of Modern Spain*, (2 vols New York, 1965), but this is now usefully supplemented by Charles J. Esdaile, *The Spanish Army in the Peninsular War* (Manchester, 1988) which is much broader than the title might suggest and explores the inter-relationships between different squabbling factions. Also important is Don W. Alexander, *Rod of Iron: French Counterinsurgency Policy in Aragon during the Peninsular War* (Wilmington, Delaware, 1985) which surveys the way in which the French army set about trying to win the guerrilla war.

Napoleon's opponents

The principal opponent of France throughout the Revolutionary and Napoleonic wars was Britain. Clive Emsley, *British Society and the French Wars 1793–1815* (1979) is an attempt to assess the impact of the wars and their demands on British society as a whole. For the internal politics of the period see A.D. Harvey, *Britain in the early nineteenth century* (1978) or any of the numerous general texts such as Ian R. Christie, *Wars and Revolutions, 1760–1815* (1982). The complex inter-relationship between politics and military policy is well rehearsed in Christopher D. Hall, *British Strategy in the Napoleonic War, 1803–15* (Manchester, 1992). Military preparation is best followed up in Richard Glover, *Britain at Bay: Defence against Bonaparte 1803–14* (1973). For the intellectual opposition to the war see J.E. Cookson, *The Friends of Peace: Anti-War Liberalism in England 1793–1815*, (Cambridge, 1982) which stresses the role of religious dissent, especially in the new manufacturing districts. For the economy during the wars by far and away the most important book is François Crouzet, *L'économie britannique et le blocus continental* (Paris, 1958). The second edition of this magisterial work (Paris, 1987) has a new, hundred page introduction surveying the recent literature and debates and providing a full bibliography of largely English texts. Phyllis Deane, 'War and Industrialisation', in J.M. Winter, ed. *War and Economic Development. Essays in Memory of David Joslin* (Cambridge, 1975) is a short, useful introduction, and there is an important, thoughtful assessment in P.K. O'Brien, 'The Impact of the Revolutionary and Napoleonic Wars, 1793–1815, on the Long-Run Growth of the British Economy', *Review*, XII (1989). John M. Sherwig *Guineas and Gunpowder: British Foreign Aid in the Wars with France 1793–1815* (Cambridge, Mass. 1969) is indispensible for anyone interested in both the British economy and the organisation and financing of the anti-French coalitions. A useful shortcut to many of these texts can be found in the essays in H.T. Dickinson, ed. *Britain and the French Revolution (1989).

The response of Prussia to the calamity of 1806 has been a popular subject for historians. Guy Stanton Ford, *Stein and the Era of Reform in Prussia 1807–1815* (Princeton, 1922; repr. Gloucester, Mass. 1965) is an old text but remains useful and can be supplemented by Peter Paret, *Yorck and the Era of Prussian Reform 1807–1815* (Princeton, 1966), an assessment of military innovation and its inter-relationship with non-military reforms, by Walter M. Simon, *The Failure of the Prussian Reform Movement 1807–1819* (New York, 1971), which looks at why the reforms – particularly agrarian and constitutional – fell short of the aspirations of the reformers, and by Marion W. Gray, *Prussia in Transition: Society and Politics under the Stein Reform Ministry of 1808* (Philadelphia, 1986), a detailed study of politics and personalities. Robert M. Berdahl, *The Politics of the Prussian Nobility: The Development of a Conservative Ideology, 1770–1848* (Princeton, 1988) covers a much wider time-span but is illuminating and valuable for the Napoleonic period.

For Russia the reader must rely largely on biographies or general texts. Significant among the former are Marc Raeff, *Michael Speran-*

sky: Statesman of Imperial Russia 1772–1839 (The Hague, 1957), Michael Jenkins, *Arakcheev: Grand Vizier of the Russian Empire* (1969), and Alan Palmer, *Alexander I: Tsar of War and Peace* (1974). P.K. Grimsted, *The Foreign Ministers of Alexander I* (Berkeley, Calif. 1969) is especially important for its revision of Russian policy at the Congress of Vienna and beyond. Of the general texts Hugh Seton-Watson, *The Russian Empire 1801–1917* (Oxford 1967) is full of detail, but easy reading; unfortunately J.N. Westwood, *Endurance and Endeavour; Russian History 1812–1986* (Oxford, 1973; 3rd edn. 1986) begins rather late for the Napoleonic period as a whole.

Austria is similarly poorly served by English-language works. W.C. Langsam, *The Napoleonic Wars and German Nationalism in Austria* (New York, 1930; repr. 1970) is still serviceable. There is a valuable section on Austria in Sheehan, *German History 1770–1866*. Chapter 4 of C.A. Macartney, *The Habsburg Empire 1790–1918* (1968) provides a useful summary and Gunther E. Rothenberg, *Napoleon's Great Adversaries: Archduke Charles and the Austrian Army 1792–1814* (1982) is an important reassessment emphasising the ability of the Archduke and the growing efficiency of his army which was Napoleon's main, regular opponent on land.

Diplomacy and international relations

The Napoleonic period has tended to lose its popularity with historians of international relations in recent years. There are useful summary essays in three recent collections: Alan Sked, ed. *Europe's Balance of Power, 1815–1848* (1979), F.R. Bridge and Roger Bullen, eds. *The Great Powers and the European States System 1815–1914* (1980), and Derek McKay and Hamish Scott, *The Rise of the Great Powers 1648–1815* (1983). For greater detail the reader is forced to turn to much older texts. R.B. Mowat, *The Diplomacy of Napoleon* (1924) is a comprehensive survey which may be supplemented by Harold C. Deutsch, *The Genesis of Napoleonic Imperialism 1801–1805* (Cambridge, Mass. 1938) and Herbert Butterfield, *The Peace Tactics of Napoleon 1806–1808* (Cambridge, 1929). Austrian foreign policy is best approached with Enno E. Kraehe, *Metternich's German Policy: Volume I, The Contest with Napoleon 1799–1814* (Princeton, 1963) and *Volume II, The Congress of Vienna 1814–1815* (Princeton, 1983). For British diplomacy see the two standard texts of C.K. Webster, *British Diplomacy 1813–1815* (1921) and *The Foreign Policy of Castlereagh*

1812–1815: Britain and the Reconstruction of Europe (1931); but there is a narrowness and glow of national pride which, while acceptable in the interwar years, has tended to date these texts. The same author also produced *The Congress of Vienna 1814–1815* (1919), also a classic in its day; Harold Nicholson, *The Congress of Vienna: A Study in Allied Unity 1812–1822* (1946) draws on this but provides a rather more lively read. There is a useful corrective view stressing European hostility to Britain in A.D. Harvey, 'European attitudes to Britain during the Revolutionary and Napoleonic Era', *History* LXIII (1978).

War and warfare

There are scores of books on individual Napoleonic campaigns and battles. Of the general surveys the most detailed and comprehensive is David Chandler's massive and magisterial *The Campaigns of Napoleon* (1967); but three other texts are also useful for their rather different perspectives: Owen Connelly, *Blundering to Glory: Napoleon's Military Campaigns* (Wilmington, Delaware, 1988) is, as the title suggests, more critical of Napoleon than many others; Gunther E. Rothenberg, *The Art of Warfare in the Age of Napoleon* (Bloomington, Indiana, 1977) is particularly good on military organisation; Geoffrey Best, *War and Society in Revolutionary Europe, 1770–1830* (1982) is refreshingly more concerned with the social impact of the wars and the new mass armies than with campaigns and battles. For the reality of a Napoleonic battle as experienced by the combatants see chapter 3 of John Keegan, *The Face of Battle: A Study of Agincourt, Waterloo and the Somme* (1976); a brilliant and original book. For the often forgotten, unglamorous, but essential question of supply and logistics, see the relevant chapters of Martin van Creveld, *Supplying War: Logistics from Wallenstein to Patton* (Cambridge, 1977). The legacy of Napoleonic warfare is well summarised in chapters 4 and 5 of Hew Strachan, *European Armies and the Conduct of War* (1983).

The Peninsular War, a Napoleonic campaign from which Napoleon was largely absent, is thoroughly surveyed in David Gates, *The Running Sore: A History of the Peninsular War* (1986) which, unlike most earlier English language studies, gives full weight to Spanish involvement rather than concentrating on Wellington's exploits. For the guerrilla conflict see Alexander's *Rod of Iron*.

Naval history is, understandably perhaps, less well covered. Michael Lewis, *A Social History of the Navy 1793–1815 (1960)* still serves as the best account of Nelson's navy. For the climactic battle of Trafalgar see David Howarth, *Trafalgar: The Nelson Touch* (1969); and for Napoleon's continuing attempt to construct a fleet capable of taking on the British see Richard Glover, 'The French Fleet, 1807–1814: Britain's Problem and Madison's Opportunity', *Journal of Modern History* XXXIX (1967). Finally it is worth recognising that even if, during the war, Britannia did rule the waves, there were many hardy seamen on the northern coast of continental Europe who refused to acknowledge this; see Patrick Crowhurst, *The French War on Trade: Privateering 1793–1815* (1989).

Maps and genealogical tables

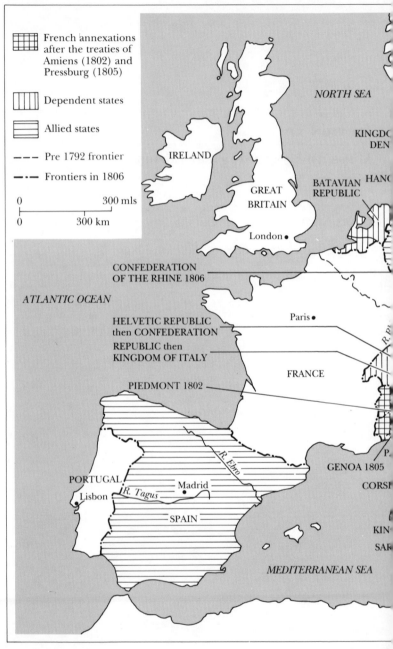

1. *Europe 1800–06*
After: Stuart Woolf, *Napoleon's Integration of Europe* (1991)

KINGDOM
OF
SWEDEN

St Petersburg

*BALTIC
SEA*

R. Dvina

Moscow

R U S S I A N

E M P I R E

R. Niemen

KINGDOM
OF
PRUSSIA

Berlin

Warsaw

R. Elbe

R. Oder

R. Vistula

R. Dnieper

Prague

A U S T R I A N

R. Dnestr

Vienna

E M P I R E

R. Danube

VENETIA
ISTRIA 1805

BLACK SEA

R. Danube

DALMATIA
1805

OTTOMAN

DOM
RURIA

me

KINGDOM
OF
NAPLES

E M P I R E

PAPAL
STATES

KINGDOM
OF SICILY

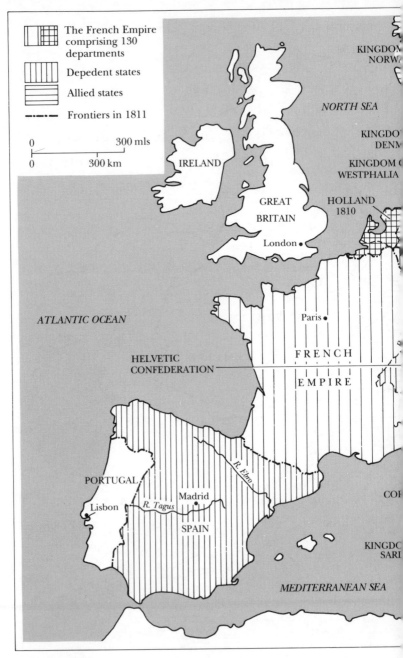

2. *Europe 1807–12*
After: Stuart Woolf, *Napoleon's Integration of Europe* (1991)

KINGDOM
OF SWEDEN

St Petersburg

BALTIC
SEA

R. Dvina

Moscow

RUSSIAN

EMPIRE

R. Niemen

KINGDOM OF PRUSSIA

Warsaw

GRAND-DUCHY
OF WARSAW
1807 | 1809

R. Elbe

R. Oder

R. Dnieper

R. Vistula

R. Dnestr

ED-
ON

HINE

AUSTRIAN

R. Danube

EMPIRE

DOM
TALY

BLACK SEA

IA

ILLYRIAN
PROVINCES 1809

OTTOMAN

ome

KINGDOM OF
NAPLES

PAPAL
STATES
1809

EMPIRE

KINGDOM OF
SICILY

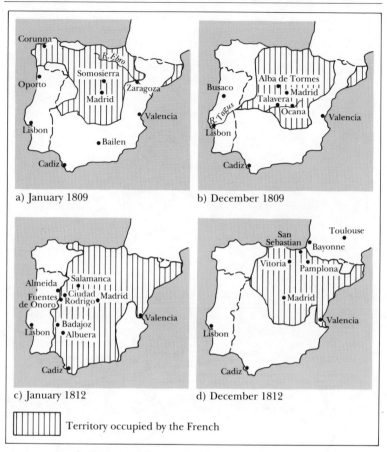

a) January 1809

b) December 1809

c) January 1812

d) December 1812

Territory occupied by the French

3. The Peninsular War, 1808–14
After: Charles J. Esdaile, *The Spanish Army in the Peninsular War* (Manchester, 1988)

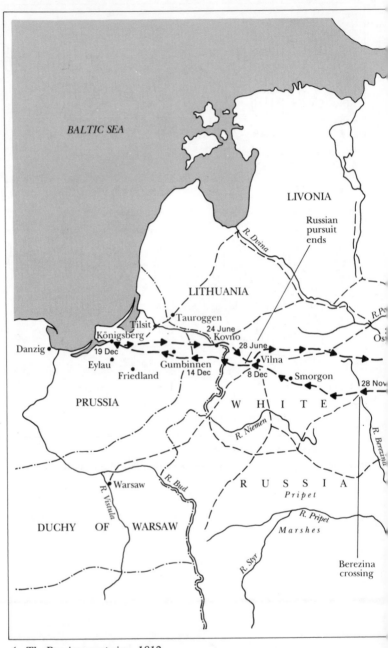

4. *The Russian campaign, 1812*
After: Antony Brett-James, 1812: *Eyewitness Accounts of Napoleon's Defeat in Russia* (1967)

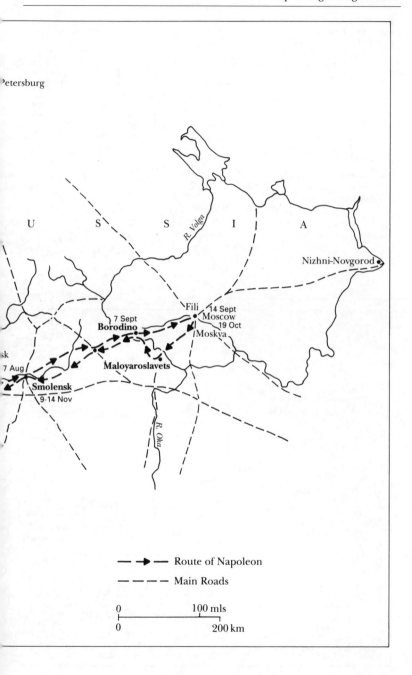

Petersburg

U   S   S   *R. Volga*   I   A

Nizhni-Novgorod

Fili   14 Sept
7 Sept   Moscow
Borodino   19 Oct
        Moskva

sk
7 Aug   **Maloyaroslavets**

Smolensk
9-14 Nov   *R. Oka*

━━▶━━ Route of Napoleon

━ ━ ━ ━ Main Roads

0   100 mls
0   200 km

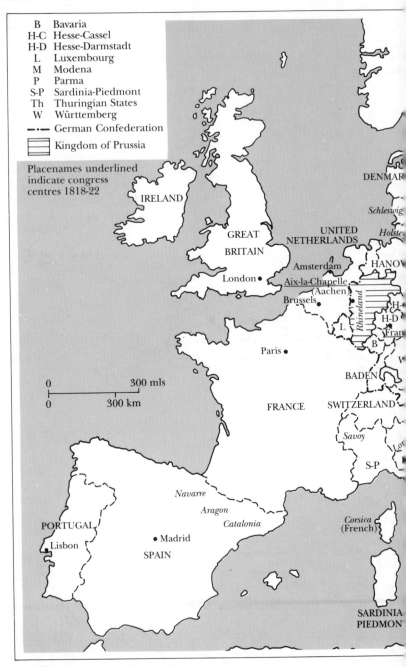

B	Bavaria
H-C	Hesse-Cassel
H-D	Hesse-Darmstadt
L	Luxembourg
M	Modena
P	Parma
S-P	Sardinia-Piedmont
Th	Thuringian States
W	Württemberg

–·–·– German Confederation

Kingdom of Prussia

Placenames underlined
indicate congress
centres 1818-22

IRELAND

GREAT
BRITAIN

London ●

DENMAR

Schleswig

Holste

UNITED
NETHERLANDS

Amsterdam

Aix-la-Chapelle
(Aachen)

Brussels ●

HANOV

Rhineland

H

H-D

Fran

L

B

W

Paris ●

BADEN

FRANCE

SWITZERLAND

Savoy

S-P

0   300 mls
0   300 km

Navarre

Aragon

Catalonia

Corsica
(French)

PORTUGAL

Lisbon

● Madrid

SPAIN

SARDINIA
PIEDMON

5. *Europe after the Congress of Vienna, 1815*

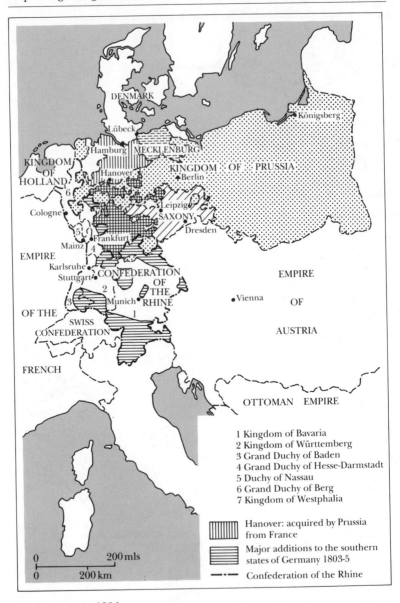

6. *Germany in 1806*
After: James Sheehan, *German History 1770–1866* (Oxford, 1990)

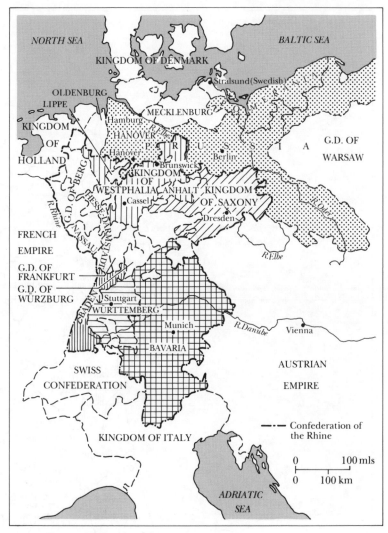

7. *Germany in 1807, following Prussia's defeat*

8. *The departments of the Empire in 1812: France*

Maps 8, 9 and 11a were based on Jacques Godechot, *Les institutions de la France sous la Révolution et l'Empire* (Paris, 1985)

Annexed during the
Revolutionary period 1790-9

—·— Frontier of the Empire

--- Department boundaries

• Principal town of department
(*chef-lieu*)

Lille
(Douai
till 1802)
NORD

AISNE
Laon

Charleville
ARDENNES

MOSELLE
Metz

MARNE
Châlons-sur-Marne

MEUSE

SEINE-
Melun
ET-

Bar-le-
Duc

Nancy
MEURTHE

Strasbourg

BAS-
RHIN

AUBE
Troyes

Chaumont

VOSGES
Epinal

Colmar

YONNE
Auxerre

HAUTE-
MARNE

HAUTE-
SAONE

Vesoul

HAUT-
RHIN

COTE-D'OR
Dijon

NIEVRE
Nevers

Besançon
DOUBS

oulins

SAONE-ET-LOIRE

ALLIER

Mâcon

Bourg

Lons-le-
Saunier
JURA

RHONE

AIN

Geneva
LEMAN

ermont-
Ferrand

-DE-DOME

LOIRE

Lyon

Montbrison

Chambéry
MONT
BLANC

ISERE

HAUTE-LOIRE
Le Puy

Valence

Grenoble

Privas

LOZERE

ARDECHE

DROME

HAUTES-
ALPES

Mende

Gap

N

GARD

VAUCLUSE

Digne

ALPES-MARITIMES

Montpellier

Nîmes

Avignon

BASSES-ALPES

BOUCHES-
DU-RHONE

Draguignan
VAR

Nice

Marseille

pignan
ALES

Bastia

CORSE
(Ajaccio)

307

9. The departments of the Empire in 1812: the Low Countries

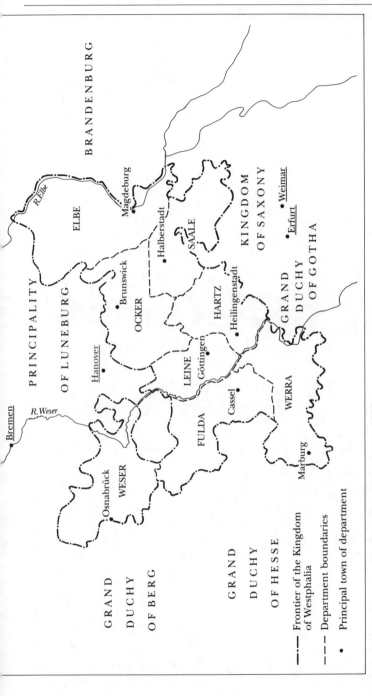

10. *The departments of the Kingdom of Westphalia, 1808*
After: Owen Connelly, *Napoleon's Satellite Kingdom* (1965)

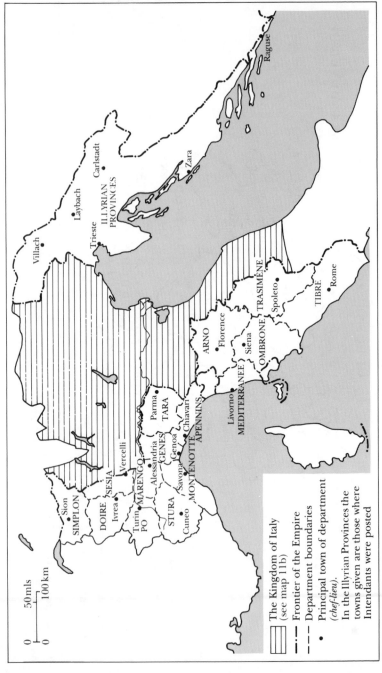

11a. *The departments of the Empire in 1812: the Italian, Swiss and Illyrian lands annexed by Napoleon between 1800–10*

The Kingdom of Italy (see map 11b)

Frontier of the Empire

Department boundaries

• Principal town of department (chef-lieu).

In the Illyrian Provinces the towns given are those where Intendants were posted

Raguse

Zara

Carlstadt

Laybach

Trieste

ILLYRIAN PROVINCES

Villach

Rome

TIBRE

Spoleto

TRASIMÈNE

OMBRONE

Siena

Florence

ARNO

MEDITERRANÉE

Livorno

APENNINS

Chiavari

Genoa

GENES

Savona

MONTENOTTE

Parma

TARO

Alessandria

MARENGO

PO

STURA

Cuneo

Turin

Ivrea

Vercelli

DOIRE

SESIA

Sion

SIMPLON

50 mls

100 km

0

0

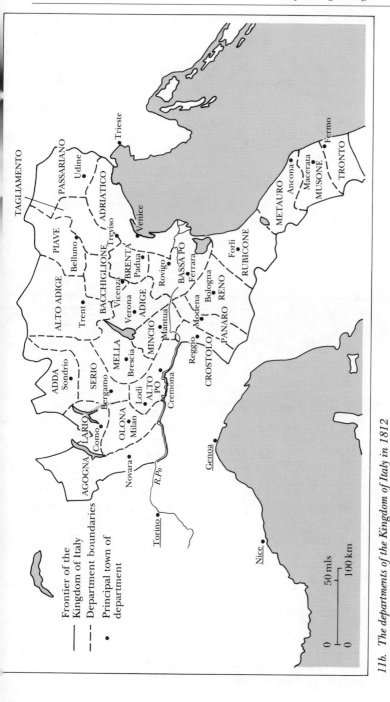

11b. *The departments of the Kingdom of Italy in 1812*
After: R. John Rath, *The Provisional Austrian Regime in Lombardy-Venetia 1814–1815* (Austin, 1969)

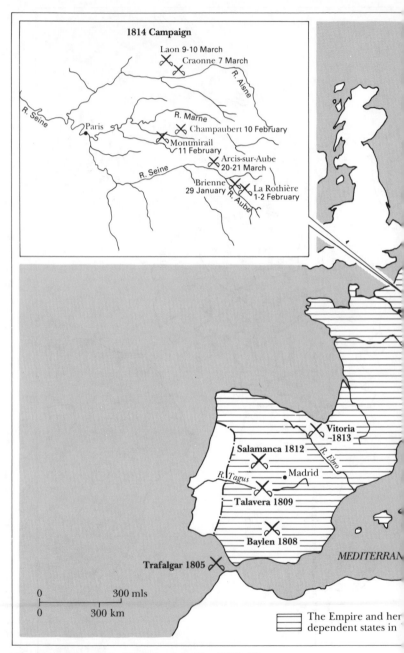

1814 Campaign

Laon 9-10 March
Craonne 7 March
R. Aisne
R. Seine
Paris
R. Marne
Champaubert 10 February
Montmirail
11 February
Arcis-sur-Aube
20-21 March
R. Seine
Brienne
29 January
La Rothière
1-2 February
R. Aube

Vitoria
~1813
Salamanca 1812
R. Ebro
R. Tagus
Madrid
Talavera 1809
Baylen 1808
Trafalgar 1805
MEDITERRAN

0   300 mls
0   300 km

The Empire and her
dependent states in

12. *Sites of the principal Napoleonic battles, 1800–15*
After: Stuart Woolf, *Napoleon's Integration of Europe* (1991)

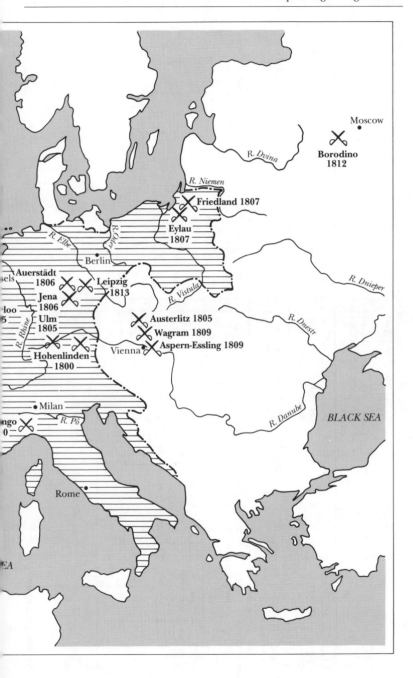

Moscow

✕
Borodino
1812

R. Dvina

R. Niemen

✕ Friedland 1807

Eylau
1807

R. Oder

Berlin

R. Elbe

R. Dnieper

Auerstädt
1806

✕ ✕ Leipzig
1813

R. Vistula

sels

Jena
1806

R. Dniestr

loo

Ulm
1805

✕ Austerlitz 1805

✕ Wagram 1809

✕ ✕ Aspern-Essling 1809

R. Rhine

✕
Hohenlinden
1800

Vienna

Milan

R. Po

R. Danube

BLACK SEA

ngo
0

✕

Rome

EA

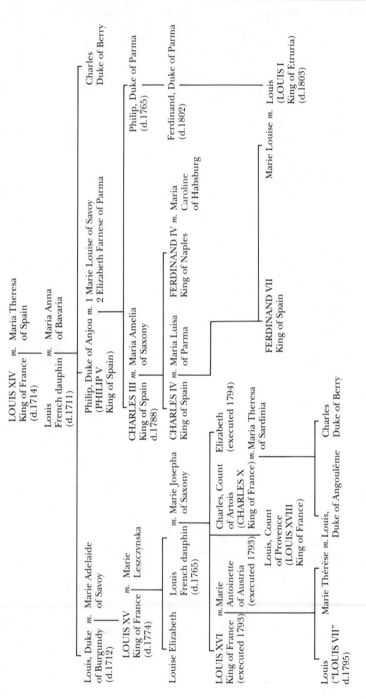

1. The Bourbon monarchs

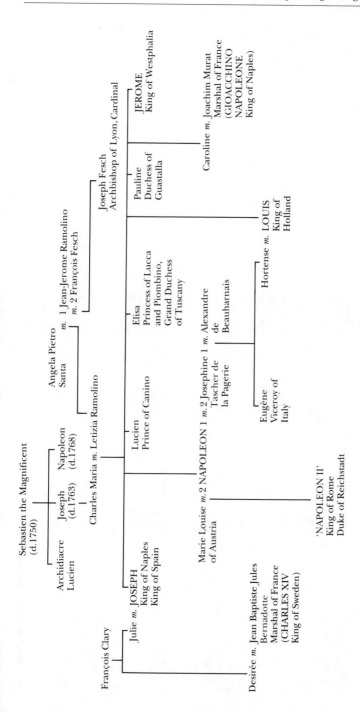

2. The Bonapartes

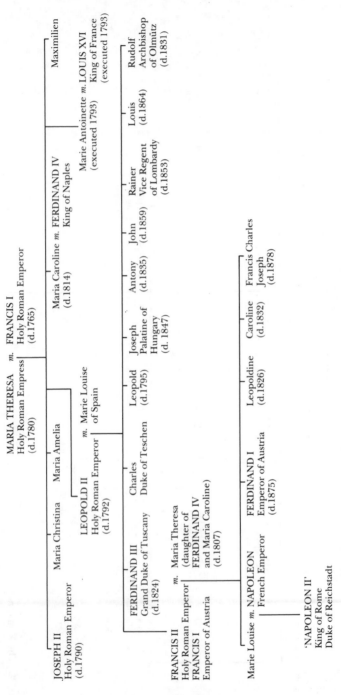

3. **The Habsburg monarchs**

Index

Readers are advised that an entry may appear more than once on a page; that references in bold indicate main entries; that since Napoleon appears on virtually every page his entry here has been sub-indexed and not every individual mention of him has been included.